STAGE 1 EXEMPTION

ACCOUNTING FUNDAMENTALS

First edition 1990
Third edition May 1991

ISBN 0 86277 736 4 (previously 0 86277 716 X)

A CIP catalogue record for this book is available
from the British Library

Published by

BPP Publishing Limited
Aldine House, Aldine Place
London W12 8AW

We are grateful to the Chartered Institute of Management Accountants, the Association of Accounting Technicians and the Chartered Association of Certified Accountants for permission to reproduce past examination questions. The suggested solutions have been prepared by BPP Publishing Limited.

CONTENTS

	Page
Preface	1
Syllabus	2
The examination paper	5
Study guide	6
A note on objective test (multiple choice) questions	12
The meaning of examiners' instructions	14
Test your knowledge: questions	16
Test your knowledge: answers	20
Specimen paper	24
Index to questions and suggested solutions	43
Questions	47
Suggested solutions	109
Objective tests: questions	225
Objective tests: solutions	246

PREFACE

BPP's range of Study Texts provides a comprehensive course of study for the examinations set by the Chartered Institute of Management Accountants. However, knowledge of the topics covered by the syllabus is only one element of examination success. Equally important are an awareness of exam technique and practice in dealing with examination style questions. BPP's range of CIMA Practice and Revision Kits has been produced to meet these needs. The kits are an ideal supplement to BPP study texts but will also be useful to students using other texts.

The main section of this Accounting Fundamentals kit contains both examination-style and objective test (multiple choice) questions. There is a bank of 68 examination-style questions arranged by topic in the order set out by the syllabus itself, including 14 easier 'basic revision questions' to get you started on each topic. All questions are provided with full suggested solutions. This is followed by objective tests containing a total of 77 multiple choice questions, also with fully worked solutions.

To put the Accounting Fundamentals paper in context, an introductory section of the kit sets out the syllabus and the paper format. A study guide on pages 6 to 11 highlights the key points in each syllabus area as an aid to study and revision. This is followed by guidance on dealing with questions in multiple choice format and a quiz to test your basic knowledge of the areas covered by the syllabus. At the end of this section we have included the Specimen Paper with full suggested solutions to indicate the scope and nature of likely examination questions.

The main question bank in the kit represents the equivalent of sitting the examination several times over. If you are able to attempt all of the questions you should be very well prepared for anything you may meet in the examination itself.

BPP Publishing
May 1991

SYLLABUS

Aim

To test the candidate's ability to:

(a) understand accounting theory;
(b) apply theory to basic financial and cost accounting practice;
(c) prepare simple accounting statements.

Content

		Ability required
1	*Accounting theory (weighting 15%)*	
	Cost and value concepts	1
	Measurement of income: capital maintenance	1
	Asset valuation alternatives: historical cost, replacement cost, net realisable value and economic value; methods of depreciation	1
	Research and development costs: capital or revenue treatment	1
	The goodwill concept	1
	Stock valuation: LIFO, FIFO, NIFO, average cost and standard cost methods	3
	Effects of changing price levels	1
2	*Objectives of financial statements (weighting 15%)*	
	User groups including shareholders, managers, employees, government, creditors, analyst-advisers and the public and their information needs	1
	Characteristics of useful information and the problems associated with its production	2
3	*Accounting with computers (weighting 10%)*	
	The role of computers in the collection, analysis and presentation of accounting data and information	1
4	*Financial accounting practice (weighting 30%)*	
	Principles and conventions of accounting	2
	Double-entry bookkeeping including books of prime entry, ledgers and control accounts	3
	Trial balance and adjustments including accruals and prepayments	3
	Treatment of provisions and reserves	3
	Preparation of non-published balance sheets and manufacturing, trading, profit and loss accounts; income and expenditure accounts	3
	Incomplete records	3

		Ability required
5	*Cost accounting practice (weighting 30%)*	
	Cost classification, elements of cost and cost behaviour in manufacturing and service organisations	2
	Materials: cost collection; control	3
	Labour: cost allocation: payroll routine	3
	Overhead cost: classification and analysis	3
	Principles of apportionment and absorption into cost centres and units; departmental accounts	3
	Marginal and absorption costing concepts	1
	Budgets and budgetary control	2
	Principles of standard costs and preparation of total cost variances for material, labour and overheads	3
	Integrated and non-integrated accounting systems	1

The syllabus printed above contains a ranking of the level of ability required in each topic, and a weighting for each syllabus area. The Institute has published the following explanatory notes on these points.

Abilities required in the examination

The rankings range from 1 to 4 and represent the following ability levels.

	Ranking for syllabus topics
Appreciation	
To understand a knowledge area at an early stage of learning, or outside the core of management accounting, at a level which enables the accountant to communicate and work with other members of the management team.	1
Knowledge	
To advise on such matters as laws, standards, facts and techniques at a level of detail appropriate to a management accounting specialist.	2
Skill	
To apply theoretical knowledge, concepts and techniques to the solution of problems where it is clear what technique has to be used and the information needed is clearly indicated.	3
Application	
To apply knowledge and skills where candidates have to determine from a number of techniques which is the most appropriate and select the information required from a fairly wide range of data, some of which might not be relevant; to exercise professional judgement and to communicate and work with members of the management team and other recipients of financial reports.	4

Study weightings

A percentage weighting is shown against each topic in the syllabus; this is intended as a *guide* to the amount of study time each topic requires.

All topics in a syllabus must be studied, as a question may examine more than one topic or carry a higher proportion of marks than the percentage study time suggested.

The weightings *do not* specify the number of marks which will be allocated to topics in the examination.

THE EXAMINATION PAPER

Paper format

Up until and including the December 1989 sitting the paper was split 60% objective testing (30 questions) and 40% longer computational and discursive questions (normally two questions). You will see later in this section that the specimen paper was in this format. However from July 1990 the split of the multiple choice questions against essay questions changed to 50 : 50. You should bear this point in mind when using the specimen paper for revision purposes.

Past papers

The Institute does not publish past question papers for the Stage 1 exemption examinations, but they have issued the specimen paper which we have reproduced later in this section. The CIMA has also made the following points which should help you in preparing for the examination.

(a) 'As the current syllabus has allowed examiners gradually to refine their approaches to their papers, it is natural to assume that some of the essay-type questions set will not necessarily be as easy as some of those in the pilot (specimen) papers. Those papers were intended to give an idea of the sort of approach taken, but that past Stage 1 papers may be a better guide.'

We have included many past Stage 1 questions in this kit to enable you to achieve the required standard.

(b) 'The exemption papers are set by the same examiners who set the Stage 1 papers and they are satisfied that the degree of difficulty is about the same.'

(c) 'There will normally be no choice of question for the essay answer.'

(d) 'The long question will usually be practically based.'

(e) 'It is worth pointing out that the Institute is usually looking for a mark of about 50% on each paper for a pass, and that candidates who do poorly on the multiple choice and well on the essay (or vice versa) may be singled out for more detailed review.'

Using this kit

The more practice you can get in answering examination-style questions, the better prepared you will be for the examination itself. But if time is limited, remember that a serious attempt at one question is more valuable than cursory attempts at two. Avoid the temptation to 'audit' the answers: complete your attempt before checking with our solution. When you have had enough practice to be confident of your grasp of the material, try a few questions under exam conditions, timing yourself against the clock.

To obtain the greatest benefit from the use of this study material you are recommended to do the following.

(a) Complete a thorough preparation of each subject before attempting the questions on that subject. Answering questions is a test of what you have learnt and also a means of practising so that you develop a skill in presenting your answers. To attempt them before you are ready is not a fair test of your proficiency and the result may discourage you.

(b) To see whether you are ready to attempt the bank of questions on a particular subject, try the basic revision question which you will find at the beginning of each section. If you can make a good attempt at this then you are ready to proceed to the remainder of the questions.

(c) Write your answers in examination conditions without referring to books, manuals or notes. Then compare the suggested solutions with your own. Look to see how many points of similarity and difference there are between them.The suggested answers are only suggestions. They are correct and complete on essentials but there is more than one way of writing an answer.

(c) Follow the subdivisions of the kit so that you use the questions to test what you can do after systematic preparation.

The questions in this kit are designed to provide a wide coverage of the syllabus. By working through the questions, you should therefore be going over all the topics you ought to learn, and assessing your ability to answer examination-style questions well.

Questions which call for a written answer are difficult to revise with, because it is human nature to be easily bored by writing out lengthy solutions. We would suggest the following as a possible remedy for this problem.

(a) You should attempt a full written solution to one or two questions, in order to gain experience and familiarity with the task of producing solutions within the timescale allowed in the examination itself.

(b) For other questions you should prepare an *answer plan*. This is a list of the points that you would put into your solution, preferably in the order that you would make them.

(c) You should then read our solution and do the following.

   (i) Make a note of points that are new to you and that you think you should learn (for example by underlining certain sentences in the solution for future reference).

   (ii) Prepare an answer plan from our own solution, to make sure that you understand the relevance to the question of the points we raise. This useful discipline will ensure that you absorb the points in the solution more thoroughly.

Notes on specific areas of the syllabus

Accounting theory

The topics embraced under this caption are suited to discussion questions. Such questions are generally unpopular with students despite the fact that marks can quite easily be gained if a methodical approach is adopted.

(a) Read the question carefully and underline key words and phrases. Note what the examiner requires and resist the temptation to give the answer to the question you would have preferred.

(b) Draw up an answer plan. This is the equivalent of your workings for a computational question. List what you expect will be the main points in each paragraph and make sure the answer will be properly structured.

(c) Write neatly and precisely. The examiner is more likely to reward short, neatly-written essays which keep to the point than lengthy scrawled ramblings.

(d) Use paragraphs and keep your sentences short.

Important areas to study include the following.

(a) (i) The *accounting equation*

Capital + liabilities = assets

(ii) The *'business equation'*. In a period

Profit = drawings + increase in net assets (after drawings)
- capital introduced in the period

These form the basis of accounts, and you should always keep them in the back of your mind.

(b) *Accounting concepts*
There are four fundamental accounting concepts.

(i) *Going concern:* an enterprise will carry on in existence for the foreseeable future.

(ii) *Accruals:* revenues and expenses should be taken into account in the period to which they relate.

(iii) *Consistency:* like items should be accounted for in the same way, even though they arise in different periods.

(iv) *Prudence:* costs should be charged, and liabilities accounted for as soon as they are recognised; income should be taken into account when its receipt is reasonably certain.

You may be examined on practical applications of these concepts. Q5 *Research and development expenditure* is such an example.

(c) *Inflation*
You are required to have a grasp of the effect of changing prices on accounts. Most accounts are prepared under the *historical cost convention*. This means that amounts shown in financial statements take no account of inflation. The consequences are as follows.

(i) If a company increases its profits from £50 to £100 in two successive years, the increase of £50 will be less in *real* terms if the value of the pound is less, in terms of what it can buy, than earlier.

(ii) The balance sheet does not reflect the *real* value of the assets of a business. For example, if an asset in 19X0 costs £50 and 19X1 costs £100 owing to inflation, it might be argued that the actual *value* of the asset purchased in 19X0 (subject to any depreciation) should reflect the current cost.

Two approaches to this problem have been CPP (current purchasing power) which adjusts all values by the retail price index and CCA (current cost accounting) which applies different price indices to individual items, to ensure real capital maintenance (ie reported profits should not include amounts needed to maintain the operating capability of the enterprise).

You might like to try Q3 *Limitations of historical cost accounting* and Q6 *Financial reporting*

(d) *'Capital' and 'revenue' expenditure*
Make sure that you can define both of these. Revise Q9 *Capital and revenue* for this essential distinction.

(e) *Users of financial information*
This topic examines the purpose of publishing accounts at all. Financial information is used by:

- those who own an enterprise
- those who run the enterprise
- those who have commercial dealings with the enterprise
- society at large, as represented by government etc.

The information requirements of these users differ. Try Q7 *Information user groups* to see how.

Financial accounting practice

Question practice is essential to acquire fluency in the figure work required. You should pay particular attention to the topics which are likely to come up time and again.

(a) *Control accounts*
Make sure you recognise the difference between a control account and a memorandum account. Entries to control accounts form part of the double entry. Entries to a memorandum account merely note things down in more detail, or in a particular order.

For example, the sales ledger control account contains *all* entries relating to debtors, together in total. The sales ledger provides a memorandum account for each individual debtor. You may sometimes have to *reconcile* differences between the sales ledger and the sales ledger control account. These are usually caused by errors, or transactions in one account not being reflected in another. In questions of this type make sure you adjust the right account: the control account or the memorandum account.

Try Q20 *C Limited*

(b) *Journal entries and suspense accounts*
Do not forget the importance of a neat layout in preparing journal entries. Bear in mind that unless the question states to the contrary, it is advisable to include narrative with each journal entry.

Questions about suspense accounts can take the form either:

(i) of a trial balance which does not balance, for which a suspense account might be useful; or

(ii) a given suspense account balance, with a list of errors in the preparation of the trial balance. Note that not all these errors affect the suspense account.

Try Q25 *In suspense*

(c) *Drawing up accounts*

Commit to memory the standard formats of manufacturing accounts; trading accounts; profit and loss accounts; balance sheets. When asked to prepare one of these statements from a mass of raw data (eg a trial balance followed by a long list of matters requiring adjustment) begin by setting down the first caption of the relevant format (for a trading account, sales; for a balance sheet, fixed assets). Search through the question for the information relevant to that caption and enter the relevant figure, by a working if necessary. Move on to the next caption and repeat the process. It is easy to be daunted by a large volume of data: this methodical procedure should enable you to pick your way through it to a reasonable solution.

Incomplete records questions

These are common, and there is usually a balancing figure to be calculated. For example, a trader may have kept no record of cash drawings or expenses; or the closing stock figure may be unknown because no stocktake was conducted. Often, as in this latter case, the problem will revolve around reconstructing the trading account. It is then essential that you should understand the basic equation of the trading account. A working in the form of an equation may save you from careless error. For example, if you are told that gross profit is a constant 20% on *cost*, the equation can be written:

Cost of sales (100) + gross profit (20) = sales (120)

It is then clear that gross profit is 20/120 x sales; sales is 120/100 x cost of sales etc. Using these ratios it will be possible to calculate the unknown figure. Similarly, if you are told that gross profit is a constant 25% on *sales* you can write the question taking sales as 100, thus:

Sales (100) = gross profit (25) + cost of sales (75)
and again the ratios can be derived.

Try Questions 29 *JB* and 30 *ABC Limited* for practice in preparing accounts.

You may be required to use simple accounting ratios to derive missing figures. For example you might be told that the number of days stock held by a business is 30 days and that the cost of sales for the year is £456,250. Assuming a 365 day year it is possible to derive a value for the average stock as follows.

$$\text{Number of days stocks held} = \frac{\text{stock value}}{\text{average cost of sales per day}}$$

$$30 = \frac{\text{stock value}}{£456{,}250 \div 365}$$

$$\therefore \text{stock value} = £37{,}500$$

Try Q51 *Stuart Limited* for some practice in dealing with simple accounting ratios.

(d) *Income and expenditure accounts*
Memorise the format of the bar trading account and the income and expenditure account itself. Set up 'T' accounts, if necessary, for bar purchases, subscriptions, cash etc. Remember that these questions are simply a form of incomplete records question.

Try Q33 *GD Sports*

(e) *Stock valuation*
This topic covers both areas of the syllabus, financial and cost accounting. You should bear in mind that financial and cost accounts are sometimes prepared for different *users*. Stock valuation is one way in which financial and cost accounts can differ.

Make sure that you are familiar with the different ways of valuing stock.

(i) FIFO (first in, first out). The price of the oldest stock items is charged out first. The value of stock at the end of a period is based on the most recent purchases.

(ii) LIFO (last in, first out). The price of the newest stock items is charged out first and so stock remaining at the end of a period is valued at 'old' prices.

(iii) Average cost. All stocks are put into a 'pool' and their costs are aggregated.

You should be able to discuss the effect each has on profits if prices fluctuate. Remember that the value of closing stock is deducted from cost of sales: the higher the value of closing stock, the lower the cost of sales, the higher the profit.

Try Q39 *Receipts and issues*

(f) *The accounts of limited companies*
The procedure in (c) above applies equally to questions which require you to prepare the accounts of limited companies. The only difference is that the formats you must memorise include certain items that would not be found in the accounts of an unincorporated business, such as dividends and share capital.

You must also be aware of certain specialised accounting transactions such as the issue of shares, the capitalisation of reserves (a 'bonus issue') and the redemption of redeemable shares. Your knowledge of the financial framework of limited companies may also be tested by a written question.

Try Q35 *STU Limited*

Cost accounting practice

(a) *Cost classification*
There are many ways of classifying costs. *Fixed costs* do not vary with the volume of production. *Variable costs*, on the other hand, depend on the number of units produced.

For example, if a manufacturing company is committed to pay rent on its premises, this is a cost incurred irrespective of production achieved. The cost of materials, however, will vary directly with the number of units produced.

Direct costs can be directly related to production. For example a manufactured unit may need an hour of labour. This is a direct cost. The cost of a supervisor's wage is *indirect*. It cannot be tied down to any particular cost unit. Try Q37 *Direct/indirect*

(b) *Absorption and marginal costing*
A key issue is the treatment of fixed indirect costs in the valuation of stock. Under absorption costing, the value of stock includes an element of fixed production overheads. Consequently, at a period end, the value of closing stock will include some of the fixed production overhead of the period. This fixed overhead absorbed in this stock is charged therefore to the profit and loss account in the *next* accounting period, when the stock is sold.

Under marginal costing, the value of stock only includes the variable costs of production. Fixed costs are *period* costs and are written off as they are incurred.

You may be asked about the differences between absorption and marginal costing. To bring this subject into focus try Q46 *Profit differences/costing methods.*

(c) *Budgeting, standard costing, variance analysis*
Be prepared to discuss the nature and function of budgets, and the process by which they are prepared. The difference between cash budgets and 'profit' budgets may be examined. You may be given information relating to a period of production and be required to work out both the profit earned and the attendant cash flows. A methodical approach is needed for this sort of question. A good example is Q61 *Budgets from variances.*

This question also raises 'variance analysis'. You need not go into too much detail, but rather you need to understand the principles of standard costs. The standard cost of an item for a period is its assumed cost. Standards can be arrived at in a number of ways. A *variance* occurs when actual costs differed from standard. Standard costs provide a means of cost control.

Try Q60 *PQR Limited*

Accounting with computers

Questions on this area are not likely to ask how a computer works, but how a computer can be used to perform accounting tasks. The emphasis will therefore be on the practical application of computer technology.
Try Q66 *Microcomputers*

A NOTE ON OBJECTIVE TEST (MULTIPLE CHOICE) QUESTIONS

Introduction

A multiple choice or objective test question consists of two elements.

(a) The *stem.* The stem sets out the problem or task to be solved. It may be in the form of a question, or it may be an unfinished statement which you have to complete.

(b) The *options.* These are the responses from which you must choose the one you believe to be correct. There is only one correct option; the other, incorrect, options are called *distractors.*

Example

An advertisement claims '80 per cent of dog owners buy Brand X'. Assuming the claim to be true, the probability that, of two dog owners chosen at random, exactly *one* buys Brand X is:

A 0.2 **B** 0.16 **C** 0.32 **D** 0.36

Discussion

The stem of the question ends at '... Brand X is'. This stem takes the form of an unfinished statement which must be completed by the student. Four options (A - D) are given and you must choose which you think is correct. In this case the correct answer is 0.32 (option C).

(a) The question above consists of a stem and *four* options. This means that there are three distractors and one correct option. The number of options may vary from one paper to another, but it will not vary within a single paper.

(b) Each option is identified by a letter A,B,C, etc. Once you have identified which you think is the correct option you must record your answer in whatever way the examiner instructs. In the specimen paper students are required to indicate their choice by circling the appropriate letter. For example, in the question above, you would place a circle 'O' around the letter C. But other methods of answering are possible, eg a tick by the appropriate letter. You should read the instructions on the question paper carefully.

(c) In some cases, option D has consisted of the words 'None of these' or 'None of the above'. If you believe that none of the options A - C is correct, you would then circle letter D. It would not be necessary in that case to submit your own calculation of what the true answer is. Indeed, the answer paper does not contain any space for calculations or workings.

One of the advantages claimed for multiple choice questions is that they remove the subjective element in marking. The special answer sheets are documents which can be read and electronically marked by computer. This means that your result on each question depends entirely on whether or not you have circled the correct option. No credit can be given for workings and, unlike with conventional questions, there is no point in submitting neat supporting calculations. Once you are satisfied that you know the correct option, draw a circle around the appropriate letter; if you later change your mind, *clearly* block out your original choice and encircle your new choice.

The use of multiple choice questions has some implications for the way you plan your study and your approach to the examination itself.

A NOTE ON OBJECTIVE TEST (MULTIPLE CHOICE) QUESTIONS

(a) Multiple choice questions are typically very short (perhaps worth one or two marks). A paper set entirely in this format would consist of some 60 to 70 questions, compared with the three to ten questions of a conventional paper. This permits the examiner to range much more widely over the syllabus. The practice of question spotting (ie revising only certain key areas of the syllabus, in the hope that the other areas will not be examined) is unwise even for a conventional examination; with a multiple choice approach, any gaps in knowledge are even more likely to be shown up.

(b) An advantage claimed for multiple choice testing is to some extent a corollary of (a) above. In conventional examinations, students are sometimes confronted with a lengthy question which they are unable to attempt (perhaps because of inadequate revision or because they can see no good way to get started or because the question is ambiguously worded). If this happens, they may fail the exam without having had enough scope to show how much they know. With multiple choice testing, failure to answer a question leads to the loss of only two marks at most. Well-prepared candidates will find they are able to show the extent of their knowledge.

(c) Multiple choice is an ideal format for testing factual knowledge and computational ability; it is much more difficult to test a student's skills in analysis and evaluation. For this reason, you will find that 50% of the marks on the paper will be allocated to conventional questions.

THE MEANING OF EXAMINERS' INSTRUCTIONS

The examinations department of the CIMA has asked the Institute's examiners to be precise when drafting questions. In particular, examiners have been asked to use precise instruction words. It will probably help you to know what instruction words may be used, and what they mean. With the Institute's permission, their list of recommended requirement words, and their meaning, is shown below.

'The following instruction words are recommended to examiners as being precise and likely to elicit the required response. The definitions given here are deliberately short and to the point rather than lengthy.

It is recommended that examiners do not ring the changes between instructions in order to be literary. If the answers to all questions in a particular paper require discussion, it is felt there is nothing against using the word 'discuss' in each requirement.'

Recommended requirement words are:

Advise/recommend	Present information, opinions or recommendations to someone to enable that recipient to take action.
Amplify	Expand or enlarge upon the meaning of (a statement or quotation)
Analyse	Determine and explain the constituent parts of
Appraise/assess/evaluate	Judge the importance or value of
Assess	See 'appraise'
Clarify	Explain more clearly the meaning of
Compare (with)	Explain similarities and differences between
Contrast	Place in opposition to bring out difference(s)
Criticise	Present the faults in a theory or policy or opinion
Demonstrate	Show by reasoning the truth of
Describe	Present the details and characteristics of
Discuss	Explain the opposing arguments
Distinguish	Specify the differences between
Evaluate	See 'appraise'
Explain/interpret	Set out in detail the meaning of
Illustrate	Use an example - chart, diagram, graph or figure as appropriate - to explain something
Interpret	See 'explain'
Justify	State adequate grounds for

THE MEANING OF EXAMINERS' INSTRUCTIONS

List	Itemise
Prove	Show by testing the accuracy of
Recommend	See 'advise'
Reconcile	Make compatible apparently conflicting statements or theories
Relate	Show connections between separate matters
State	Express
Summarise	State briefly the essential points (dispensing with examples and details)
Tabulate	Set out facts or figures in a table.

Requirement words which will be avoided

Examiners have been asked to avoid instructions which are imprecise or which may not specifically elicit an answer. The following words will *not* be used.

Comment	
Consider	as candidates could do this without writing a word
Define	in the sense of stating exactly what a thing is, as CIMA wishes to avoid requiring evidence of rote learning
Enumerate	list is preferred
Identify	
Outline	as its meaning is imprecise. The addition of the word 'briefly' to any of the suggested action words is more satisfactory
Review	
Specify	
Trace	

TEST YOUR KNOWLEDGE: QUESTIONS

1 What is the business equation?

2 Define capital expenditure and revenue expenditure.

3 Distinguish between trade discounts received and settlement discounts received. What is the correct accounting treatment for each?

4 What accounting treatment should be adopted where it is found that a fixed asset's useful life has been estimated incorrectly?

5 At what amount should stocks normally be valued?

6 List five possible methods of establishing the cost of a stock item which is continually being purchased and sold.

7 List four fundamental accounting concepts.

8 What differences are apparent between the accounts of a non-trading organisation and those of a business?

9 Distinguish between:

(a) an ordinary share;
(b) a preference share;
(c) a cumulative preference share.

10 List four capital reserves.

11 Define:

(a) shareholders' funds;
(b) equity shareholders' funds.

12 List four differences between debentureholders and shareholders.

13 Distinguish between authorised, issued, called up and paid up share capital.

14 Distinguish between a reserve and a provision.

15 What is a rights issue?

16 What is the difference between overhead allocation and overhead apportionment?

17 Distinguish between a fixed cost and a variable cost.

18 What is the primary difference between marginal and absorption costing?

19 What is 'contribution'?

20 What is a manufacturing account?

21 Why are cash budgets useful?

22 Name four types of performance standard.

23 What are the two types of cost accounting system, and what is the main difference between them?

24 If a company reduces its selling prices by 20% to 80/100 of their former level, but increases its sales volumes by 20% as a consequence of the price reduction, then profits will be unchanged. True or false?

25 If a company introduces automation into its work practices, so that:

(i) unit variable costs fall, but
(ii) fixed costs increase substantially, so that
(iii) profitability at current sales volumes remains unchanged,

then the decision to automate would have been irrelevant to the future profitability of the company.
True or false?

26 Which account is the odd one out?

A Motor vehicles
B Office furniture and equipment
C Freehold land and buildings
D Plant and machinery
E Stock of materials.

27 If a purchases return of £48 has been wrongly posted to the debit of the sales returns account, but had been correctly entered in the suppliers account, the totals of the trial balance would show:

A the credit side to be £48 more than the debit side
B the debit side to be £48 more than the credit side
C the credit side to be £96 more than the debit side
D the debit side to be £96 more than the credit side
E that both sides were equal in value.

28 The total of the discounts column on the debit side of the cash book, recording cash discounts deducted by customers when paying their accounts, is posted to:

A the debit of the discounts received account
B the credit of the discounts received account
C the debit of the discounts allowed account
D the credit of the discounts allowed account
E nowhere, it is a memorandum column only.

29 You have received a cheque for £285 from a customer, in settlement of his account of £300 from which a cash discount of £15 had been deducted, have banked it and made all the correct entries in your books. The cheque was then returned to you by the bank marked R/D. You would now make the following entries in your books.

A debit bank account £285, debit discount received account £15 and credit the debtors account £300
B credit bank account £285, credit discount received account £15 and debit the debtors account £285
C credit bank account £270, credit discount allowed account £15 and debit the debtors account £285
D credit bank account £285, credit discount allowed account £15 and debit the debtors account £300
E debit bank account £270, debit discount received account £15 and credit the debtors account £285.

(*Note:* R/D means 'refer to drawer'. The cheque has 'bounced'.)

30 The following information relates to a company's year-end stock of finished goods.

	Direct costs of materials and labour	*Production overheads incurred*	*Expected selling and distribution overheads*	*Expected selling price*
	£	£	£	£
Stock category 1	2,470	2,100	480	5,800
Stock category 2	9,360	2,730	150	12,040
Stock category 3	1,450	850	290	2,560
	13,280	5,680	920	20,400

At what amount should finished goods stock be stated in the company's balance sheet?

A £13,280
B £18,730
C £18,960
D £19,650

31 At 31 December 19X5 the provision for doubtful debts in the books of X Ltd included a specific provision for a balance owed by Mr Y. In 19X6 Mr Y was declared bankrupt and X Ltd wishes to write off the balance as a bad debt. The journal entry required is:

A	DEBIT	Bad and doubtful debts expense account
	CREDIT	Debtors control account
B	DEBIT	Bad and doubtful debts expense account
	CREDIT	Provision for doubtful debts account
C	DEBIT	Provision for doubtful debts account
	CREDIT	Bad and doubtful debts expense account
D	DEBIT	Provision for doubtful debts account
	CREDIT	Debtors control account

32 Which one of the following occurrences might explain the existence of a credit balance on an individual debtor's account?

A The bookkeeper failed to make a posting from the returns inwards book to the debtors ledger
B The debtor took advantage of a settlement discount and paid less than the full amount invoiced
C The bookkeeper failed to post an invoice from the sales day book to the debtors ledger
D The bookkeeper posted a total from the returns inwards book to the debtors control account twice by mistake.

33 A company's usage of raw materials during a year was £24,700. Direct labour costs amounted to £38,900, production overheads to £12,600 and administration overheads to £6,800. Opening work in progress was £3,900 and closing work in progress was £4,300.

In the company's manufacturing account, factory cost of finished goods produced is:

A £75,800
B £76,600
C £82,600
D £83,400

34 A public company's ordinary share capital consists of 10,000,000 50p shares, issued at a premium of 20p each. They are currently being traded on the stock exchange at a price of 90p. The company has just announced a 12% final ordinary dividend for 19X6.

The total amount of the net dividend paid out by the company will be:

A £600,000
B £840,000
C £1,080,000
D £1,200,000

35 A textile company makes two products: normal ties and bow ties. The manufacture is split into two processes, cutting and stitching. Wages in the cutting process are £50,000 per annum. In the stitching process, annual wages are £30,000. Manufacturing overheads, which are to be apportioned between departments on the basis of wages costs were £100,000 for the year. The costs in each department are apportioned to the company's product lines as follows.

	Cut	*Stitch*
Bow tie	75%	55%
Normal tie	25%	45%

The production overhead cost attributable to bow ties is:

A £46,875
B £58,500
C £67,500
D £121,500

36 What is an applications package? Give examples of such packages.

TEST YOUR KNOWLEDGE: ANSWERS

1 The business equation is

$$P = I + D - C$$

where P = profit for period
I = increase in net assets over the period (after taking account of drawings)
D = drawings in period
C = new capital injected during period

2 Capital expenditure is expenditure which results in the acquisition of fixed assets or an improvement in their earning capacity.

Revenue expenditure is expenditure incurred either in the day-to-day running of the business (eg administration expenses or distribution expenses) or to maintain the existing earning capacity of fixed assets.

3 Trade discount received is a reduction in the cost of goods purchased, usually because of large or frequently recurring orders. The accounting treatment is to deduct the discounts from the cost of purchases in the *trading* account.

Settlement discount received is a discount awarded for prompt payment of debts. The accounting treatment is to include the discount as a credit in the *profit and loss* account.

4 The asset's remaining net book value should be depreciated over its remaining useful life, as newly estimated.

5 At the lower of their cost and their net realisable value.

6 Possible methods include FIFO, LIFO, average cost, standard cost, NIFO.

7 Going concern; accruals; consistency; prudence.

8 Differences include:
income and expenditure account vs profit and loss account;
surplus/deficit for period vs profit/loss for period;
accumulated fund vs proprietor's capital/share capital;
usually no trading account for non-trading organisations (but sometimes, say, a bar trading account).

9 (a) Ordinary shares carry no right to a fixed dividend but are entitled to all profits left after payment of any preference dividend.

(b) Preference shares carry the right to a fixed dividend, in priority to any dividends on ordinary shares. They usually have priority over ordinary shares for the return of capital in a liquidation. They do not usually carry voting rights.

(c) If a company issues cumulative preference shares it must make good any arrears of preference dividend before paying any ordinary dividend.

10 Share premium account; revaluation reserve; capital redemption reserve; debenture redemption reserve.

11 (a) Shareholders' funds = net assets (or share capital plus reserves).
(b) Equity shareholders' funds = ordinary share capital plus all reserves.

12 Shareholders are members of a company, while debentureholders are creditors; shareholders receive dividends (an appropriation of profit), while debentureholders receive interest (an expense charged against revenue); debentureholders can enforce payment of interest by legal action, while shareholders cannot enforce payment of dividends; debentures are often secured on company assets, while shares are not.

13 Authorised share capital: the maximum amount of share capital that a company is empowered to issue.

Issued share capital: the amount of share capital that has been issued to shareholders.

Called up share capital: the amount the company has asked shareholders to pay, for the time being, on shares issued to them.

Paid up share capital: the amount of the called up share capital which the shareholders have actually paid for.

14 A reserve is an appropriation of distributable profits for a specific purpose, while a provision is an amount charged against revenue as an expense.

15 A rights issue is an issue of shares for cash, usually for less than the prevailing market value, to existing shareholders.

16 Overhead allocation is the allotment of whole items of overhead cost to a cost centre or cost unit. Overhead apportionment is the sharing out of overhead costs over a number of different cost centres or cost units, using an appropriate basis.

17 A fixed cost remains constant over a range of output. A variable cost increases or decreases as the level of output rises or falls.

18 Marginal costing includes only variable production overheads in the valuation of finished goods; absorption costing includes fixed production overheads as well.

19 Contribution is the difference between sales value and the marginal or variable cost of sales.

20 A manufacturing account is an account where the costs of producing finished goods are accumulated.

21 The usefulness of cash budgets is that they enable management to make any forward cash planning decisions that may be needed, such as advising their bank of estimated overdraft requirements or strengthening their credit control procedures to ensure that debtors pay more quickly.

22 Ideal, expected, current and basic.

23 There are two types of cost accounting system - interlocking and integrated. Interlocking accounts contain separate ledgers for cost accounts and for financial accounts. Integrated accounts combine both financial and cost accounts in one system of ledger accounts.

24 False. The problem should be considered in terms of contribution, and it is helpful to use algebra.

Let the current sales price be	s
the variable unit cost be	v
and the sales quantity be	q

Total contribution = contribution per unit x volume of sales
= (s - v)q
= qs - qv.

With the reduction in sales price to 0.8s and the increase in sales volume to 1.2q, total contribution would be:

(0.8s - v)1.2q = 0.96qs - 1.2qv.

Total contribution would be less, because sales revenue would fall (qs to 0.9qs) and total variable costs would rise (qv to 1.2qv).

25 False. Although total contribution and profits are unchanged at the current sales volume, the automation will have important consequences for any increase or fall in sales demand in the future, because the *ratio of contribution to sales has increased.* An increase in sales volume will now result in a faster rate of increase in profits (just as a fall in sales volume would reduce profitability at a faster rate).

26 E; the only current asset: the rest are fixed assets (except for specialised businesses, such as car dealers, furniture suppliers etc).

27 D; a purchase return should be a credit entry. Since it has been debited to the wrong account, and in addition a debit entry has been made in the suppliers account, debits must exceed credits by 2 x £48 = £96.

28 C; the discounts allowed in the cash book provide the data for the posting to the discounts allowed account. (The double entry is debit discounts allowed, credit debtors).

29 D; the original entries (debit cash £285, debit discounts allowed £15, credit debtors £300) are reversed, as indicated in D.

30 B; because 1 is valued at cost to date of £4,570 (cost exceeds net realisable value) but 2 and 3 are valued at net realisable value of £11,890 and £2,270 respectively (costs to date less provision for all losses, ie £200 on 2 and £30 on 3).

31 D; because the debt is already fully provided for and there is therefore no further profit and loss effect; this entry is purely to tidy up the balance sheet.

32 C; because the subsequent posting of a cash payment would not be matched with a debit entry created by an invoice posting.

33 A; £(24,700 + 38,900 + 12,600 + 3,900 - 4,300) the only irrelevant figure is administration overheads, which are not part of cost of sales.

34 A; because the dividend has been expressed as a percentage, the amount payable is 12% x 50p x 10,000,000. If it had been expressed as 12p *per share*, £1.2m would have been payable.

35

	Cut		Stitch		Total
	£		£		£
Production overheads	62,500	(50/80)	37,500	(30/80)	100,000
Bow ties	46,875	(75%)	20,625	(55%)	67,500
Normal ties	15,625	(25%)	16,875	(45%)	32,500
	62,500		37,500		100,000

(*Note:* the wages cost was not supposed to be part of the computation.)

36 Applications packages are ready-made programs written to perform a particular job. A distinction can be made between the following.

(a) *Specific-purpose packages*, such as payroll system packages, sales ledger system packages, and purchase ledger system packages, which are designed to carry out a specific task. The system can be used as soon as the master files have been set up by the user.

(b) *More general purpose packages*, which perform a general type of processing but can be adapted to suit the user's specific needs - eg a spreadsheet package or a database package can be adapted to a variety of user applications.

Packages include:

(a) accounting application packages (eg payroll, sales ledger, nominal ledger);
(b) spreadsheet packages (eg Lotus 123);
(c) database packages (eg DBase III, RMS/38 etc);
(d) word processing packages (eg Wordstar, Wordcraft);
(e) modelling packages (eg for financial modelling, or operational research models such as critical path analysis models, linear programming models);
(f) audit packages, to help auditors with audit work.

SPECIMEN PAPER: RUBRIC

Time allowed three hours

Attempt all questions

Instructions to candidates

1. Enter your examination number on the front of the answer book. Your name must not appear anywhere.

2. State XAF on the line marked subject. The full title of the paper is not required.

3. Attempt all questions.
   Section A carries 60 marks.
   Section B carries 40 marks.

4. Candidates are advised that allocation of the marks between the two sections does not indicate the Institute's assessment of the amount of time that is required to answer the two types of question. Candidates are advised to devote no more than 75 minutes to the multiple choice questions.

5. Use the special answer sheet provided for section A. Begin the answer to each question in section B on a separate page.

6. Answer the questions in section B using:

   * effective arrangement and presentation
   * clarity of explanation
   * logical argument
   * clear, concise and lucid English.

> *Tutorial note:* remember that the allocation of marks in the examination has now changed to 50% for each section. We have left the marks as shown in the specimen paper so that you can judge the relative weightings for this particular set of questions.

SPECIMEN PAPER: OBJECTIVE TEST QUESTIONS

Section A

Each of the questions numbered from 1 to 30 inclusive, given below, has only one correct answer. On the special answer sheet provided, you are required to place a circle 'O' around the letter (either A, B, C or D) that gives the correct answer.

If you wish to change your mind about an answer, block out your first attempt and then encircle another letter. If you do not indicate clearly your final choice, or if you encircle more than one letter, no marks will be awarded for the question concerned.

You are advised to spend no more than 75 minutes on this section.

1 **Capital expenditure is expenditure on:**

- A the purchase of fixed assets
- B working capital
- C the issue of share capital
- D the preliminary expenses of the formation of a limited company

2 **When a business is purchased, any amount paid in excess of the total of the assets, minus the liabilities, taken over is called:**

- A capital employed
- B share premium
- C goodwill
- D working capital

3 **'The quantity in stock is added to the quantity purchased, the value of the quantity in stock is added to the cost of the quantity purchased, and the first total is then divided into the second total.'**

The method of pricing material issues from stores described above is called

- A next in, first out
- B last in, first out
- C average cost
- D standard cost

4 **The effect of a period of inflation on monetary assets (eg cash, debtors) and real or tangible assets (eg land, buildings, plant, stock) is, in general, likely to be that**

- A both monetary and real assets will maintain their purchasing power
- B real assets will maintain their purchasing power but monetary assets will lose some of theirs
- C monetary assets will maintain their purchasing power but real assets will lose some of theirs
- D both monetary and real assets will lose some of their purchasing power

5 'Relevancy, understanding, reliability, completeness, objectivity, timeliness and comparability' are:

A accepted by the accountancy profession to be the desirable characteristics of useful information
B required by the Companies Act 1985 to apply to the financial statements of limited companies
C required of companies listed on a recognised stock exchange by the Fourth Directive of the European Economic Community Commission
D conditions imposed by the International Monetary Fund on the financial statements of the central banks of nations applying for loans, or for the extension of loans

6 'A system in which the cost accounts are distinct from the financial accounts, the two sets of accounts being kept continuously in agreement by the use of control accounts or made readily reconcilable by other means.'

This statement from the CIMA Official Terminology describes:

A joint accounts
B integrated accounts
C concurrent accounts
D interlocking accounts

7 The CIMA Official Terminology defines 'classification' as:

A the assignment of data to the codes contained in an accounting manual
B the arrangement of items in logical groups having regard to their nature or to the purpose to be fulfilled
C a system of symbols designed to be applied to a set of items, to give a brief accurate reference, facilitating entry, collation and analysis
D the division of data between two or more headings on an equitable basis

8 The 'accrual' concept in accounting means that

A revenue and profits are not anticipated, but are recognised by inclusion in the profit and loss account only when realised in the form either of cash or of other assets the ultimate cash realisation of which can be assessed with reasonable certainty
B revenues and costs are matched one with the other and dealt with in the profit and loss account of the period to which they relate irrespective of the period of receipt or payment
C every entry in the financial accounts involves the recording of simultaneous receiving and giving of value by an entity
D there is a consistency of treatment of like items (accounting bases and policies) within each accounting period and from one period to the next

9 What effect will a year-end adjustment for a prepaid revenue expense have on the balance sheet and profit and loss account?

A To reduce profit and reduce current assets
B To reduce profit and reduce current liabilities
C To increase profit and increase current liabilities
D To increase profit and increase current assets

10 A credit balance of £2,000 brought down on X Limited's account in the books of Y Limited means that

A Y Limited has sold to X Limited goods worth £2,000
B X Limited owes Y Limited £2,000
C Y Limited owes X Limited £2,000
D X Limited has sold to Y Limited goods worth £2,000

11 If a purchase return of £100 had been wrongly posted to the debit of the sales return account, but had been correctly entered in the supplier's account, the totals of the trial balance would show

A the debit side to be £200 more than the credit side
B the debit side to be £100 more than the credit side
C the credit side to be £100 more than the debit side
D the debit and credit sides to be equal in value

12 The total of the discounts column on the debit side of the cash book, recording cash discounts deducted by customers when paying their accounts, is posted to

A the debit of the discount allowed account
B the credit of the discount allowed account
C the debit of the discount received account
D the credit of the discount received account

13 When a transaction is credited to the correct ledger account but debited incorrectly to printing and stationery account instead of to plant and machinery account, the error is known as:

A an error of principle
B an error of commission
C an error of omission
D a compensating error

14 The interest on a company's debentures:

A may only be paid when there is a profit, and is debited to profit and loss account
B may only be paid when there is a profit, and is debited to appropriation account
C must be paid even if there is no profit, and is debited to appropriation account
D must be paid even if there is no profit, and is debited to profit and loss account

15 A statement of business assets and liabilities at a particular moment in time is called a

A trial balance
B balance sheet
C profit and loss account
D source and application of funds statement

16 Working capital is

A share capital plus reserves
B liquid assets plus stocks
C current assets minus current liabilities
D current assets minus stocks

17 Your bank statement shows a balance at the year end of £260 overdrawn. The statement includes bank charges of £1,041 which have not been entered in your cash book. There are also unpresented cheques totalling £645, and cash paid in of £97 which has been entered in your cash book but not yet been credited by the bank. The bank balance which should appear in your balance sheet should be:

A £233 in hand
B £260 overdrawn
C £288 in hand
D £808 overdrawn

18 A document sent by X to Y which lists the items which Y has bought from X, with their prices and values, is called by X a

A credit note
B delivery note
C purchase invoice
D sales invoice

19 The imprest system is a system whereby

A the bank statement and the cash book are reconciled regularly
B a trial balance is taken out every month
C a petty cashier is reimbursed regularly for his payments
D a 'book value' of stock is calculated by using the average percentage rate of gross profit on sales

20 A company manufactures and sells a single product. When it manufactures and sells 100 units per year its total costs and total sales are £10,000 and £11,000 respectively. When it manufactures and sells 101 units per year its total costs and total sales become £10,049.50 and £11,110.00 respectively. The marginal cost of manufacturing and selling one unit of product is

A £49.50
B £99.50
C £100.00
D £110.00

21 The standard quantity of material X to be used in manufacturing one unit of product Y is 10 kgs and the standard price is £2 per kg. The budgeted quantity of product Y to be manufactured in a period was 1,000 units. The actual quantity manufactured during that period was 900 units, the quantity of material X used was 9,600 kgs and the actual price paid for material X was £2.10 per kg. The total cost variance for material X during that period was

A £160 adverse
B £800 favourable
C £1,200 adverse
D £2,160 adverse

22 A fixed budget is one which

A is a plan for capital expenditure in monetary terms
B is designed to remain unchanged irrespective of the volume of output or turnover attained
C deals with income and/or expenditure applicable to a particular function
D by recognising the difference in behaviour between fixed and variable costs in relation to fluctuations in output, turnover, or other variable factors such as number of employees, is designed to change appropriately with such fluctuations

23 Cost allocation is

A the division of costs amongst two or more cost centres in proportion to the estimated benefit received, using a proxy, eg square metres
B the collection of costs attributable to cost centres and cost units using the costing methods, principles and techniques prescribed for a particular business entity
C the charging of discrete identifiable items of cost to cost centres or cost units
D the process of attributing cost to cost centres or cost units resulting from cost allocation and cost apportionment

24 An accountant has expressed an opinion that, in preparing the year-end financial statements, a computer cannot perform the following tasks:

1 calculate prepayments and accruals
2 prepare a list showing the age of debtors
3 calculate the depreciation charge
4 decide whether or not the accounts are to be prepared on a going concern basis

Which of these tasks can the computer **not** perform?

A 1 and 2 only
B 4 only
C 3 and 4 only
D all of them

25 Consider whether the following accounting operations can be performed on a computer

1 keeping a register of plant and machinery
2 writing up a cash book
3 writing up a nominal ledger
4 preparing the weekly wages payroll

Which of these tasks can be done on a computer?

A 4 only
B 1 and 4 only
C 1,2 and 4 only
D all of them

26 The accounting concept of capital maintenance means that

A the share capital of a limited company may not be returned to the shareholders unless either a new issue of shares is made for cash or a transfer is made out of profits that are available for distribution to a capital redemption reserve, of an amount equal to the value of the share capital redeemed
B in the case of certain fixed assets whose nature requires large and expensive repairs every few years to maintain them in good condition, the intervening years shall all bear a proportion of the cost by means of an annual charge which is credited to a repairs and maintenance equalisation provision
C the figure of profit from which cash dividends may be payable to shareholders shall allow for the impact of price changes on the funds needed to continue the existing business and maintain its operating capability
D the return on capital employed of a business shall be at least equal to the rate of interest which it is required to pay on its loan capital

27 The economic value of an asset is

A the net value that would be received if the assets were sold in an arms-length transaction in a free competitive market
B the net cash flows which the asset should earn during the remainder of its life discounted at the appropriate cost of capital
C the historical cost of the asset multiplied by the proportional increase in the retail price index since its purchase
D the cost of replacing an asset, when substantial technological change has occurred since its purchase, by a modern equivalent asset incorporating this technological change

28 Fungible assets are assets which

A are substantially indistinguishable one from another
B appear in the balance sheet but have no realisable value
C do not have a physical identity
D are readily convertible into cash

29 Stocks of finished products should normally be valued at

A total cost (prime cost plus manufacturing, administration, selling and distribution costs)
B the lower of prime cost or net replacement value
C selling prices minus direct selling costs (eg commission, discounts, carriage, packing)
D the lower of prime cost plus production and other overhead which is required to bring the product to its present location and condition or the net realisable value of the separate items of stock

30 The following passage describes in words a formula for calculating one of the methods of depreciation:

The original cost of a fixed asset minus the estimated realisable value at the end of its life is apportioned to each year of its estimated life in proportion to the estimated life (in years) of the asset plus one year and minus the number of years the asset has been in use, divided by the total of all the years that the asset is expected to be in use.

The method of depreciation described is

A straight-line
B diminishing (reducing) balance
C double declining balance
D the sum of the years' digits

Total marks available for section A: 60

Objective test: answer sheet

Section A

1	A	B	C	D
2	A	B	C	D
3	A	B	C	D
4	A	B	C	D
5	A	B	C	D
6	A	B	C	D
7	A	B	C	D
8	A	B	C	D
9	A	B	C	D
10	A	B	C	D
11	A	B	C	D
12	A	B	C	D
13	A	B	C	D
14	A	B	C	D
15	A	B	C	D
16	A	B	C	D
17	A	B	C	D
18	A	B	C	D
19	A	B	C	D
20	A	B	C	D
21	A	B	C	D
22	A	B	C	D
23	A	B	C	D
24	A	B	C	D
25	A	B	C	D
26	A	B	C	D
27	A	B	C	D
28	A	B	C	D
29	A	B	C	D
30	A	B	C	D

Section B

Answer both questions (20 marks each)

1. **ABC**

The trial balance of ABC public limited company at 31 December 1984 was as follows.

	Dr £'000	*Cr* £'000
Ordinary share capital		500
Retained profit		500
Fixed assets at cost	810	
Depreciation provision		170
Material stock at actual cost	100	
Work in progress at standard cost	10	
Finished goods stock at standard cost	200	
Debtors	120	
Cash at bank	110	
Creditors for materials		40
Taxation due		90
Proposed dividend		50
	1,350	1,350

The following summarised transactions occurred during the year to 31 December 1985.

1. Invoiced credit sales were £1,000,000 at actual selling prices.
2. The standard manufacturing cost of the finished goods sold was £700,000.
3. £990,000 was received in cash from debtors.
4. Invoiced credit purchases of materials for stock amounted to £420,000.
5. £415,000 was paid in cash to creditors for materials.
6. Issues of direct materials from material stock amounted to £410,000 at actual cost, £400,000 at standard cost.
7. Direct wages paid in advance amounted to £104,000. This included an adverse variance of £4,000.
8. Depreciation for the year was £80,000, and was apportioned as follows.

	£
Manufacturing	60,000
Distribution	10,000
Administration	10,000

9. Manufacturing overhead paid in cash amounted to £156,000. There was a favourable variance of £5,000 on manufacturing overhead. Standard manufacturing overhead charged to work in progress was £221,000.
10. The standard cost of finished goods manufactured and handed over by the factory to the finished goods storekeeper was £720,000.

11. The following amounts were paid in cash.

	£
Distribution costs	80,000
Administration expenses	100,000
Fixed assets purchased	70,000
Taxation due	90,000
Proposed dividend	50,000
Interim dividend	25,000

You are given the following additional information.

12. In its ledger the company keeps the material stock account at actual cost and the work in progress and finished goods stock accounts at standard manufacturing cost.

13. Standard manufacturing cost includes direct materials, direct wages and manufacturing overhead (including the apportionment of depreciation).

14. Total cost variance accounts are kept in the ledger for materials, wages and manufacturing overhead, but not for distribution costs and administration expenses.

You are required to enter the information given above in the appropriate accounts in the company's ledger and to show the closing trial balance at 31 December 1985.

(20 marks)

2. **DEF**

DEF Limited was incorporated and commenced trading on 1 January 1985. The company's trial balance at 31 December 1985 was as follows.

	Dr £'000	*Cr* £'000
Ordinary share capital		500
Fixed assets at cost	400	
Debtors	80	
Cash at bank	46	
Creditors		25
Purchases of materials	304	
Manufacturing wages	118	
Manufacturing overhead	210	
Distribution costs	152	
Administration expenses	215	
Sales		1,000
	1,525	1,525

You are given the following information.

1 The company manufactures and sells a single product. During 1985 120,000 units of product were manufactured and 100,000 units sold.

2. Materials issued to the factory during 1985 cost £244,000.

3. A physical stocktaking of materials and finished products confirmed that the book stocks were correct.

4. Work in progress at the year end consisted of 4,000 units of partly-finished product in the factory. These units were 50% completed in all respects.

5. Depreciation of fixed assets (which were all purchased on 1 January 1985) is to be calculated at the rate of 10% per annum on cost, and is to be apportioned between manufacturing, distribution and administration in the ratio of 8:1:1.

6. Stocks of finished products and work in progress are to be valued at the appropriate proportion of manufacturing cost, which consists of materials, manufacturing wages and manufacturing overhead (including the apportionment of depreciation).

7. A provision of 5% of the year-end debtors is to be created for doubtful debts. This item is to be treated as a distribution cost.

8. Prepayments and accruals at 31 December 1985 were as follows.

	Prepayments £'000	*Accruals* £'000
Manufacturing wages		4
Manufacturing overhead		2
Distribution costs	1	1
Administration expenses	2	3

9. Provision is to be made at the year end for corporation tax at the rate of 50% of the net profit, and a proposed dividend of 10% on the ordinary share capital.

You are required to prepare a profit and loss account for DEF Limited for the year ended 31 December 1985 and a balance sheet at that date, not necessarily in the form required by the Companies Acts.

(20 marks)

Section A

1 A This is (roughly) the definition of capital expenditure.

2 C Again, the question comprises a definition, this time of purchased goodwill.

3 C

4 B Monetary assets decline in purchasing power in periods of inflation (eg £1 will buy less in one year's time than it will now).

5 A

6 D

7 B

8 B

9 D Current assets are increased (a prepayment is similar to a debtor).

10 C D is incorrect because the credit balance may have arisen for some reason other than the purchase of goods (eg the £2,000 may represent rent owed by Y to his landlord X).

11 A The supplier's account would be correctly debited £100. There would then be two debit entries and no credit. Debits would exceed credits by £200. (The returns should have been credited to the purchases returns account).

12 A The double entry is to debit discount allowed (an expense in the P & L account) and credit debtors (to reduce amounts owing from them).

13 A

14 D Debenture interest is not an appropriation, because debenture holders are creditors, not owners of the business.

15 B A trial balance includes expenses and revenues as well as assets and liabilities.

16 C

17 D The bank reconciliation is as follows.

	£	£
Balance per bank statement		(260) o/d
Bank charges not in cash book	1,041	
Outstanding lodgement	97	
		1,138
		878
Unpresented cheques		645
Unadjusted balance per cash book		233

But to arrive at the balance sheet figure, the cash book should be adjusted to take account of bank charges. The balance sheet figure will be £233 - £1,041 = £808 overdrawn.

18 **D**

19 **C**

20 **A** The marginal cost of the last unit is £10,049.50 - £10,000, £10,000 being the cost of producing the previous 100 units. The sales figures would only be relevant if we were discussing marginal *revenue*.

21 **D**

	£
Actual expenditure on material X (9,600 x £2.10)	20,160
Standard expenditure (900 x 10 x £2)	18,000
Variance (adverse)	2,160

22 **B**

23 **C**

24 **B** Task 4 is a problem calling for the exercise of human judgement.

25 **D**

26 **C**

27 **B**

28 **A** For example, items of stock; or shares held as an investment.

29 **D**

30 **D**

Section B

Tutorial note: Question 1 is very lengthy, requiring the preparation of 21 ledger accounts and the subsequent extraction of a trial balance. It is reasonably straightforward provided you understand the point of note 12. This means that transfers from raw materials stock account to work in progress account, and from work in progress account to finished goods account, must be at *standard* manufacturing cost. As you will see in the suggested solution, this means that a variance emerges in the materials stock account, because materials are initially debited to the account not at standard cost, but at actual purchase price.

The main complication in question 2 is the valuation of closing stocks of work in progress and finished goods. The approach is to calculate the total manufacturing costs incurred in the year and the number of units produced. It is then possible to calculate the cost of producing a single unit. Note that the number of units produced includes not only the 120,000 fully completed units, but also 4,000 units of work in progress. As each of these units is 50% complete, they are equivalent to 2,000 fully completed units and are valued accordingly.

1. **ABC**

ORDINARY SHARE CAPITAL

	£'000		£'000
		Balance b/f	500

RETAINED PROFIT

	£'000		£'000
		Balance b/f	500

FIXED ASSETS COST

	£'000		£'000
Balance b/f	810	Balance c/f	880
Cash at bank (11)	70		
	880		880

FIXED ASSETS DEPRECIATION

	£'000		£'000
Balance c/f	250	Balance b/f	170
		Overhead accounts (8)	80
	250		250

MATERIALS STOCK

	£'000		£'000
Balance b/f	100	Work in progress (6)	400
Creditors (4)	420	Materials variance (6)	10
		Balance c/f	110
	520		520

WORK IN PROGRESS

	£'000		£'000
Balance b/f	10	Finished goods (10)	720
Materials stock (6)	400	Balance c/f	11
Direct wages (7)	100		
Manufacturing overhead (9)	221		
	731		731

FINISHED GOODS

	£'000		£'000
Balance b/f	200	Cost of sales (2)	700
Work in progress (10)	720	Balance c/f	220
	920		920

DEBTORS

	£'000		£'000
Balance b/f	120	Cash at bank (3)	990
Sales (1)	1,000	Balance c/f	130
	1,120		1,120

CASH AT BANK

	£'000		£'000
Balance b/f	110	Creditors for materials (5)	415
Debtors (3)	990	Direct wages (7)	104
		Manufacturing overhead (9)	156
		Distribution overhead (11)	80
		Administration overhead (11)	100
		Fixed assets cost (11)	70
		Taxation due (11)	90
		Dividends (11)	75
		Balance c/f	10
	1,100		1,100

CREDITORS FOR MATERIALS

	£'000		£'000
Cash at bank (5)	415	Balance b/f	40
Balance c/f	45	Materials stock (4)	420
	460		460

TAXATION DUE

	£'000		£'000
Cash at bank (11)	90	Balance b/f	90

DIVIDENDS

	£'000		£000
Cash at bank (11)	75	Balance b/f	50
		Balance c/f	25
	75		75

SALES

	£'000		£'000
		Debtors (1)	1,000

COST OF SALES

	£'000		£'000
Finished goods (2)	700		

MATERIALS VARIANCE

	£'000		£'000
Materials stock (6)	10		

DIRECT WAGES

	£'000		£'000
Cash at bank (7)	104	Work in progress (7)	100
		Direct wages variance (7)	4
	104		104

DIRECT WAGES VARIANCE

	£'000		£'000
Direct wages (7)	4		

MANUFACTURING OVERHEAD

	£'000		£'000
Depreciation (8)	60	Work in progress (9)	221
Cash at bank (9)	156		
Manufacturing o'hd variance (9)	5		
	221		221

DISTRIBUTION OVERHEAD

	£'000		£'000
Depreciation (8)	10	Balance c/f	90
Cash at bank (11)	80		
	90		90

ADMINISTRATION OVERHEAD

	£'000		£'000
Depreciation (8)	10	Balance c/f	110
Cash at bank (11)	100		
	110		110

MANUFACTURING OVERHEAD VARIANCE

	£'000		£'000
		Manufacturing overhead	5

TRIAL BALANCE AT 31 DECEMBER 1985

	£'000	£'000
Ordinary share capital		500
Retained profit		500
Fixed assets cost	880	
Fixed assets depreciation		250
Materials stock	110	
Work in progress	11	
Finished goods	220	
Debtors	130	
Cash at bank	10	
Creditors for materials		45
Dividends	25	
Sales		1,000
Cost of sales	700	
Materials variance	10	
Direct wages variance	4	
Distribution overhead	90	
Administration overhead	110	
Manufacturing overhead variance		5
	2,300	2,300

2. **DEF**

PROFIT AND LOSS ACCOUNT
YEAR ENDED 31 DECEMBER 1985

	£'000	£'000
Sales		1,000
Purchases	304	
Manufacturing wages (118 + 4)	122	
Manufacturing overhead (210 + 2 + (W1) 32)	244	
	670	
Less closing stock:		
Materials (304 - 244)	(60)	
Work in progress (W2)	(10)	
Finished goods (W2)	(100)	
Cost of sales (100,000 units at (W2) £5)		(500)
Gross profit		500
Distribution costs (W3)	160	
Administration expenses (215 + 3 - 2 + (W1) 4)	220	
		(380)
Net profit before tax		120
Taxation at 50%		(60)
Profit after tax		60
Dividend (10% x 500)		(50)
Retained profit for the year		10

BALANCE SHEET AS AT 31 DECEMBER 1985

	Cost £'000	*Dep'n* £'000	*Net* £'000
Fixed assets	400	40	360
Current assets			
Stocks			
Materials	60		
Work in progress	10		
Finished goods	100		
		170	
Debtors (less provision)		76	
Prepayments		3	
Cash at bank		46	
		295	
Current liabilities			
Trade creditors		25	
Accruals		10	
Taxation		60	
Dividend		50	
		145	
Net current assets			150
			510
Capital and reserves			
Ordinary share capital			500
Retained profit			10
			510

Workings

1. *Depreciation*

Charge for year : 10% x £400,000 =	£40,000
Apportioned:	
manufacturing (80%)	£32,000
distribution (10%)	£ 4,000
administration (10%)	£ 4,000

2. *Valuation of work in progress and finished goods stock*

Units of production in year:	
completed units	120,000
partially completed (4,000 x 50%)	2,000
	122,000

Total manufacturing costs in year per trading account were £670,000 - £60,000 = £610,000

Each unit of production therefore had a manufacturing cost of $\frac{£610,000}{122,000} = £5$

Valuation

Finished goods	(20,000 x £5)	= £100,000
Work in progress	(4,000 x 50% x £5)	= £ 10,000

3. *Distribution costs*

	£'000
Per trial balance	152
Depreciation (W1)	4
Provision for doubtful debts (5% x £80,000)	4
Accrual	1
Prepayment	(1)
	160

INDEX TO QUESTIONS AND SUGGESTED SOLUTIONS

		Question	Suggested solution
	ACCOUNTING THEORY AND OBJECTIVES OF FINANCIAL STATEMENTS		
	Basic principles		
1	*Basic revision question: Prudence*	49	111
2	Definitions (CIMA Stage 1)	49	112
3	Limitations of historical cost accounting (CIMA Stage 1)	49	113
4	Estimation/depreciation (CIMA Stage 1)	49	114
5	Research and development expenditure (CIMA Stage 1)	50	114
6	Financial reporting (CIMA Stage 1)	50	115
7	Information user groups (CIMA Stage 1)	50	116
8	Information needs of creditors (CIMA Stage 1)	50	117
9	Capital and revenue (CIMA Stage 1)	50	118
10	Engineering	51	119
11	Closing stock	51	120
	FINANCIAL ACCOUNTING PRACTICE		
	Ledger accounting and control accounts		
12	*Basic revision question: RBD*	52	120
13	AB the sole trader (CIMA Stage 1)	53	121
14	Plant and machinery (CIMA Stage 1)	53	123
15	Bramwell factors	54	124
16	Journal entries (CIMA Stage 1)	55	125
17	XYZ Limited (CIMA Stage 1)	55	126
18	Ledger accounts with control accounts	56	127
19	Nostla Products Limited	57	128
20	C Limited (CIMA Stage 1)	59	129
	Bank reconciliations		
21	*Basic revision question: Rex Limited*	60	131
22	JC Limited (CIMA Stage 1)	60	131
	Suspense accounts		
23	*Basic revision question: Timber products*	62	132
24	RST	63	133
25	In suspense (CIMA Stage 1)	64	135

INDEX TO QUESTIONS AND SUGGESTED SOLUTIONS

		Question	Suggested solution
Incomplete records			
26	*Basic revision question: Herbert Howell*	65	136
27	Miss Teek	66	138
28	Byrd	67	141
29	JB (CIMA Stage 1)	68	145
30	ABC Limited (CIMA Stage 1)	70	146
Income and expenditure accounts and company accounts			
31	*Basic revision question: Profit forecast*	72	151
32	HB Tennis club (CIMA Stage 1)	73	152
33	GD Sports (CIMA Stage 1)	74	153
34	Tallis Limited	75	156
35	STU Limited (CIMA Stage 1)	77	159
COST ACCOUNTING PRACTICE			
Cost classifications			
36	*Basic revision question: Cost behaviour*	79	163
37	Direct/indirect (CIMA Stage 1)	79	165
Materials and stocks			
38	*Basic revision question: Rosebowl Hotel*	79	166
39	Receipts and issues (CIMA Stage 1)	80	167
40	Materials control	80	168
41	Component X (CIMA Stage 1)	80	169
Absorption and marginal costs			
42	*Basic revision question: Job costing*	81	170
43	SP (CIMA Stage 1)	81	171
44	Apportionment (CIMA Stage 1)	82	172
45	Abacus Limited (CIMA Stage 1)	84	174
46	Profit differences/costing methods (CIMA Stage 1)	85	176
47	LMN Limited (CIMA 1 Stage 1)	86	178
48	Fixed overheads (CIMA Stage 1)	86	180
Manufacturing and departmental accounts			
49	*Basic revision question: Abcoll Limited*	87	182
50	Manufacturing Limited (CIMA Stage 1)	88	183
51	Stuart Limited (CIMA Stage 1)	90	186
52	Dick Turnip	91	191
53	Smith Plc (CIMA Stage 1)	92	194

	Question	Suggested solution
Budgets and budgetary control		
54 *Basic revision question: Honecker*	94	197
55 Cash budgets	95	198
56 Flexible budget (CIMA Stage 1)	96	199
57 Single product (CIMA Stage 1)	97	201
Standard costing		
58 *Basic revision question: Mycost Limited*	98	202
59 AR Limited (CIMA Stage 1)	98	203
60 PQR Limited (CIMA Stage 1)	100	206
61 Budgets from variances (CIMA Stage 1)	101	207
Integrated and non-integrated accounting systems		
62 *Basic revision question: Integrated accounting system*	103	211
63 Integrated (CIMA Stage 1)	103	212
64 Interlocking Limited	106	214
ACCOUNTING WITH COMPUTERS		
65 *Basic revision question: Checklist*	107	217
66 Microcomputers (CIMA Stage 1)	107	218
67 Matrix form (CIMA Stage 1)	107	219
68 Spreadsheets and databases (CIMA Stage 1)	107	221
OBJECTIVE TESTS		
Quiz 1	225	246
Quiz 2	228	247
Quiz 3	231	249
Quiz 4	234	251
Quiz 5	237	253
Quiz 6	239	255
Quiz 7	242	257

QUESTIONS

1 **BASIC REVISION QUESTION: PRUDENCE**

(a) Given that prudence is the main consideration, briefly discuss under what circumstances, if any, revenue might be recognised when:

(i) goods have been acquired by the business which it confidently expects to resell very quickly;
(ii) a customer places a firm order for goods;
(iii) goods are delivered to the customer;
(iv) the customer is invoiced for goods;
(v) the customer pays for the goods;
(vi) the customer's cheque in payment for the goods has been cleared by the bank.

(b) Explain briefly how the prudence concept might be applied:

(i) to the valuation of stocks;
(ii) to the valuation of debtors;
(iii) to the valuation of land and buildings.

2 **DEFINITIONS (15 marks)**

In producing accounts, it is essential that they should be comparable with accounts of the same company for previous years to identify trends. In order to try and ensure this, the accounting profession identified four fundamental accounting concepts and included them in a statement of standard accounting practice. These were:

(a) the going concern concept;
(b) the accruals concept;
(c) the consistency concept; and
(d) the prudence concept.

Required

Explain any *three* of the above concepts with an example to illustrate *each* answer.

3 **LIMITATIONS OF HISTORICAL COST ACCOUNTING (15 marks)**

Describe the main limitations of preparing balance sheets and profit and loss accounts on an historical cost accounting basis in times of inflation.

4 **ESTIMATION/DEPRECIATION (15 marks)**

The writing down of fixed asset values over the life of the asset is a time-consuming, costly exercise, which, because of the use of estimates, serves no useful purpose.

You are required to criticise this statement with reference to accounting concepts and capital maintenance theories.

5 **RESEARCH AND DEVELOPMENT EXPENDITURE (15 marks)**

(a) Explain the three classifications of research and development expenditure. (6 marks)

(b) Discuss the treatment of research and development expenditure with special reference to the fundamental concepts of accounting. (9 marks)

6 **FINANCIAL REPORTING (15 marks)**

The Corporate Report identified many different user groups of accounting information.

With regard to the particular needs of shareholders, *you are required:*

(a) to describe their information needs; (6 marks)

(b) to explain how changing price levels affect the information provided and discuss the steps which may be taken to ensure that their information needs continue to be satisfied despite such changes. (9 marks)

7 **INFORMATION USER GROUPS (15 marks)**

Different users of accounting information each have different information needs in addition to the basic fundamental accounting details which are produced by companies in their annual reports.

You are required to identify six main user groups. Give brief details of their information needs to show how those needs differ.

8 **INFORMATION NEEDS OF CREDITORS (15 marks)**

What are the information needs of trade creditors and other lenders to a company?

To what extent are these needs satisfied by the publication of a company's accounts?

9 **CAPITAL AND REVENUE (10 marks)**

In the context of period profit measurement, consistent classification is required of both income and expenditure between capital and revenue items.

Required

(a) Distinguish between capital and revenue items, illustrating your answer with examples. (6 marks)

(b) Explain the importance of the consistency concept in relation to this distinction. (4 marks)

10 ENGINEERING (16 marks)

You are the accountant to a medium size engineering company, and are presented with the following information relating to the valuation of part of the stock held by that company at the year end.

	Historical cost	*Replacement cost*	*Net realisable value*
	£	£	£
Sheet steel	8,000	9,500	8,600
Iron bars	7,600	6,750	7,000
Electrical circuits	12,400 *	16,000	13,100
	28,000	32,250	28,700

* The historical cost valuation of the electrical circuits has been reached as follows.

	£	£
Purchases during the year		
250 at £30 =		7,500
300 at £35 =		10,500
200 at £40 =		8,000
		26,000
Issues		
200 at £40 =	8,000	
160 at £35 =	5,600	
		13,600
Closing stock		12,400

You are required:

(a) to state what principles should be applied to the valuation of the stock; and (6 marks)

(b) to explain clearly what value you, as the accountant, would place on stock. (10 marks)

11 CLOSING STOCK (19 marks)

An evaluation of a physical stock count on 30 April 19X2 in respect of the financial year ending on that date at Cranfleet Commodities has produced a figure of £187,033.

The firm's book keeper has approached you, as the accountant, for assistance in dealing with the following matters to enable him to arrive at a final figure of closing stock for inclusion in the annual accounts.

(i) 320 components included at their original cost of £11 each can now be bought in for only £6 each due to overproduction by the manufacturer. This drop in price is expected to be only temporary and the purchase price is expected to exceed its original figure within 12 months. Cranfleet Commodities intends to continue selling the existing stock at the present price of £15 each.

(ii) It has been discovered that certain items which had cost £5,657 have been damaged. It will cost £804 to repair them after which they can be sold for £6,321.

(iii) On one stock sheet a sub-total of £9,105 has been carried forward as £1,095.

(iv) 480 units which cost £1.50 each have been extended at £15.00 each.

(v) The firm has sent goods with a selling price of £1,500 (being cost plus 25%) to a customer on a sale or return basis. At 30 April 19X2, the customer had not signified acceptance, but the goods have not been returned, and consequently had not been included in the physical stock count.

(vi) Included in stock were goods bought on credit for £4,679 from Byfleet Enterprises. At 30 April 19X2, Cranfleet Commodities had not paid this account.

(vii) Byfleet Enterprises had also sent some free samples (for advertising purposes only). These have been included in stock at their catalogue price of £152.

You are required, taking account of such of the above facts as are relevant, to calculate a closing stock figure for inclusion in the 19X2 annual accounts of Cranfleet Commodities, giving reasons for the action you have taken in each individual case.

12 BASIC REVISION QUESTION: RBD

The ledger of RBD & Co included the following account balances.

	At 1 June 19X4	*At 31 May 19X5*
	£	£
Rents receivable: prepayments	463	517
Rent and rates payable:		
prepayments	1,246	1,509
accruals	315	382
Creditors	5,258	4,720
Provision for discounts on creditors	106	94

During the year ended 31 May 19X5 the following transactions had arisen.

	£
Rents received by cheque	4,058
Rent paid by cheque	7,491
Rates paid by cheque	2,805
Creditors paid by cheque	75,181
Discounts received from creditors	1,043
Purchases on credit	*to be derived*

Required

Post and balance the appropriate accounts for the year ended 31 May 19X5, deriving the transfer entries to profit and loss account, where applicable.

13 AB THE SOLE TRADER (15 marks)

AB, a sole trader, commenced trading on 1 January 19X0. He has provided you with the following details of his telephone costs.

Quarterly rental payable in advance on 1 January, 1 April, 1 July and 1 October	£15
Telephone calls payable in arrears	£
January to March 19X0 paid 1 April 19X0	159
April to June 19X0 paid 1 July 19X0	211
July to September 19X0 paid 1 October 19X0	183

He is to prepare his first accounts to 31 October 19X0 and estimates that the total cost of his calls for October 19X0 will be £74.

AB also pays rent quarterly in advance for his premises and has made payments as follows.

	£
1 January 19X0	600
1 April 19X0	750
1 July 19X0	750
1 October 19X0	750

You are required:

(a) to prepare AB's ledger accounts for telephone and rent for the period from 1 January 19X0 to 31 October 19X0, showing clearly the amounts to be transferred to his profit and loss account for the period together with any balances carried forward on 31 October 19X0; (9 marks)

(b) to explain the accruals concept in relation to profit measurement theory. (6 marks)

14 PLANT AND MACHINERY (20 marks)

A company keeps its plant and machinery account in its ledger at net book value (cost minus depreciation), and the balance on this account at 31 October 19X4 was £38,125. This was made up of plant purchased at cost on the dates given below.

	£
30 April 19X4	10,000
31 January 19X3	5,000
31 July 19X2	20,000
31 October 19W9	15,000
30 April 19W5	30,000
31 October 19W4	40,000

Depreciation is calculated at the rate of 10% per annum on cost commencing on the date of purchase and continuing to the date of sale or disposal, except that depreciation must not exceed 100% of cost. Any profit or loss on sale or disposal is shown as a separate item from depreciation in the profit and loss account.

The following transactions occurred during the year ended 31 October 19X5.

(i) 31 January 19X5 - sold plant which originally cost £10,000 on 30 April 19W5 for £400 in cash
(ii) 30 April 19X5 - purchased plant costing £8,000
(iii) 31 July 19X5 - scrapped plant which originally cost £5,000 on 31 October 19W9
(iv) 31 October 19X5 - scrapped plant which originally cost £10,000 on 31 October 19W4.

Required

(a) Write up the plant and machinery account (at net book value) in the company's ledger for the year ended 31 October 19X5 carrying down a balance on that date and showing clearly the depreciation charge and any profit or loss on sale or disposal for the year. (15 marks)

(b) Give the entries in the balance sheet at 31 October 19X5 for plant and machinery showing cost, depreciation and net book value. (5 marks)

15 BRAMWELL FACTORS (17 marks)

You are preparing the annual accounts of Bramwell Factors for the year 19X2. The following matters have to be taken into account at 31 December.

(a) The provision for discounts allowed to debtors, which at present has a balance of £229.53 needs to be reduced to £157.40.

(b) Debts totalling £64.80 are now known to be bad and must be written off. However, an amount of £21.44 written off as a bad debt in the previous year has now been recovered in full, but the cheque has not yet been paid into the bank or posted to the accounts.

(c) Owing to an oversight, discount has been allowed to a credit customer on the gross invoiced amount of £80.00 at the rate of 10%. A rate of 6% should have been used.

(d) Electricity accrued amounts to £36.71 whilst insurance premiums of £22.45 have been prepaid.

(e) In October 19X2 the business employees received a general wages increase, backdated to July 19X2. There are now amounts of wages arrears, totalling £126.55, payable to former employees who left shortly before the wages award was announced and who have not yet been traced. It has been decided that the wage packets will be opened and the cash paid back into the bank until those ex-employees can be found.

(f) Amounts earned by employees in the last week of December 19X2 but not due to be paid until January 19X3, comprise wages £464.12 and salaries £301.70.

(g) During 19X2 the exterior of the warehouse was repainted at a cost of £5,000. The whole of this amount was wrongly debited to premises account. It is the policy of Bramwell Factors to provide depreciation on the closing balances of fixed assets and this has already been done. The annual rate of depreciation on premises is 2%, calculated on the straight line basis and assuming no residual value.

(h) In December 19X2, Bramwell Factors had bought goods on credit from Conbrec Limited for £452.10 and had sold goods on credit to that same company for £163.04. These sums have been correctly posted to their respective accounts. These accounts are to be settled in contra at 31 December 19X2 and the remaining balance by cheque in January 19X3.

Required

Prepare suitable entries in the journal of Bramwell Factors to record each of the above matters at 31 December 19X2. (Your entries should also include items affecting the cash and bank accounts).

16 JOURNAL ENTRIES (15 marks)

The following is a list of transactions in which M Limited was involved.

(i) On 27 January M Limited sold on credit to N Limited goods to the value of £20,000.

(ii) On 31 January M Limited drew a three months' bill of exchange on N Limited for £20,000 which N Limited accepted.

(iii) On 1 February M Limited discounted this bill with its bank and received £19,250.

(iv) On 5 February M Limited purchased on credit from P Limited goods to the value of £10,000.

(v) On 6 February P Limited drew a three months' bill of exchange on M Limited for £10,000, which M Limited accepted.

(vi) On 7 February P Limited discounted this bill with its bank and received £9,625.

(vii) On 30 April the bank informed M Limited that N Limited had dishonoured the bill by non-payment. The bank exercised its right of recourse against the drawer and debited M Limited's bank account with the value of the bill.

(viii) On 6 May M Limited paid the bill originally drawn on it by P Limited.

(ix) On 7 May N Limited went into liquidation.

(x) On 23 September the liquidator of N Limited paid a first and final dividend of 30 pence in the £ to the unsecured creditors.

You are required to show the journal entries (including cash items) for the above transactions in the books of M Limited.

17 XYZ LIMITED (15 marks)

The following details relate to the payroll of XYZ Limited for the week ended 27 October 19X0.

	£
Net wages paid	34,000
PAYE deducted	16,500
National Insurance	
Employees	2,900
Employers	3,300

The company pays its employees £5.00 per hour plus an overtime premium of £2.50 per hour in excess of the normal working week.

A summary of the employees' time sheets for the same week shows the following.

Hours worked on customers' jobs	8,260
Hours worked on company capital expenditure	1,300
Non productive hours	940
	10,500

The figure for hours worked on customers' jobs includes 80 hours overtime which was worked at the specific request of a customer, who has agreed to pay for the overtime premium.

You are required:

(a) to show the journal entry for the wages of the company for week ended 27 October 19X0 including an appropriate narrative; (7 marks)

(b) to explain the treatment of costs incurred on the company's capital expenditure and the implications for profit measurement. (8 marks)

18 LEDGER ACCOUNTS WITH CONTROL ACCOUNTS (20 marks)

The following balances on accounts appeared in a company's ledger at 30 September 19X1.

	£
Debtors ledger control	63,158
Creditors ledger control	32,000
Provision for bad debts	3,158
Provision for discount receivable	800
Provision for discount allowable	1,500

During the year to 30 September 19X2 the following summarised transactions occurred.

	£
Sales on credit	550,000
Purchases on credit	276,000
Sales returns	6,000
Purchases returns	4,000
Cash received from customers (excluding bad debt recovered)	514,268
Cash paid to suppliers	258,100
Discount allowed to customers	12,790
Discount received from suppliers	5,900
Bad debts written off against the provision	4,100
Amount recovered from debtor whose debt had been written off as bad in previous years	542
Debtor and creditor accounts settled by setting-off one against the other	4,000

The company's policy is to pass all transactions for bad debts written off and recovered through the provision for bad debts account, and to make the provision at the year end equal to 5% of the debtors. The company also makes provisions for discounts allowable equal to 2½% of the year end debtors minus the provision for bad debts, and for discount receivable equal to 2½% of the year end creditors.

You are required to enter the above information in the following ledger accounts, to carry down the balances at 30 September 19X2 and, in the case of (c), (d) and (e), to show the amount transferred to profit and loss account.

(a) Debtors ledger control.
(b) Creditors ledger control.
(c) Provision for bad debts.
(d) Discount receivable.
(e) Discount allowable.

19 NOSTLA PRODUCTS LIMITED (17 marks)

Nostla Products Limited includes in its accounting system a purchases ledger control account and a sales ledger control account. The company's trial balance at 30 November 19X8 included the following entries.

	Dr £	*Cr* £
Purchases ledger control account	1,242	24,647
Sales ledger control account	39,650	941

The following is a summary of the company's transactions with its suppliers and customers during the year ended 30 November 19X9.

	£
Goods purchased and received from supplier	
Gross invoice value before trade discounts	210,786
Net invoice price after trade discounts	176,410
Goods returned to suppliers	
Gross invoice value before trade discounts	16,476
Net invoice price after trade discounts	15,113
Amounts due to suppliers	
Total full amount	163,300
Settled by payment of	159,400
Goods sold to customers	
Gross invoice value before trade discounts	344,700
Net invoice price after trade discounts	310,690
Goods returned from customers	
Gross invoice value before trade discounts	7,600
Net invoice price after trade discounts	6,764
Amounts due from customers	
Full amount	307,610
Settled by receipt of	306,540
Customers' debts written off as irrecoverable	970

It has been decided to create a provision for doubtful debts at 30 November 19X9 of 2½% of the total amount due from customers indebted to the company; there was no provision for doubtful debts in the trial balance at 30 November 19X8.

At 30 November 19X9 both the purchases ledger and the sales ledger included accounts with J Dyke.

	£
Purchases ledger	1,630 credit
Sales ledger	1,268 debit

It has been decided to set off J Dyke's balance in the sales ledger against his balance in the purchases ledger.

The purchases ledger at 30 November 19X9 included the following accounts with debit balances.

	£
G Graham	930
L Brooke	420

The sales ledger at 30 November 19X9 included the following accounts with credit balances.

	£
P Hilltop	230
H Pumpkin	83
K Bunson	500

Required

(a) Prepare the following accounts for the year ended 30 November 19X9 in the books of Nostla Products Limited.

Purchases ledger control account.
Sales ledger control account.

Note: the balances outstanding on 30 November 19X9 should be brought down.

(b) (i) Show the journal entry for the creation of the provision for doubtful debts at 30 November 19X9.

Note: the journal narrative is required.

(ii) Explain the relationship between the provision for doubtful debts and the sales ledger control account.

20 C LIMITED (15 marks)

The sales ledger control account of C Limited is shown below.

Sales ledger control

	Dr £		*Cr* £
Balance b/d	70,814.16	Balance b/d	1,198.73
Sales	54,738.36	Sales returns	2,344.39
Dishonoured cheque	607.15	Payments received	68,708.27
Debt collection fees	108.81	Contra	378.82
		Bad debts written off	474.16
Balance c/d	1,194.26	Balance c/d	54,358.37
	127,462.74		127,462.74

A listing of the individual customer balances in the sales ledger gives the following totals.

Debits	£55,136.65	Credits	£1,194.26 (used above)

The following facts have been discovered.

1. No entries have been made in the sales ledger for the debt collection charges or bad debts written off.
2. A credit balance of £673.46 has been taken as a debit balance in the listing of the customer balances.
3. The sales day book has been over-added by £500.00
4. The account of the customer who settled by contra was debited with £378.82
5. A balance on a customer's account of Debit £347.58 has been entered on the listing of balances as Debit £374.85.
6. The sales returns day book had been under-added by £10.00
7. The dishonoured cheque has been entered in the sales ledger as credit £601.75.

Required

(a) Correct the sales ledger control account (commencing with the closing balances given) and reconcile the listing of the individual balances to the new sales ledger control account balances. (12 marks)

(b) Explain the purposes of control accounts. (3 marks)

21 BASIC REVISION QUESTION: REX LIMITED

According to the cash book of Rex Limited the company has an overdrawn credit balance at the bank of £380 on 30 June 19X5, but this is not borne out by the bank statement of the same date. An investigation into the difference yields the following information.

(a) A standing order for a charitable subscription of £40 had been paid by the bank on 29 June but no entry had been made in the cash book.

(b) A cheque paid for advertising on 10 June for £179 had been entered in the cash book as £197.

(c) Cheques for £1,037 sent to creditors on 30 June were not paid by the bank until 6 July.

(d) Cheques received from customers amounting to £1,680 were paid into the bank on 30 June but were not credited by the bank until 1 July.

(e) On 20 June a cheque for £114 was received from a customer in settlement of an invoice for £120. An entry of £120 had been made in the cash book.

You are required:

(a) to prepare a bank reconciliation (calculating the balance per the bank statement);

(b) to explain how a company may have reduced its bank balance during an accounting period but still have earned a profit for that same period.

22 JC LIMITED (15 marks)

JC Limited uses a computerised accounting system to record its transactions and produce a trial balance. The trial balance which was produced by the system at 31 March 19X0 showed that the bank balance was £12,879 overdrawn, but the bank statement which is reproduced below showed a balance on the same date of £5,467 credit. A bank account control report was printed by the accountant of JC Limited so that the transactions could be compared.

JC LIMITED
COMPUTERISED ACCOUNTING SYSTEM
CONTROL REPORT
BANK ACCOUNT CODE 99 TRANSACTIONS FROM 1.3.X0 TO 31.3.X0

Date		*Dr*	*Cr*	*Bal*
		£	£	£
1.3.X0	Balance			4,201
2.3.X0	J Smith & Sons	1,405		
	White Brothers	697		6,303
4.3.X0	Brown & Co	234		6,537
7.3.X0	543987		279	
	543988		1,895	
	543989		11,987	(7,624)
10.3.X0	J Lake	1,386		(6,238)
12.3.X0	543990		1,497	
	543991		547	
	543992		296	(8,578)
17.3.X0	Grey Enterprises	2,569		
	Hunt Lodges	34		
	B Black	643		(5,332)
24.3.X0	543993		2,305	(7,637)
31.3.X0	543994		5,242	(12,879)

The bank statement for the same month was as follows.

STATEMENT OF ACCOUNT

NATTOWN BANK — 31 March 19X0

March		*Dr*	*Cr*	*Bal*
		£	£	£
1	Balance			3,529
3	Counter credit		2,489	6,018
4	543986	237		5,781
6	Counter credit		2,102	7,883
7	Bank charges	195		
	543988	1,895		5,793
9	Counter credit		234	6,027
11	543985	68		5,959
13	Brown & Co cheque dishonoured	234		
	543989	1,197		4,528
14	Counter credit		1,486	6,014
17	543990	1,497		
	543992	296		4,221
23	Counter credit		5,332	9,553
25	Standing order: rates	4,029		5,524
27	543991	57		5,467
31	Balance			5,467

The balances on 1 March 19X0 were reconciled, the difference being partly due to the following cheques which were unpresented on that date.

Cheque	543984	£1,512
	543985	£68
	543986	£237

You are required

(a) to prepare a bank reconciliation statement at 31 March 19X0; (12 marks)

(b) to list three reasons why bank reconciliation statements should be prepared regularly. (3 marks)

23 BASIC REVISION QUESTION: TIMBER PRODUCTS

The trial balance as at 30 April 19X7 of Timber Products Limited was balanced by the inclusion of the following debit balance.

Difference on trial balance suspense account £2,513

Subsequent investigations revealed the following errors.

(i) Discounts received of £324 in January 19X7 have been posted to the debit of the discounts allowed account.

(ii) Wages of £2,963 paid in February 19X7 have not been posted from the cash book.

(iii) A remittance of £940 received from K Mitcham in November 19X6 has been posted to the credit of B Mansell Limited.

(iv) In December 19X6, the company took advantage of an opportunity to purchase a large quantity of stationery at a bargain price of £2,000. No adjustments have been made in the accounts for the fact that three quarters, in value, of this stationery was in stock on 30 April 19X7.

(v) A payment of £341 to J Winters in January 19X7 has been posted in the personal account as £143.

(vi) A remittance of £3,000 received from D North, a credit customer, in April 19X7 has been credited to sales.

The draft accounts for the year ended 30 April 19X7 of Timber Products Limited show a net profit of £24,760.

Timber Products Limited has very few personal accounts and therefore does not maintain either a purchase ledger control account or a sales ledger control account.

Required

(a) Prepare the difference on trial balance suspense account showing, where appropriate, the entries necessary to correct the accounting errors.

(b) Prepare a computation of the corrected net profit for the year ended 30 April 19X7 following corrections for the above accounting errors.

(c) Outline the principal uses of trial balances.

24 RST (17 marks)

The draft final accounts of RST Limited for the year ended 30 April 19X5 showed a net profit for the year after tax of £78,263.

During the subsequent audit, the following errors and omissions were discovered. At the draft stage a suspense account had been opened to record the net difference.

(a) Trade debtors were shown as £55,210. However:
   (i) bad debts of £610 had not been written off;
   (ii) the existing provision for doubtful debtors, £1,300, should have been adjusted to 2% of debtors;
   (iii) a provision of 2% for discounts on debtors should have been raised.

(b) Rates of £491 which had been prepaid at 30 April 19X4 had not been brought down on the rates account as an opening balance.

(c) A vehicle held as a fixed asset, which had originally cost £8,100 and for which £5,280 had been provided as depreciation, had been sold for £1,350. The proceeds had been correctly debited to bank but had been credited to sales. No transfers had been made to disposals account.

(d) Credit purchases of £1,762 had been correctly debited to purchases account but had been credited to the supplier's account as £1,672.

(e) A piece of equipment costing £9,800 and acquired on 1 May 19X4 for use in the business had been debited to purchases account. (The company depreciates equipment at 20% per annum on cost.)

(f) Items valued at £2,171 had been completely omitted from the closing stock figure.

(g) At 30 April 19X5 an accrual of £543 for electricity charges and an insurance prepayment of £162 had been omitted.

(h) The credit side of the wages account had been under-added by £100 before the balance on the account had been determined.

Required

Using relevant information from that given above, you are required to do the following.

(a) Prepare a statement correcting the draft net profit after tax. (13 marks)

(b) Post and balance the suspense account. (Note: the opening balance of this account has not been given and must be derived.) (4 marks)

25 IN SUSPENSE (15 marks)

The trial balance of MLN plc was extracted on 30 September 19X9 and showed the following totals.

Debit	£1,605,668	Credit	£1,603,623

A suspense account was opened and used to record the difference until it could be investigated but the company continued to prepare its draft accounts by applying the prudence concept to the treatment of the suspense account balance.

After investigation the following facts emerged.

1. Discounts allowed of £1,248 had not been entered in the sales ledger control account.

2. A credit sale of £857 to SEC Limited had not been entered in the sales day book.

3. A contra entry between the sales and purchases ledgers had been entered in the control accounts as follows.

Debit sales ledger control	£731
Credit purchase ledger control	£731

4. An invoice of £54 for telephones had been entered in the telephone account as £45 but was correctly entered in the creditors account.

5. Bank charges of £66 had been correctly entered in the expense account but had not been entered in the cash book.

6 One of the pages of the purchase day book had been incorrectly totalled as £11,269 instead of £11,629.

7. During the year a fixed asset was sold for £740. Its original cost was £3,600 and its net book value at the date of disposal was £800. The only entry made was to debit the proceeds of sale to the bank account.

Required

(a) Record in the suspense account the effects of correcting 1 to 7 above. (5 marks)

(b) Reconcile the difference between the balance on the sales ledger control account in the original trial balance and the sum of the individual customer balances in the sales ledger; the original control account balance was £327,762. (5 marks)

(c) Prepare a statement of adjusted net profit showing both the original net profit of £412,967 as given by the draft accounts and the net profit after correcting items 1 to 7 above. (5 marks)

26 BASIC REVISION QUESTION: HERBERT HOWELL

The following trial balance has been extracted from the ledger of Herbert Howell, a sole trader, as at 31 May 19X9, the end of his most recent financial year.

HERBERT HOWELL
TRIAL BALANCE AS AT 31 MAY 19X9

	Dr £	*Cr* £
Property, at cost	90,000	
Equipment, at cost	57,500	
Provisions for depreciation (as at 1 June 19X8)		
property		12,500
equipment		32,500
Stock, as at 1 June 19X8	27,400	
Purchases	259,600	
Sales		405,000
Discounts allowed	3,370	
Discounts received		4,420
Wages and salaries	52,360	
Bad debts	1,720	
Loan interest	1,560	
Carriage out	5,310	
Other operating expenses	38,800	
Trade debtors	46,200	
Trade creditors		33,600
Provision for bad debts		280
Cash on hand	151	
Bank overdraft		14,500
Drawings	28,930	
13% loan		12,000
Capital, as at 1 June 19X8		98,101
	612,901	612,901

The following additional information as at 31 May 19X9 is available.

(a) Stock as at the close of business was valued at £25,900.

(b) Depreciation for the year ended 31 May 19X9 has yet to be provided as follows.

Property - 1% using the straight line method.
Equipment - 15% using the straight line method.

(c) Wages and salaries are accrued by £140.

(d) 'Other operating expenses' include certain expenses prepaid by £500. Other expenses included under this heading are accrued by £200.

(e) The provision for bad debts is to be adjusted so that it is 0.5% of trade debtors as at 31 May 19X9.

(f) 'Purchases' include goods valued at £1,040 which were withdrawn by Mr Howell for his own personal use.

Required

Prepare Mr Howell's trading and profit and loss account for the year ended 31 May 19X9 and his balance sheet as at 31 May 19X9.

27 MISS TEEK (18 marks)

Miss Anne Teek runs a market stall selling old pictures, china, copper goods and curios of all descriptions. Most of her sales are for cash although regular customers are allowed credit. No double entry accounting records have been kept, but the following information is available.

SUMMARY OF NET ASSETS AT 31 MARCH 19X8

	£	£
Motor van		
Cost		3,000
Depreciation		2,500
Net book value		500
Current assets		
Stock	500	
Debtors	170	
Cash at bank	2,800	
Cash in hand	55	
	3,525	
Less current liabilities		
Creditors	230	
Net current assets		3,295
		3,795

Additional information

1. Anne bought a new motor van in January 19X9 receiving a part exchange allowance of £1,800 for her old van. A full year's depreciation is to be provided on the new van, calculated at 20% on cost.

2. Anne has taken £50 cash per week for her personal use. She also estimates that petrol for the van, paid in cash, averages £10 per week.

3. Other items paid in cash were as follows.

Sundry expenses	£24
Repairs to stall canopy	£201

4. Anne makes a gross profit of 40% on selling prices. She is certain that no goods have been stolen but remembers that she appropriated a set of glasses and some china for her own use. These items had a total selling price of £300.

5. Trade debtors and creditors at 31 March 19X9 are £320 and £233 respectively, and cash in hand amounts to £39. No stock count has been made and there are no accrued or prepaid expenses.

A summary of bank statements for the twelve months in question shows the following.

	£
Credits	
Cash banked (all cash sales)	7,521
Cheques banked (all credit sales)	1,500
Dividend income	210
	9,231
Debits	
Purchase of motor van	3,200
Road fund licence	80
Insurance on van	323
Creditors for purchases	7,777
Rent	970
Sundry	31
Accountancy fees (re current work)	75
Bank overdraft interest (six months to 1 October 19X8)	20
Returned cheque (bad debt)	29
	12,505

The bank statement for 1 April 19X9 shows an interest charge of £27.

You are required to prepare Anne's trading and profit and loss account for the year to 31 March 19X9, and a balance sheet as at that date.

(Assume a 52 week year.)

28 BYRD (17 marks)

Old Mr Byrd has run his corner shop in one of London's twilight areas for many years. On 30 September 19X0, vandals looted his shop, taking all his stock and the till float of £75. Fortunately the windows had been boarded up and only minor damage was done to the premises themselves.

Mr Byrd was fully insured against theft and he has asked you to help him formulate an insurance claim. Investigations on your part reveal the following.

(a) Net assets on 1 January 19X0 were as follows.

	£	£
Fixtures and fittings:		
cost	900	
accumulated depreciation	400	
net book value		500
Stock		2,700
Debtors		430
Prepayments (rates)		30
Cash in bank		2,140
Cash float in till		30
Trade creditors		1,650
Accrued electricity		40

(b) Bank statements for the nine months from 1 January show the following.

	£
Receipts	
Cash and cheques banked	20,060
Investment income	182
	20,242

	£
Payments	
Trade creditors	17,850
Rent (1 Jan - 31 Dec)	1,200
Electricity	155
Insurance: theft	45
life	107
Telephone	83
	19,440

(c) The following were paid in cash from the till.

	£
Trade creditors	2,400
Drawings (per month)	295

(d) Mr Byrd's gross profit margin on sales has averaged 20% in recent years.

(e) The fixtures and fittings are now thought to be worth only £200.

(f) A cheque for £52, in respect of the telephone bill for the quarter ending 29 September 19X0, is not shown on the bank statements until 3 October.

(g) Rates for the period 1 April - 1 October amount to £75 and have not yet been paid.

(h) Trade debtors and creditors amounted to £270 and £1,900 respectively on 30 September 19X0.

Required

(a) Prepare Mr Byrd's trading and profit and loss account for the nine months to 30 September 19X0.

(b) Prepare the balance sheet as at 30 September 19X0.

29 JB (20 marks)

JB, a sole trader, does not maintain a set of ledgers to record his accounting transactions. Instead he relies on details of cash receipts/payments, bank statements and files of invoices. He started business on 1 June 19X7 with private capital of £5,000 which comprised a second hand van valued at £1,500 and £3,500 cash which he deposited in a business bank account on that date. He has not prepared any accounts since he commenced trading and you have agreed to prepare his first set of accounts for him in respect of the 18 months ended 31 December 19X8.

You have discovered the following.

1. A summary of his cash transactions from his cash book for the period was as follows.

		£	£
Receipts	Capital introduced	3,500	
	Cash sale receipts	21,250	
	Sale of motor van	850	
			25,600
Payments	Cash paid to bank	21,350	
	Cash purchases	2,160	
	Postage and stationery	474	
	Motor expenses	919	
			24,903
Cash in hand at 31 December 19X8			697

2. A summary of his bank statements shows the following.

		£	£
Receipts	Cash paid into bank	21,190	
	Bank loan	4,500	
	Credit sale receipts	1,955	
			27,645
Payments	Purchase of goods	7,315	
	Office equipment	1,280	
	Motor van	4,000	
	Drawings	5,400	
	Rent and rates	1,850	
	Light and heat	923	
			20,768
Balance at 31 December 19X8			6,877

3. The office equipment was purchased on 1 October 19X7.

4. The new motor van was purchased on 1 April 19X8 to replace the original second hand van which was sold on the same date.

5. JB expects the office equipment to last five years but to have no value at the end of its life. The motor van bought on 1 April 19X8 is expected to be used for three years and to be sold for £700 at the end of that time.

6. The cost of goods unsold on 31 December 19X8 was £1,425. JB thought he would sell these for £2,560 with no item being sold for less than its original cost.

7. On 31 December 19X8 JB owed £749 for goods bought on credit and was owed £431 for goods sold on credit. Of these amounts £189 was due from/to XEN Limited which is both a customer and supplier of JB. A contra settlement arrangement has been agreed by both JB and XEN Limited.

8. Rent and rates paid includes an invoice for £1,200 for the rates due for the year to 31 March 19X9.

9. No invoice was received for light and heat in respect of November and December 19X8 until 25 February 19X9. This showed that the amount due for the three months ended 31 January 19X9 was £114.

10. The bank loan was received on 1 January 19X8. Interest is charged at 10% per annum on the amount outstanding.

You are required to prepare JB's trading and profit and loss account for the period ended 31 December 19X8 and his balance sheet at that date in vertical form.

30 ABC LIMITED (35 marks)

The balance sheet of ABC Limited at 31 October 19X6 was as follows.

	£'000	£'000	£'000
Fixed assets at cost		4,000	
Less depreciation provision		1,550	
			2,450
Current assets			
Material stock		1,400	
Work in progress		400	
Finished goods stock		2,500	
Debtors	1,000		
Less bad debts provision	50		
		950	
Prepayments: rates	37		
fire insurance	2		
		39	
Cash at bank		582	
Cash in hand		2	
		5,873	
Current liabilities			
Creditors for materials	490		
Accruals: wages	23		
rent	10		
Corporation tax 19X5/X6	480		
Proposed dividends	560		
		1,563	
			4,310
			6,760
Share capital and reserves			
Ordinary shares of £0.50, fully paid			4,000
Retained profit			2,760
			6,760

On 17 September 19X7 a fire destroyed all the financial records of ABC Limited. The bank statement for the year ended 31 October 19X7 showed the following.

	£'000	£'000
Balance at 31 October 19X6		587
Cash banked		13,768
		14,355
Less payments		
Creditors for materials	5,328	
Wages	1,418	
Rent for eleven months ended 31 August 19X7	110	
Rates for the year ending 31 March 19X8	108	
Fire insurance for the year ending 31 January 19X8	24	
Manufacturing overheads	2,458	
Administration costs	1,906	
Selling and distribution costs	1,403	
Fixed assets purchased on 30 April 19X7	1,000	
Corporation tax for 19X5/X6 (final settlement of liability originally estimated at £480,000)	500	
Dividends	560	
		14,815
Balance at 31 October 19X7		460

You ascertain the following information.

1. Unpresented cheques, all made out to creditors for materials, were £5,000 at 31 October 19X6 and £7,000 at 31 October 19X7.

2. The only cash received was from debtors. Out of this, £3,000 was taken to pay administration costs. Cash in hand at 31 October 19X7 was £1,000. There were no cash sales.

3. Discounts allowed and received cannot be ascertained and should be ignored. During the year debts amounting to £30,000 were written off against the provision as bad. Good debtors at 31 October 19X7 were £1,200,000. It is the company's practice to have a year end bad debts provision of 5% of the good debts.

4. Creditors for materials at 31 October 19X7 (after deducting the unpresented cheques) amounted to £460,000. No debtors and creditors accounts were set off by contra during the year.

5. At 31 October 19X7 there were accrued wages of £5,000.

6. A physical stocktaking at 31 October 19X7 gave the following figures.

	£'000
Material stock	1,700
Work in progress	300
Finished goods stock	3,000

7. Fixed assets are to be depreciated at the rate of 10% per annum on cost from the date of purchase to the date of disposal.

8. The following items are to be apportioned between manufacturing, administration and selling according to the ratios given below.

	Manufacturing	*Administration*	*Selling*
Depreciation	80%	10%	10%
Bad debts	–	–	100%
Rent	75%	20%	5%
Rates	75%	20%	5%
Fire insurance	85%	10%	5%

9. A provision of £600,000 is to be made for corporation tax on the year's profit.

10. A provision is to be made for a proposed final dividend of £0.08 per share.

Required

(a) Prepare ABC Limited's profit and loss account for the year ended 31 October 19X7. (19 marks)

(b) Prepare the balance sheet at that date. (16 marks)

31 BASIC REVISION QUESTION: PROFIT FORECAST

The directors of the company by which you are employed as an accountant have received the forecast profit and loss account for 19X3 which disclosed a net profit for the year of £36,000.

This is considered to be an unacceptably low figure and a working party has been set up to investigate ways and means of improving the forecast profit.

The following suggestions have been put forward by various members of the working party.

(1) 'Every six months we deduct income tax of £10,000 from the debenture interest and pay it over to the Inland Revenue. If we withhold these payments, the company's profit will be increased considerably.'

(2) 'I see that in the three months August to October 19X3 we have forecast a total amount of £40,000 for repainting the exterior of the company's premises. If, instead, we charge this amount as capital expenditure, the company's profit will be increased by £40,000.'

(3) 'In November 19X3, the replacement of a machine is forecast. The proceeds from the sale of the old machinery should be credited to profit and loss account.'

(4) 'There is a credit balance of £86,000 on general reserve account. We can transfer some of this to profit and loss account to increase the 19X3 profit.'

(5) 'The company's £1 ordinary shares, which were originally issued at £1 per share, currently have a market value of £1.60 per share and this price is likely to be maintained. We can credit the surplus £0.60 per share to the 19X3 profit and loss account.'

(6) 'The company's premises were bought many years ago for £68,000, but, following the rise in property values, they are now worth at least £300,000. This enhancement in value can be utilised to increase the 19X3 profit.'

You are required as the accounting member of the working party, to comment on the feasibility of each of the above suggestions for increasing the 19X3 forecast profit.

32 HB TENNIS CLUB (15 marks)

The HB tennis club was formed on 1 April 19X0 and has the following receipts and payments account for the six months ended 30 September 19X0.

Receipts	£	*Payments*	£
Subscriptions	12,600	Purchase of equipment	4,080
Tournament fees	465	Groundsman's wages	4,520
Bank interest	43	Rent and business rates	636
Sale of club ties	373	Heating and lighting	674
Life membership fees	4,200	Postage and stationery	41
		Court maintenance	1,000
		Tournament prizes	132
		Purchase of club ties	450
		Balance c/d	6,148
	17,681		17,681

Notes

1. The annual subscription fee is £300. On 30 September there were five members who had not paid their subscription, but this money was received on 4 October 19X0.

2. The equipment is expected to be used by the club for five years, after which time it will need to be replaced. Its estimated scrap value at that time is £50.

3. During the six months, the club purchased 100 ties printed with its own design. Forty of these ties remained unsold at 30 September 19X0.

4. The club had paid business rates in advance on 30 September 19X0 of £68.

5. The club treasurer estimates that the following amounts should be accrued for expenses.

	£
Groundsman's wages	40
Postage and stationery	12
Heating and lighting	53

6. The life membership fees received relate to payments made by four families. The scheme allows families to pay £1,050 which entitles them to membership for life without further payment. It has been agreed that such receipts would be credited to income and expenditure in equal instalments over ten years.

You are required

(a) to prepare the club's Income and Expenditure account for the six months ended 30 September 19X0; (8 marks)

(b) to prepare the club's balance sheet at 30 September 19X0. (7 marks)

33 GD SPORTS (20 marks)

The GD Sports Club committee has recently asked if you would prepare the club accounts for the year ended 31 March 19X8. You have agreed and have found that they do not keep any accounting records other than notes concerning the subscriptions of members and the amounts paid for expenses. During discussions with the club committee you discover the following matters.

(a) The club does not have a bank account and conducts all its transactions in cash, any surplus being paid into a building society account. Interest credited to this account for the year to 31 March 19X8 was £350.

(b) A summary of the payments for the year is as follows.

	£
Deposit to building society account	250
Purchase of dartboards	100
Heat/light	262
Repairs to snooker tables	176
Bar creditors	7,455
Rental of premises	1,000
Club match referees' fees and expenses	675
Trophies, etc (treated as an expense)	424
Refreshments for visiting teams	235

(c) The club has 100 members who each pay an annual subscription of £5. However, on 31 March 19X7 ten members had already paid their subscriptions for 19X7/X8.

On 31 March 19X8 two members who had not been seen in the club since August 19X7 had not paid subscriptions for 19X7/X8 and it has been decided that the amount due be written off and that their names be removed from the list of members.

(d) The club has only two sources of income from club members: subscriptions and bar sales. A profit margin of 30% of selling price is normally applied to determine bar selling prices but during the year £397 of goods were sold at cost.

(e) The club has the following other assets and liabilities.

	1 April 19X7	*31 March 19X8*
	£	£
Equipment	4,000	?
Building society account	4,600	5,200
Bar stocks	840	920
Bar creditors	630	470
Cash in hand	nil	nil
Creditor for heat/light	34	41

(f) Equipment is depreciated at 10% of the value of equipment held on 31 March each year.

You are required to prepare the following.

(a) A bar trading account for the ended 31 March 19X8. (8 marks)
(b) An income and expenditure account for the year ended 31 March 19X8. (7 marks)
(c) A balance sheet at 31 March 19X8. (5 marks)

34 TALLIS LIMITED (25 marks)

The following balances were extracted from the books of Tallis Limited, retailers of midgets, fidgets and didgets, as of 30 June 19X5.

		£'000
25p ordinary shares		210
8% £1 preference shares		100
12% debentures		200
General reserve		40
Retained profits 1 July 19X4		52
Freehold property:	cost	300
	depreciation 1 July 19X4	8
Plant and equipment:	cost	275
	depreciation 1 July 19X4	121
Stock		149
Provision for doubtful debts 1 July 19X4		23
Purchases		2,785
Sales		3,400
Discounts allowed		9
Debenture interest		12
Wages and salaries		214
Light and heat		27
Rates and insurance		65
Printing, postage and stationery		53
Sundry expenses		18
Legal fees		16
Preference dividend		8
Bank overdraft charges		11
Suspense		97
Bank overdraft		14
Cash in hand		3
Debtors		280
Creditors		154

You are also given the following information.

(a) The suspense account consists of the following balances.

	£'000
Proceeds of the issue of a further 80,000 ordinary shares	40
Proceeds of the sale of old equipment	3
Less consideration for purchase of H Purcell & Co	140
	97

(b) Tallis placed the following values on the assets of H Purcell & Co which they took over.

	£'000
Plant and equipment	80
Stock	30

All the stock taken over was sold by Tallis before the year end.

(c) During the year the company disposed of equipment which had cost £35,000 and had a written down value of £4,000. The depreciation charge for the year is to be 25% of the cost (or valuation) of plant and equipment owned at 30 June 19X5.

(d) At the time of purchase the buildings were thought to constitute one third of the value of the freehold premises and were estimated to have a fifty year life. The depreciation charge for the year is to be based on these figures. The premises were revalued at £500,000 on 30 June 19X5 and this revaluation is to be reflected in the accounts.

(e) Stock in hand on 30 June 19X5 consisted of the following.

Item	*Quantity*	*Cost price per unit*	*Selling price per unit*	*Future marketing cost per unit*
		£	£	£
Midget	10,000	6	10	2
Fidget	20,000	4	8	1
Didget	9,000	5	7	3

(f) There have been no bad debts during the year but it is thought that the doubtful debts provision should be adjusted to 5% of total debtors.

(g) It is estimated that an amount of £8,000 was owed for electricity as at 30 June 19X5 and rates and insurance included £48,000 paid in respect of the calendar year 19X5.

(h) The directors wish to provide for the following.

(i) A final dividend of 5p per ordinary share.
(ii) The audit fee, estimated to be £15,000.
(iii) A transfer to general reserve of £30,000.

(i) All shares in issue were fully paid and ranked for dividends at 30 June 19X5. The debentures were in issue for the whole year.

You are required to prepare the following.

(a) The trading, profit and loss and appropriation account for the year to 30 June 19X5.

(b) A balance sheet as at that date.

35 STU LIMITED (35 marks)

The following trial balance was extracted from the books of STU Limited at 31 January 19X8.

	Dr	*Cr*
	£	£
Land at cost	59,950	
Buildings at cost	48,000	
Fixtures at cost	23,110	
Motor vehicles at cost	40,100	
Provision for depreciation		
Buildings		26,670
Fixtures		12,713
Motor vehicles		24,060
Trade debtors and creditors	15,748	7,620
Provision for doubtful debts		889
Wages and salaries	18,891	
Sales		164,751
Purchases	73,501	
Returns in	921	
Returns out		434
Carriage in	3,810	
Administration expenses	7,233	
Selling and distribution expenses	4,515	
Stock at cost (1 February 19X7)	9,906	
Bank	4,693	
Cash	470	
10% debenture 19Y2 (issued in 19X3)		20,000
Debenture interest	1,000	
Directors' fees	10,100	
Discount allowed	1,528	
Discount received		2,027
Interim dividend	2,540	
Ordinary shares of £1 each, fully paid		40,000
Share premium		10,000
Retained profits (1 February 19X7)		16,852
	326,016	326,016

Notes

(a) The company depreciates all fixed assets held at the end of the year as follows.

Buildings	2% per annum on cost
Fixtures	10% per annum on cost
Motor vehicles	20% per annum on the reducing balance

No depreciation has yet been provided for the year ended 31 January 19X8.

(b) During the year a motor vehicle originally purchased on 1 February 19X4 for £6,000 was sold for £1,300; the only entries made in respect of this transaction were to debit bank and credit the motor vehicles at cost account with the sale proceeds.

(c) On 3 February 19X8 the company carried out a physical stocktake with the following results.

Category	*Code*	*Quantity*	*Cost each* £	*Net realisable value (each)* £
A	101	50	12.00	13.00
A	102	62	8.00	10.00
A	103	34	7.00	6.00
B	501	1,200	1.50	2.00
B	502	1,600	3.00	2.50
B	503	2,250	2.50	5.00

The following transactions occurred between 1 February 19X8 and 3 February 19X8.

	Category	*Code*	*Quantity*
Receipts	A	102	15
	B	501	200
Sales	A	101	24
	B	503	220

(d) £68 owed by a customer is to be written off as a bad debt against the provision.

(e) The provision for doubtful debts is to be equal to 2.5% of the amounts owed by trade debtors.

(f) On 31 January 19X8 selling and distribution expenses prepaid amounted to £559 and administration expenses accrued were £741.

(g) The directors propose that a final dividend of 4 pence per share be paid.

(h) Corporation tax is to be provided at 30% of net profit.

Required

(a) Prepare a trading and profit and loss account of STU Limited for the year ended 31 January 19X8, based upon the information given above. *A balance sheet is not required.* (25 marks)

(b) Accounts are usually prepared in accordance with the going concern concept. Why is this concept important and how does its use affect the final accounts of a business? (5 marks)

(c) Describe briefly how the day to day recording of accounting transactions is dealt with by microcomputer accounting packages. (5 marks)

36 BASIC REVISION QUESTION: COST BEHAVIOUR

(a) In economics, variable costs are often described as curvilinear whereas within cost accounting it is usual to assume variable costs have a linear function.

You are required to sketch two separate diagrams depicting:
(i) a curvilinear variable cost;
(ii) a linear variable cost.

(b) Explain and show by drawing two separate diagrams what is meant by:
(i) a semi variable cost;
(ii) a stepped fixed cost;
and give one example of each.

37 DIRECT/INDIRECT (15 marks)

(a) Distinguish between, and give an example of:
(i) direct costs; and
(ii) indirect costs. (3 marks)

(b) The valuation of finished goods stocks and work in progress in a company manufacturing a range of products requires costs to be collected and classified according to the functions of the organisation.

You are required:

(i) to describe the procedures necessary to collect the indirect costs of a manufacturing company; (8 marks)
(ii) to explain the procedures used to ascertain the cost of stocks and work in progress in such organisations. (4 marks)

38 BASIC REVISION QUESTION: ROSEBOWL HOTEL

The following account is kept for material X, used by the maintenance firm working for the Rosebowl Hotel.

Date	*Receipts*			*Issues*			*Balance*	
	Quantity	*Value*	£	*Quantity*	*Value*	£	*Quantity*	*Value* £
Oct 1							100	150
Oct 8	300	£1.52	456				400	606
Oct 9	200	£1.55	310				600	916
Oct 11				250				
Oct 12				150				

Required

(a) Value the issues of October 11 and 12 using each of the following methods FIFO, LIFO, weighted average.

(b) Under each of the above three methods show the value of the closing stock.

(c) In time of inflation which of the valuation methods will show the higher profit figure in the accounts? Give reasons.

39 RECEIPTS AND ISSUES (15 marks)

A and B are in business, buying and selling goods for resale. Neither of them are accountants but A has read a book on stock control whereas B has purchased a software package for daily stock records. During September 19X9 the following transactions occurred.

September 1	Balance brought forward	Nil
September 3	Bought 200 units at £1.00 each	
September 7	Sold 180 units	
September 8	Bought 240 units at £1.50 each	
September 14	Sold 170 units	
September 15	Bought 230 units at £2.00 each	
September 21	Sold 150 units	

A prepares the stores ledger card using the LIFO method and B uses the same data to test the software package which uses the weighted average method of pricing.

Required

(a) Show the ledger cards as they would appear for each method (calculations should be made to two decimal places of £1.00). (10 marks)

(b) Comment on the effect on profits of using each method of valuing stock. (5 marks)

40 MATERIALS CONTROL (20 marks)

(a) Briefly note the steps taken from reaching a re-order level to charging materials to a job.

(b) Suggest lines along which a continuous stocktaking could be organised.

41 COMPONENT X (20 marks)

On 1 January 19X7 a company had 200 units of component X in its stores which were valued in its books at the original cost of £50 per unit. The following purchases were then made.

8 January	600 units at £58 each
3 February	400 units at £64 each
11 March	600 units at £72 each
3 April	200 units at £73 each

Issues of the component to the factory during the first three months of 19X7 were as follows.

16 January	400 units
12 February	600 units
23 March	200 units

Required

(a) Prepare the stores ledger account for component X showing the receipts, issues and stock in hand in both quantities and values when issues are priced in accordance with the weighted average price method. (12 marks)

(b) Describe briefly two other methods of pricing material issues from stock.

What effect on the company's reported profit would the application of one of these methods have as compared to the existing weighted average price method? (8 marks)

42 BASIC REVISION QUESTION: JOB COSTING

The following information is available for Job 4321, which is being produced at the request of a customer.

	Department A	*Department B*	*Department C*
Materials consumed	£4,000	£1,000	£1,500
Direct labour:			
wage rate per hour	£3	£4	£5
Direct labour hours	300	200	400

In accordance with company policy the following are chargeable to jobs.

Fixed production overhead	£5 per direct labour hour
Fixed administration overhead	80% total production cost
Profit mark-up	20% margin on selling price

Required

(a) Distinguish briefly between job costing and batch costing.

(b) Calculate the total cost and selling price of Job 4321.

43 SP (20 marks)

SP plc is engaged mainly in retailing fashion and leisure wear, camping equipment and protective clothing. The company's head office and warehouse are located on the east coast and the 50 shops it operates are divided into three divisions as follows.

Division	*No of shops*
North west	16
West	13
South	21

Servicing of the shops is undertaken from the head office for:

- personnel and staff training
- window display, sales promotion and advertising
- warehousing and distribution - no goods are delivered direct to the shops from the manufacturers.

Costs for the three service functions are budgeted for the next financial year, as shown below, and it is desired to determine methods of apportioning these costs to the three retailing divisions.

	Personnel and staff training	*Window display sales promotion and advertising*	*Warehousing and distribution*
	£'000	£'000	£'000
Wages	40	65	140
Transport	9	30	115
Other costs	8	135	30

Other information available from the budget for the next financial year is as follows.

	North west	*West*	*South*	*Total*
	£'000	£'000	£'000	£'000
Sales	2,760	2,320	4,120	9,200
Cost of goods sold	1,154	978	1,668	3,800
Branch wages	422	358	645	1,425
Divisional administration	45	45	53	143

Required

(a) Prepare a statement showing how you would apportion the costs of the service functions to each of the retailing divisions.

(b) Explain, in a brief report, why you have selected the bases of apportionment that you have used in (a) above and state any limitations.

44 APPORTIONMENT (20 marks)

A company manufactures and sells two products, X and Y, whose selling prices are £100 and £300 respectively, and each product passes through two manufacturing processes, A and B. In process A, product X takes two hours per unit and product Y takes four hours. In process B, product X takes one hour per unit, and product Y takes three hours. Labour in process A is paid £4 per hour, and in process B £5 per hour.

The two products are made out of materials P,Q and R and the quantities of each material used in making one unit of each product is as follows.

	Product X	*Product Y*
Material P	37 lbs	93 lbs
Material Q	10	240
Material R	20 sq.ft	75 sq.ft

Material prices are £1 per lb for P, £2.40 per dozen for Q and £0.20 per square foot for R.

Salesmen are paid a commission of 5% of sales. The packing materials are £1 for X and £4 for Y. Costs of transporting the goods to the customer are £2 for X and £5 for Y.

Other annual costs are as follows.

		£	£
Indirect wages:	process A	25,000	
	process B	40,000	
	stores	20,000	
	canteen	10,000	
			95,000
Indirect materials:	process A	51,510	
	process B	58,505	
	stores	1,310	
	canteen	8,425	
			119,750
Rent and rates			450,000
Depreciation of plant and machinery			140,000
Power			50,000
Insurance:	fire on buildings		3,750
	workmen's compensation at 2% of wages		12,000
Heating and lighting			4,500
Advertising			90,000

A royalty of £1 is payable on product X. The annual quantities sold are 15,000 units of X and 10,000 units of Y.

Other relevant information is as follows.

Cost centre	*Area in square feet*	*Book value of plant and machinery* £	*Horse-power of machinery* %	*Direct labour hours*	*Number of employees*	*Number of stores issue notes*
Process A	100,000	1,000,000	80	70,000	40	10,000
Process B	50,000	200,000	20	45,000	30	5,000
Stores	100,000	150,000			10	
Canteen	50,000	50,000			5	
	300,000	1,400,000	100	115,000	85	15,000

Required

(a) Prepare a production overhead analysis and apportionment sheet, showing clearly the bases of apportionment used. (10 marks)

(b) Calculate appropriate rates of overhead recovery for processes A and B. (2 marks)

(c) Calculate the full (absorption) cost of making and selling one unit of each product. (6 marks)

(d) Calculate the unit profit or loss for each product. (2 marks)

45 ABACUS LIMITED (20 marks)

Abacus Limited has analysed its current product cost with the following results.

	£ per unit
Direct materials	4.50
Direct wages	6.00
Variable overhead	3.25
Fixed overhead	5.25
	19.00

During October 19X0 the number of units produced was 9,200. This was 800 units more than the quantity sold. The opening stock of finished goods at the beginning of October 19X0 was 250 units.

The product has a selling price of £23.00.

You are required

(a) to prepare a profit statement for October 19X0,

(i) using absorption costing, and
(ii) using marginal costing,

from the information given above; (8 marks)

(b) to explain the difference in the profits given by the two systems. (4 marks)

(c) The company uses the following standard costs established at the start of the year, to monitor its performance.

	£ per unit
Direct materials	4.40
Direct wages	5.85
Variable overhead	3.35
Fixed overhead	5.40
	19.00

The fixed overhead cost per unit is based on a monthly production of 10,000 units.

Calculate the following total cost variances.

(i) Direct materials.
(ii) Direct wages.
(iii) Overhead. (8 marks)

46 PROFIT DIFFERENCES/COSTING METHODS (35 marks)

DEF Limited, a company having a year end of 31 December, makes a single product which it sells to consumers for £34. The current costs of the product are as follows.

	£
Direct labour (2 hours at £4.50)	9
Direct materials	10
Direct expenses	2
Overhead	8
	29

Overhead is absorbed into product costs on the basis of direct labour hours used to produce each unit, and this year's overhead is based on an annual production of 80,000 units.

For many years the company has produced its budgets and forecasts using absorption (total) costing but the managing director has recently returned from a conference on cost control where he has heard that marginal (variable) costing is better.

The following information relates to next year.

1. Costs are expected to increase as follows.

	%
Direct labour rates	4
Direct materials	5
Direct expenses	7
Fixed overhead	12.5

2. Opening stocks are expected to be 4,500 units valued at current costs, with annual production remaining at 80,000 units arising evenly during the year.

3. Sales are expected to be as follows.

Six months to 30 June	39,000 units at £34 each
Six months to 31 December	42,000 units at £36 each

(a) *You are required* to prepare forecasts for next year for each half year separately and the annual total, based on the information given above showing sales, costs, and profit, using:
(i) absorption costing;
(ii) marginal costing.
Explain the difference between the total profit given by each method. (15 marks)

(b) Explain:
(i) the term 'under/over absorption of fixed overhead cost?
(ii) the conditions which cause either an under or over absorption of fixed overhead cost to occur;
(iii) why most organisations have no choice but to accept these conditions. (10 marks)

(c) Cost accounting classifies costs in a different way to financial accounting. Why is this and how does this difference affect the use of an integrated accounting system? (10 marks)

47 LMN LIMITED (15 marks)

LMN Limited has the following budgeted overhead costs and related data for the year to 31 March 19X9.

	Machining	*Assembly*	*Finishing*
Overhead costs	£175,500	£56,450	£98,750
Number of employees	16	7	12
Labour hours	32,540	14,000	26,000
Machine hours	30,000	2,400	nil
Wages cost	£142,400	£43,600	£91,500
Material cost	£94,500	£32,560	£43,575

During September 19X8 Job 123 was completed. Direct costs and related data were as follows.

	Machining	*Assembly*	*Finishing*
Material cost	£1,369	£124	£93
Labour costs	£608	£90	£251
Labour hours	52	30	70
Machine hours	147	25	nil

Required

(a) Calculate an appropriate overhead absorption rate for *each* of the *three* departments (to the nearest £0.01) giving reasons for your choice of method. (6 marks)

(b) Use these rates to calculate the following.

(i) The total cost of Job 123.
(ii) The selling price if a gross profit of 40% on selling price is applied.

(5 marks)

(c) Explain the difference between the valuation of stock under an absorption costing system and under a marginal costing system. (4 marks)

48 FIXED OVERHEADS (20 marks)

The valuation of stocks in a manufacturing and trading company is dependent on a number of factors, not least of which is the company's policy concerning its treatment of fixed overhead costs, which is an important part of a company's cost accounting procedures.

Required

(a) Discuss the principles of marginal and absorption costing, explaining clearly the difference between them. (10 marks)

(b) Explain the use of predetermined rates to absorb overhead costs into product costs. (10 marks)

Use numerical examples to illustrate your answers, for which *eight* of the total marks are available.

49 BASIC REVISION QUESTION: ABCOLL LIMITED

From the information given below you are required to prepare the manufacturing, trading and profit and loss account of Abcoll Limited for the year ended 31 December 19X5.

Balances at 31 December 19X4

	£
Authorised and issued share capital	
Ordinary shares of £1 each fully paid	100,000
Reserves	1,000
Creditors	57,400
Fixed assets (cost £60,000)	39,000
Stocks	
Raw materials	25,000
Work in progress, valued at prime cost	5,800
Finished goods	51,000
Debtors	35,000
Cash at bank	2,000
Administration expenses prepaid	600

The following transactions occurred during 19X5.

Invoiced sales, less returns	243,000
Cash received from debtors	234,700
Discounts allowed	5,400
Bad debts written off	1,100
Invoiced purchases of raw materials, less returns	80,000
Payments to creditors	82,500
Discounts received	1,700
Factory wages paid	33,300
Manufacturing expenses paid	61,900
Administration expenses paid	16,200
Selling and distribution expenses paid	16,800
Payment for purchase of fixed assets	30,000

Balances at 31 December 19X5

Fixed assets (cost £90,000)	60,000
Stocks	
Raw materials	24,000
Work in progress	5,000
Finished goods	52,000
Administration expenses accrued	1,100
Factory wages accrued	700
Selling and distribution expenses prepaid	1,200

The following information is given.

(a) Depreciation of fixed assets is to be apportioned between manufacturing, administration and selling in the proportions of 7: 2: 1.

(b) Discounts allowed and bad debts written off are to be regarded as selling and distribution expenses.

(c) Discounts received are to be credited to administration expenses.

(d) Taxation is to be ignored.

50 MANUFACTURING LIMITED (40 marks)

You are the chief accountant of Manufacturing Limited, a company which manufactures and sells a single product. At 31 May 19X6, the company's balance sheet is expected to be as follows.

	£'000	£'000
Fixed assets		
Cost	2,900	
Depreciation	1,250	
		1,650
Current assets		
Stock		
Materials (56,000 lbs)	560	
Work in progress	10	
Finished products (12,000 units)	720	
Debtors		
April sales	800	
May sales	1,000	
Fixed administration expenses prepaid	15	
Cash at bank	699	
	3,804	
Current liabilities		
Creditors for materials: May purchases	160	
Fixed administration expenses accrued	20	
Taxation	250	
Proposed dividend	150	
	580	
Net current assets		3,224
		4,874
Share capital and reserves		
Ordinary shares of 25p each, fully paid		3,000
Retained profits		1,874
		4,874

The following information is available.

1. The selling price of the product during June and July 19X6 will be unchanged at £100 per unit. The marketing director estimates that 11,000 units should be sold in June and 9,000 units in July. All sales are on credit, and debtors are required to pay their accounts during the second month following the month of sale. Annual sales will be 120,000 units.

2. Only one kind of material is used in manufacturing the product, and 2 lbs of this material are used in making one unit. The purchase price of the material will be unchanged at £10 per lb. During the two months all purchases are on credit, and the company pays creditors during the month following the month of purchase. The managing director requires material stocks to be reduced to 50,000 lbs at the end of June and 40,000 lbs at the end of July.

3. Only one grade of direct labour is employed, and it takes four hours to manufacture one unit of product. The wage rate will be unchanged at £4 per hour during June and July.

4. The following variable costs per unit will be payable in the month in which they are incurred.

	£
Variable manufacturing costs, incurred when the product is manufactured	5
Variable distribution costs, incurred when the product is sold	5

5. The managing director requires finished product stocks to be built up to 20,000 units at the end of July 19X6. Production is to be equal during each of the two months.

6. Work in progress will be unchanged in quantity and value during the period.

7. A unit of finished product will be valued for balance sheet purposes during the period at the total of direct materials, direct labour, variable manufacturing cost and £19 for the yearly average of fixed manufacturing cost (including depreciation). No administration expenses or distribution costs, whether variable or fixed, are to be included.

8. Fixed assets costing £100,000 are expected to be purchased for cash on 1 June 19X6. The company's policy is to depreciate its fixed assets at the rate of 10% per annum on cost on a strict time basis, and the depreciation for a month, which is to be regarded as a fixed cost, is to be divided between manufacturing, administration and distribution in the ratio 8:1:1. For this purpose, all months are to be regarded as of equal length. No fixed assets will be depreciated more than 100% of cost during the period.

9. The following cash payments other than to creditors or for the purchase of fixed assets, wages or variable costs, are expected to be made.

	June	*July*
	£	£
Taxation	250,000	
Proposed dividend		150,000
Fixed manufacturing costs	170,000	170,000
Fixed administration expenses	196,500	196,500
Fixed distribution costs	97,500	97,500

It is to be assumed that the settlement of debtors' and creditors' accounts will occur on the due dates.

10. Accrued and prepaid fixed administration expenses at the month ends should be as follows.

	June	*July*
	£	£
Accrued	22,000	24,000
Prepaid	16,000	17,000

11. Provision is to be made each month for corporation tax at the rate of 50% of net profit. No provision for dividends is to be made.

You are required to prepare the following, in vertical and columnar form, for internal use only.

(a) Forecast profit and loss accounts for each of the months of June and July 19X6, including the manufacturing and trading results and appropriation of profits. (25 marks)

(b) Forecast balance sheets at the end of each of the two months. (15 marks)

51 STUART LIMITED (35 marks)

Stuart Limited, a manufacturing and trading company, makes up its accounts to 30 September each year. The company operates a standard costing system and from these cost standards the management accountant produces a flexible budget expressed in costs per unit of output for presentation to senior management. An extract from this report for the year to 30 September 19X8 is as follows.

Number of units produced and sold	10,000	12,000
	£	£
Cost per unit		
Direct materials	6.00	6.00
Direct labour	9.00	9.00
Manufacturing overhead	7.50	7.40
Administration overhead	4.00	3.90
Selling overhead	2.50	2.48
	29.00	28.78

The budgeted production and sales quantity for the year to 30 September 19X8 was planned at 10,500 units, but actual production was 11,000 units.

Actual sales were 10,250 units for a total revenue of £512,400.

The cost accountant has calculated that the total cost variances for the year are as follows.

Direct materials	£4,420 adverse
Direct labour	£3,840 adverse
Overhead	£6,900 favourable

The overhead variance can be further analysed as follows.

Manufacturing	£5,400 adverse
Administration	£9,250 favourable
Selling	£3,050 favourable

The company values its stocks of raw materials at cost and finished goods at standard absorption cost. Because of the nature of its production process there is no work in progress stock.

The stocks of raw materials are always maintained at 500 units (each unit being used to produce one item of the finished product) and on 1 October 19X7 were valued at £3,000. Stocks of finished goods on 1 October 19X7 comprised 260 items which were valued at £5,482.

During the year an interim dividend of two pence per ordinary share was paid which totalled £22,000. The company is financed by ordinary shares of 25 pence each (all issued at par) and retained profits. A final dividend of a further three pence per ordinary share is proposed.

The taxation charge for the year is £64,500. There is no adjustment to be made in respect of previous years.

The debtors payment period (year end debtors divided by sales multiplied by 366 days) is 45 days and the creditors payment period for raw materials (year end creditors divided by raw material purchases multiplied by 366 days) is 60 days.

The company's ratio of current assets to current liabilities is 1.7:1.

The balance sheet valuation of fixed assets at 30 September 19X8 is £327,000.

Required

(a) Prepare the company's actual manufacturing, trading, profit and loss, and appropriation accounts for the year ended 30 September 19X8 and the company's balance sheet at that date in as much detail as possible from the above information. (26 marks)

(b) Calculate the value of finished goods stock at 30 September 19X8:
(i) using standard marginal costs; and
(ii) using average actual costs for the year; (4 marks)

(c) Comment on the acceptability of using standard costs as the basis of stock valuation. (5 marks)

52 DICK TURNIP (22 marks)

Dick Turnip commenced trading on 1 April 19X8 as Highwayman Stores, retail stationers and confectioners, with an initial capital of £3,000 which was utilised in the opening of a business bank account.

All receipts and payments are passed through the bank account. The following is a summary of the items credited in the business cash book during the year ended 31 March 19X9.

	£
Purchase of fixtures and fittings	
Stationery department	2,600
Confectionery department	1,500
Staff wages	
Stationery department	2,200
Confectionery department	1,540
Rent for the period 1 April 19X8 to 30 April 19X9	1,300
Rates for the year ended 31 March 19X9	570
Electricity	370
Advertising	1,100
Payments to suppliers	53,550
Drawings	5,000

The purchases during the year under review were as follows.

	£
Stationery department	26,000
Confectionery department	29,250

The above purchases do not include goods costing £500 bought by the business and then taken by Mr Turnip for his own domestic use. The figure of £500 is included in payments to suppliers.

The gross profit in the stationery department is at the rate of 20% of sales, whilst in the confectionery department it is 25% of sales. In both departments, sales each month are always at a uniform level. The policy of Mr Turnip is to have the month end stocks in each department just sufficient for the following month's sales. The prices of all goods bought by Highwayman Stores have not changed since the business began.

Total trade debtors at 31 March 19X9 amounted to £9,000.

At 31 March 19X9 electricity charges accrued due, amounted to £110.

In August 19X8 Mr Turnip and his sister, Mrs Green, received legacies from their late mother's estate of £5,000 and £4,000 respectively. Both legacies were paid into the bank account of Highwayman Stores; Mrs Green has agreed that her legacy should be an interest free loan to the business.

Mr Turnip has decided that expenses not incurred by a specific department should be apportioned to departments as follows.

(i) Rent and rates: according to floor area occupied
(ii) Electricity: according to consumption
(iii) Advertising: according to turnover

Two thirds of the business floor space is occupied by the stationery department whilst three quarters of the electricity is consumed by that department. All the floor space of the business is allocated to a department.

It has been decided that depreciation on fixtures and fittings should be provided at the rate of 10% of the cost of assets at the year end.

Required

(a) A trading and profit and loss account for the year ended 31 March 19X9 for:
 (i) the stationery department; and
 (ii) the confectionery department.

(b) A balance sheet at 31 March 19X9.

53 SMITH PLC (40 marks)

The trial balance of Smith plc at 31 December 19X6 was as follows.

		Dr £'000	*Cr* £'000
Ordinary shares of £0.50 each fully paid			5,000
Retained profit at 1 January 19X6			13,980
Fixed assets at cost		20,000	
Stocks at 1 January 19X6			
Materials		1,531	
Work in progress:	product X	25	
	product Y	60	
Finished products:	X	875	
	Y	3,900	
Debtors		5,000	
Bad debts provision			255
Cash at bank and in hand		150	
Creditors			1,320
Sales:	product X		24,000
	product Y		16,000
Purchases of materials		11,400	
Manufacturing wages:	product X	3,141	
	product Y	1,564	
Production overhead expenses		7,674	
Distribution costs		3,715	
Administrative expenses		4,520	
		63,555	63,555

Further information

1. Materials issued from stores during 19X6 were as follows.

		£
Direct:	product X	6,410,000
	product Y	4,785,000
Indirect:	manufacturing	105,000

A physical stocktaking at 31 December 19X6 valued materials stock at £1,600,000. Any difference with book stocks is to be regarded as a production overhead expense.

2. Movements in respect of products X and Y during 19X6 were as follows.

	Products	
	X	*Y*
	units	units
Stocks at 1 January 19X6	35,000	65,000
Manufactured during 19X6	640,000	160,000
	675,000	225,000
Sold during 19X6	600,000	200,000
Stock at 31 December 19X6	75,000	25,000

3. Work in progress at 31 December was valued as follows.

	£'000
Product X	50
Product Y	30

4. Finished product stocks at 31 December 19X6 were valued as follows.

	£'000
Product X	1,875
Product Y	1,500

5. Depreciation for 19X6 was £2,000,000 and is to be apportioned as follows.

	£
Production	1,600,000
Distribution	200,000
Administration	200,000

6. The bad debts provision is to be adjusted to 5% of debtors. Any increase or decrease is to be regarded as a distribution cost.

7. Prepayments and accruals at 31 December 19X6 were as follows.

	Prepayments	*Accruals*
	£'000	£'000
Manufacturing wages: product X		64
product Y		31
Production overhead expenses	10	200
Distribution costs	5	95
Administrative expenses	30	110

8. Production overhead expenses (including the proportion of depreciation) are to be divided between the products in proportion to manufacturing wages.

9. Distribution costs (including the proportion of depreciation and any adjustment of the bad debts provision) are to be divided between the products in proportion to the quantities sold during 19X6.

10. Administrative expenses (including the proportion of depreciation) are to be divided between the products in proportion to the quantities of fully completed products manufactured during 19X6.

11. Provision is to be made for corporation tax at the rate of 40% of the net profit, and for a proposed dividend of 15 pence per share.

Required

(a) Prepare for internal use only, in tabular and columnar form, a profit and loss account for the year ended 31 December 19X6, showing the amount of profit or loss before tax for each product and the amount of retained profit for the year. (25 marks)

(b) The profit for the year has been calculated according to the historic cost principle. Describe two other principles which may be used to calculate profit.

(15 marks)

54 BASIC REVISION QUESTION: HONECKER

Honecker manufacturers very strong bricks for walls and security installations.

Each brick is sold for £20. In 19Y0 60,000 bricks were produced of which 50,000 were sold. Budgeted and actual costs for the period were as follows.

	Budget	*Actual*
Direct production costs per brick	£10	£10
Variable factory overhead per brick	£4	£4
Fixed overheads	£72,000	£78,000
Variable selling expenses, per brick	£1	£1
Fixed selling expenses	£10,000	£10,000

Fixed overheads are absorbed on the basis of normal production. There was no opening stock at the beginning of the year, as 19Y0 was Honecker's first year in production.

Required

(a) Draw up a statement calculating the net profit for 19Y0.

(b) What would the profit have been if marginal costing had been used?

(c) What affect on your answer in (a) above would there be if there had been an adverse direct production cost variance of £0.50 per unit, and a favourable variable selling cost variance of £0.25 per brick?

(d) Honecker decides to monitor his cash flow. He also wishes to draw up a budget for 19Y1, his second year of trading.

He estimates that sales will increase to 100,000 bricks, and he assumes that closing stocks at the end of 19Y1 will be 20,000 bricks. (There will be no closing stocks of raw materials.)

Sales and costs arise evenly over the year. Debtors for sales pay three months in arrears. Variable production overheads are paid three months in arrears. All other costs are paid as they occur.

Selling prices and unit costs are to remain the same as in 19Y0, with the exception of fixed production overhead which increases to £80,000 in total.

Honecker at the end of 19Y0 has an overdraft of £10,000.

Prepare, showing your workings:

(i) a production budget for 19Y1 (in bricks);
(ii) a cash budget for 19Y1, indicating Honecker's bank balance at the end of the year.

55 CASH BUDGETS (30 marks)

Cash budgets for months 1,2 and 3 are given.

You are required to prepare, using the information supplied, cash budgets for months 4,5 and 6 in the format shown.

CASH BOOK

	Month 1	2	3	4	5	6
	£	£	£	£	£	£
Balance b/f	(12,705)	(10,215)	100			
Receipts						
Debtors	15,700	16,000	6,000			
Issue of ordinary shares						
Sale of plant						
	2,995	5,785	6,100			
Payments						
Creditors for materials	12,000	4,500	4,350			
Wages	600	575	595			
Overhead	610	610	615			
Debenture interest						
Taxation						
Dividends						
Purchase of plant						
Repayment of debentures						
	13,210	5,685	5,560			
Balance c/f	(10,215)	100	540			
	2,995	5,785	6,100			

Note: balances in brackets represent bank overdrafts.

You are given the following information.

1. Material cost is expected to be 75% of invoiced sales.

2. Debtors are given two months' credit.

3. Creditors for materials allow the company one month's credit.

4. No discounts received or allowed, bad debts or items settled by contra are expected.

5. Three quarters of wages earned each month are paid in that month and the remaining quarter in the following month.

6. Overhead expenses are paid, half in the month in which they are incurred and half in the following month.

7. Items other than above are dealt with completely in the month shown in the table of data below.

8. Other relevant information is as follows.

	Month					
	1	*2*	*3*	*4*	*5*	*6*
	£	£	£	£	£	£
Invoiced sales	6,000	6,200	6,800	7,200	8,400	12,000
Material stocks						
Increase					700	
Decrease		300	100			
Wages earned	560	580	600	640	700	960
Overhead incurred	600	620	610	630	630	640
Debenture interest paid						1,000
Taxation paid				10,000		
Dividends paid						500
Plant purchased						1,945
Ordinary shares issued at par						35,000
Plant sold				200		
Debentures repaid						20,000

56 FLEXIBLE BUDGET (20 marks)

(a) Explain what is meant by the terms 'fixed budget' and 'flexible budget' and state the main objective of preparing flexible budgets. (5 marks)

(b) (i) Prepare a flexible budget for 19X6 for the overhead expenses of a production department at the activity levels of 80%, 90% and 100%, using the information listed below. (12 marks)

1. The direct labour hourly rate is expected to be £3.75.

2. 100% activity represents 60,000 direct labour hours.

3. *Variable costs*

Indirect labour	£0.75 per direct labour hour
Consumable supplies	£0.375 per direct labour hour
Canteen and other welfare services	6% of direct and indirect labour costs

4. Semi-variable costs are expected to correlate with the direct labour hours in the same manner as for the last five years which was as follows.

Year	*Direct labour hours*	*Semi-variable costs* £
19X1	64,000	20,800
19X2	59,000	19,800
19X3	53,000	18,600
19X4	49,000	17,800
19X5	40,000 (estimate)	16,000 (estimate)

5. Fixed costs are as follows.

	£
Depreciation	18,000
Maintenance	10,000
Insurance	4,000
Rates	15,000
Management salaries	25,000

6. Inflation is to be ignored.

(ii) Calculate the budget cost allowance for 19X6 assuming that 57,000 direct labour hours are worked. (3 marks)

57 SINGLE PRODUCT (25 marks)

A company which manufactures and sells a single product drew up a budget for the year ended 31 December 19X6 based upon production and sales quantities of 100,000 units of the product.

The company used a system of standard costing, and the standards for 19X6 for one unit of product were as follows.

Direct materials:	quantity used	10 lbs
	price per lb	£3
Direct labour:	time taken	5 hrs
	rate per hour	£4
Variable overheads		£10

The selling price used in the 19X6 budget was £100 per unit, and the budgeted annual fixed overheads were £2,000,000.

The actual results for the year ended 31 December 19X6 were as follows.

Quantity of product manufactured and sold		100,000 units
Unit selling price		£100
Direct materials:	total quantity used	1,020,000 lbs
	price per lb	£3
Direct labour:	total time taken	500,000 hours
	rate per hour	£4.20
Total variable overheads		£990,000
Total fixed overheads		£2,030,000

During the year ended 31 December 19X5 selected actual results were as follows.

Quantity of product manufactured and sold	80,000 units
Direct material total cost variance	£1,000 Favourable
Direct labour total cost variance	£90,000 Adverse

Required

(a) Prepare a budgeted profit and loss account for the year ended 31 December 19X6. (3 marks)

(b) Prepare an actual profit and loss account for the year ended 31 December 19X6. (3 marks)

(c) Prepare a statement reconciling the budgeted profit and loss account for 19X6 with the actual profit or loss using total variances calculated according to standard absorption costing principles. (9 marks)

(d) Comment briefly on the trends revealed by a comparison of figures for 19X5 and 19X6 in respect of the cost of direct materials and direct labour. Briefly suggest some possible causes for these trends. (10 marks)

58 BASIC REVISION QUESTION: MYCOST LIMITED

(a) Briefly explain the term 'standard cost'.

(b) Outline the benefits which a company may obtain from a standard costing system.

(c) Discuss the problems which may arise in the development and operation of a standard costing system.

59 AR LIMITED (35 marks)

AR Limited is a company which provides a shuttle airline service from London to Manchester. In addition to the flight services, it has a souvenir shop and cafeteria at each of its airstrips. The company operates a standard cost accounting system for its flight services and its standard cost card for each flight is as follows.

	£
Direct wages of pilot and crew	60.00
Indirect labour costs	12.00
Fuel cost	440.00
In-flight catering	50.00
Indirect material cost	18.00
	580.00
Ground services costs absorbed	120.00
Standard cost per flight	700.00

The ground services costs are absorbed into the standard flight costs using an overhead absorption rate of 200% of direct wages. This rate comprises 60% of direct wages for variable ground services costs and 140% for fixed ground services costs. The 140% is calculated assuming an annual number of 2,000 flights.

During the year ended 31 March 19X1, the company made 1,900 flights and flight ticket receipts amounted to £2,400,000 of which £105,000 related to advance ticket sales. The amount of advance ticket sales received in the year to 31 March 19X0 was £97,000.

An extract from the company's trial balance at 31 March 19X1 showed the following.

		Dr £	*Cr* £
Cafeteria sales			480,000
Souvenir sales			72,000
Opening stock at 1 April 19X0:	cafeteria	16,000	
	souvenirs	3,000	
Purchases:	cafeteria	233,000	
	souvenirs	44,000	

Closing stocks at 31 March 19X1 were valued as follows.

Cafeteria	£15,000
Souvenirs	£5,000

At the end of each accounting period the management accountant of the company prepares a report which shows the variances for the current period and the year to date in respect of flight services. An extract from this report for the year to 31 March 19X1 shows the following.

	Total variance £	
Direct wages of pilot and crew	12,000	Adverse
Indirect labour costs	3,000	Favourable
Fuel cost	63,000	Adverse
In-flight catering	15,000	Favourable
Indirect material cost	2,000	Adverse
Ground services costs: fixed element	14,000	Adverse
Ground services costs: variable element	15,000	Adverse

All of these costs are wholly variable except for the ground services costs which are semi-variable costs.

You are required:

(a) to prepare a profit statement of AR Limited in as much detail as possible for the year ended 31 March 19X1, showing the actual results of the company separately for flight services, cafeteria services, souvenir services and in total, using a columnar marginal costing format; (25 marks)

(b) to state what is meant by the term 'standard cost' and to discuss the use of standard costing techniques in a non-manufacturing environment such as that of AR Limited. What benefits arise from the use of such a system? (10 marks)

60 PQR LIMITED (15 marks)

The following data have been extracted from the budget records of PQR Limited for the year to 31 December 19X8.

Budgeted production volume for the year was 8,000 units.

	Annual level of activity				
Units of output	6,000	7,000	8,000	9,000	10,000
	£	£	£	£	£
Production costs					
Raw materials (variable)	36,000	42,000	48,000	54,000	60,000
Operatives' wages (variable)	21,000	24,500	28,000	31,500	35,000
Indirect costs					
Supervisor's salary (fixed)	11,500	11,500	11,500	11,500	11,500
Power (fixed)	7,500	7,500	7,500	7,500	7,500
Power (variable)	6,000	7,000	8,000	9,000	10,000
Heat/light (fixed)	1,000	1,000	1,000	1,000	1,000
Heat/light (variable)	4,500	5,250	6,000	6,750	7,500
Factory rates (fixed)	40,000	40,000	40,000	40,000	40,000

All fixed costs are expected to accrue evenly during the year.

During the quarter ended 31 March 19X8 the actual production quantity was 1,875.

Costs incurred were as follows.

	£
Production costs	
Raw materials	11,400
Operatives' wages	6,540
Indirect costs	
Supervisor's salary	2,900
Power	3,675
Heat/light	1,756
Factory rates	10,050

Required

(a) Calculate the standard costs and total variances for each of the cost elements in respect of the quarter ended 31 March 19X8. (10 marks)

(b) List the factors which should be considered when setting material cost standards. (5 marks)

61 BUDGETS FROM VARIANCES (40 marks)

ABC Limited, a manufacturing and trading company, operates a standard costing system. The standard costs which are used to calculate the variances are taken from the company's standard cost card for the year. The appropriate data for the year to 30 September 19X8 were as follows.

	£/unit
Direct materials (5 litres)	10.00
Direct labour (4 hours)	16.00
Direct expenses	4.00
	30.00
Production overhead	20.00
Production cost	50.00
Profit	30.00
Selling price	80.00

During the year the company operated at standard efficiency but actual production costs differed from standard costs due to differences in prices paid.

The following total cost variances arose during the year.

	£	
Direct materials	4,900	Favourable
Direct labour	7,840	Adverse
Direct expenses	490	Favourable
Production overhead	4,150	Adverse

Budget production was 10,000 units but actual production was 9,800 units and sales were 9,750 units. All sales were made at the standard selling price of £80 per unit.

At 30 September 19X8, there were 700 units of the finished product in stock valued at £34.00 each (stocks are valued at standard variable production cost based on the average expected cost for the year).

The company is considering its plans for the year to 30 September 19X9. The following data have emerged from discussions.

1. Sales are expected as follows.

October - December 19X8	2,100 units
January - March 19X9	4,800 units
April - June 19X9	1,500 units
July - September 19X9	3,000 units

2. Stocks of finished units held at the end of December, March and June are to be equal to one third of the following quarter's sales. At the end of September 19X9 such stocks are to be 960 units.

3. Direct material prices are expected to be greater than the average actual price paid in the year to 30 September 19X8 by the following percentages.

October 19X8 - March 19X9	3%
April 19X9 - September 19X9	4%

Direct materials are received in the month of production and paid for one month later. Consequently, no raw material stocks are held.

4. Direct wage rates from 1 January 19X9 are expected to be 8% above the average actual rate paid during the year ended 30 September 19X8. No change is expected until that date. Direct wages are paid in the month in which they are incurred.

5. Direct expenses are not expected to change for the year to 30 September 19X9. They will continue to be incurred at the same rate per unit of output as they were in the year to 30 September 19X8. They are paid in the quarter following the quarter in which they are incurred.

6. An analysis of the production overhead incurred in the year to 30 September 19X8 confirmed that 80% was fixed, the remaining 20% varying in proportion to output. This was as expected in the standard costs shown above. The variable overhead per unit is expected to be 5% higher than the average variable overhead cost incurred in the year to 30 September 19X8. This increase is to be effective from 1 October 19X8. All production overhead costs are paid in the month following that in which they are incurred except for 10% of the fixed overhead cost which relates to depreciation.

7. Selling prices are to remain at £80.00 per unit of output until 1 April 19X9 when they are to increase to £90.00 per unit for the remainder of the year. All sales are on credit; 50% are settled in the same quarter as the sale, 45% in the following quarter, and the remainder are bad debts.

Required

(a) (i) Prepare a production budget in terms of units to be produced for the quarter ending 31 March 19X9. (5 marks)

(ii) Prepare columnar profit and loss accounts for each of the six month periods ending 31 March 19X9 and 30 September 19X9 and for the year in total (all figures to the nearest £). (20 marks)

(iii) Show the cash budget for the quarter January to March 19X9, assuming an opening balance at the beginning of January 19X9 of £124,678 overdrawn. (5 marks)

(b) Explain how a microcomputer spreadsheet package might be used to produce the budgets of a company such as ABC Limited. What are the advantages of using a spreadsheet for this type of work? (10 marks)

62 BASIC REVISION QUESTION: INTEGRATED ACCOUNTING SYSTEM

(a) Briefly explain what is meant by 'an integrated accounting system', and explain its advantages over alternative systems.

(b) Give journal entries for entering the following transactions in an integrated accounting system.
Note: ignore narratives.

	£
Purchases of raw materials on credit	10,000
Raw materials issued to production	6,000
Maintenance materials issued	1,000
Cash paid for indirect production wages	2,000
Depreciation of machinery used for production	4,000
Absorption of production overhead	7,000

63 INTEGRATED (20 marks)

A company operates an integrated system of financial and cost accounts on a computer, using a system of numerical code numbers for this purpose. The code numbers consist of five digits, of which (reading from left to right) the first two indicate the relevant account in the financial ledger, the second two indicate the relevant account in the cost ledger, and the fifth digit indicates whether the item is a debit or a credit.

In the financial ledger the accounts for material stock, finished goods and work in progress show the values obtained on a physical stocktaking at the end of the financial year, and are not kept on a running basis. In the cost ledger these accounts are kept on a running basis, and should always show up to date values. The material stock account is kept at actual cost, and the finished goods stock and work in progress accounts at standard cost. No accounts for capital, retained profit, fixed assets, debtors and creditors are kept in the cost ledger.

Some of the numbers indicating the relevant account in the financial ledger (the first two digits) are as follows.

Not entered in financial accounts	00
Fixed assets	10
Depreciation provision	15
Material stock	20
Work in progress	21
Finished goods stock	22
Debtors	23
Bad debts provision	24
Cash at bank	25
Creditors	30
Sales	40
Purchases of materials	50
Wages	51
Office salaries	52
Office expenses	53
Advertising, selling and distribution expenses	54
Depreciation charge	55
Discounts received	56
Discounts allowed	57
Change in bad debts provision	58

Some of the numbers indicating the relevant account in the cost ledger (the second two digits) are as follows.

Not entered in cost accounts	00
Manufacturing overhead	01
Administration overhead	02
Marketing, selling and distribution overhead	03
Material stock	20
Work in progress	21
Finished goods stock	22
Sales	40
Manufacturing cost of goods sold	41
Direct material total variance	50
Direct labour total variance	51
Manufacturing overhead total variance	52
Administration overhead total variance	53
Marketing etc overhead total variance	54

The last digit of the five consists of the following.

Debits	0
Credits	1

During a year the following summarised transactions occurred.

			£'000
1	Purchase of materials on credit amounted to		4,910
	which was allocated as follows.		
	Taken into material stock		4,400
	Indirect materials:	manufacturing	210
		administration	200
		marketing, selling and distribution	100
2	Creditors were paid in cash		4,975
	after deducting cash discounts of		125
	These discounts are regarded as an administration item for costing purposes.		
3	Wages were paid in cash		1,969
	and were allocated as follows.		
	Direct, at standard		1,110
	Indirect, at actual:	manufacturing	600
		administration	100
		marketing, selling and distribution	150
	Difference		9
4	Office salaries were paid in cash		1,430
	and were allocated as follows.		
	Indirect:	manufacturing	300
		administration	880
		marketing, selling and distribution	250

		£'000
5	Office expenses were paid in cash	150
	and were apportioned as follows.	
	Indirect: manufacturing	25
	administration	105
	marketing, selling and distribution	20
6	Advertising, selling and distribution expenses were paid in cash	900
7	The depreciation charge for the year was calculated at	300
	and was allocated to: manufacturing	240
	administration	30
	marketing, selling and distribution	30
8	Materials issued from stores at actual cost amounted to	4,847
	and were allocated as follows.	
	Direct, at standard	4,440
	Indirect, at actual: manufacturing	300
	administration	60
	marketing, selling and distribution	55
	Difference	8
9	Manufacturing overhead at standard on direct work done amounted to	1,665
	The balance on the account was written off.	
10	Completed finished goods were transferred from the factory to the finished goods stock, valued at standard manufacturing cost of	7,150
11	Bad debts written off against the provision amounted to	10
12	The bad debts provision was increased by	15
	This increase is to be regarded as a marketing, selling and distribution item for costing purposes.	
13	Sales on credit amounted to	10,000
14	The standard manufacturing cost of the goods sold was	6,500
15	Cash received from debtors	9,555
	after deducting cash discounts of	245
	These discounts are regarded as an administration item for costing purposes.	
16	The excess or deficit of actual total overhead when compared with standard total overhead was as follows.	
	Administration — Deficit	5
	Marketing, selling and distribution — Excess	20
17	Fixed assets were purchased for cash for	250

You are required to journalise the summarised transactions given above, using the appropriate code numbers. You are not to use the titles of the accounts in your journal entries. Narratives need not be given.

64 INTERLOCKING LIMITED (20 marks)

The trial balance of Interlocking Limited at 31 December 19X2 was as follows.

	£
Capital: authorised and issued	
10,000 £1 ordinary shares	10,000
Fixed assets	4,000
Debtors	1,600
Materials	2,000
Work in progress	2,100
Finished goods	1,900
Creditors	2,000
Bank	400

The transactions during January 19X3 were as follows.

Materials purchases (credit)	1,500
Sales (credit)	2,500
Operating expenses	1,200
Wages	1,000
Discounts allowed	120
Discounts received	100
Creditors' payments	1,600
Debtors' payments	2,750
Issues of raw materials	3,000
Issues of finished goods	2,000
Production to finished goods	4,200
Production capitalised	500

Depreciation is taken as 1% per month on fixed assets and £100 is charged as notional rent in the cost accounts.

You are required to prepare the following.

(a) All the ledger accounts.
(b) The cost profit and loss account.
(c) The financial profit and loss account.
(d) The trial balance as at 31 January 19X3.

65 BASIC REVISION QUESTION: CHECKLIST (20 marks)

The accounts manager of a business rang up the data processing manager one day and said:

'It's in the back of my mind that we might be needing some new software packages soon. Obviously I'll be in touch before making any decisions, but I wonder if there is some sort of checklist available, listing points to consider when choosing a package? Any package, not just accounting ones. Can you help?'

The data processing manager turns this query over to you; you are required to draw up a checklist for the accounts manager to use.

66 MICROCOMPUTERS (15 marks)

Microcomputers are being used by many organisations of varying sizes either to prepare their accounts or to assist the managers of an organisation to control its activities.

(a) Describe how a microcomputer accounting package may be used to deal with accounting transactions. (10 marks)

(b) What are the advantages of using such accounting packages instead of a manual system? (5 marks)

67 MATRIX FORM (10 marks)

(a) What is the general name often given to computer programs specifically designed to use the matrix form and in what ways can a computer use such a form? (4 marks)

(b) Explain how such computer programs can be applied in accounting. (6 marks)

68 SPREADSHEETS AND DATABASES (15 marks)

Spreadsheets and databases are commonly used by accountants.

You are required to explain the following.

(a) The difference between a database and a spreadsheet. (5 marks)

(b) How a database might be used to record details of an organisation's fixed assets. (5 marks)

(c) How a spreadsheet might be used in the preparation of budgets. (5 marks)

SUGGESTED SOLUTIONS

1 BASIC REVISION QUESTION: PRUDENCE

(a) (i) A sale must never be recognised before the goods have even been ordered. There is no certainty about the value of the sale, nor when it will take place, even if it is virtually certain that the goods will be sold.

(ii) A sale must never be recognised before the customer places an order. Even though the order will be a specific quantity of goods at a specific price, it is not yet certain that the sale transaction will go through. The customer may cancel the order, or the supplier might be unable to deliver the goods as ordered.

(iii) A sale will be recognised when delivery of the goods is made only when:
1. the sale is for cash, and so the cash is received at the same time; or
2. the sale is on credit and the customer accepts delivery (eg by signing a delivery note).

(iv) The critical event for a credit sale is usually the dispatch of an invoice to the customer. There is then a legally enforceable debt, payable on specified terms, for a completed sale transaction.

(v) The critical event for a cash sale is both when delivery takes place and the cash is received at the same time. It would be too cautious or 'prudent' to await cash payment for a credit sale transaction before recognising the sale, unless the customer is a high credit risk and there is serious doubt about his ability or intention to pay.

(vi) It would again be over-cautious to wait for clearance of the customer's cheque before recognising sales revenue. Such a precaution would only be justified in cases where there is a very high risk of the bank refusing to honour the cheque.

(b) (i) Stocks should be valued at the lower amount of
1. cost; or
2. net realisable value (ie their sale value, net of further costs which would be incurred to make them ready for sale). In the case of unfinished work in progress, where there is a foreseeable loss on the completed job, the cost of the work to date should be reduced by the amount of the foreseeable loss.

(ii) Where appropriate, a *provision* should be made for doubtful debts.

(iii) Where the market value of land and buildings has risen, and so exceeds their purchase cost, it might be appropriate to revalue the assets in the balance sheet of the business. For example, if a property which cost £200,000 has risen in value to £280,000, but only on condition that the increase in market value is likely to be permanent.

It would not be appropriate, however, to claim a realised profit on revaluation of the property, since there has been no sale, and there is no prospect of a cash benefit from the increase in property value until it is eventually sold. However, the profit *would be* realised when (and if) the property is sold.

2 DEFINITIONS

(a) The *going concern concept* assumes that the company will continue in operational existence for the foreseeable future. Thus, the company's assets can be recorded in the accounts at the value to the company and not at break up valuation. This will often result in a significant difference in valuation, especially where assets are unlikely to be of value to any other business, for example specially adapted premises, tools etc.

In addition, where a business is not a going concern and therefore accounts are prepared on the assumption that the business will be dissolved, extra costs (for example bad debt and stock obsolescence provisions, liquidators' fees, reorganisation costs) must be allowed for.

An example of the use of the going concern concept is the capitalisation of development expenditure and amortisation over its expected economic life.

(b) The *accruals concept* is also described as the matching concept. Revenue and expenditure are matched under this concept and recorded in the accounts when earned or incurred, rather than on the associated cash movement, provided that it is prudent so to treat them.

This allows most obviously for credit sales, but also results in the identification of stock at the end of each accounting period rather than writing all purchases off to the trading account. Only purchases which result in a sale recorded in the period or are used for promotional or similar purposes should be matched with sales for the period. Therefore, if purchased goods still on hand at the period end are of saleable quality and the company will still be trading in the next period (ie the prudence and going concern concepts are satisfied), then any unsold goods can be treated as current assets and their value can be deducted from purchases and opening stock.

(c) The *consistency concept* provides that similar items should be treated in the same way from year to year in accounts. When the accounting treatment changes, comparatives should also be restated to facilitate comparisons. This makes it easier to establish trends, one of the principal uses of accounts by investors and analysts.

Additionally, profit should not be open to manipulation by managers to avoid tax, boost bonuses, investment analysis ratios etc by choosing the most beneficial accounting treatment instead of that which is most apt.

An example of the application of this concept is the requirement to publish the policies for depreciating different classes of fixed asset, eg motor vehicles depreciated over four years on a straight line basis, and to apply these policies.

(d) The *prudence concept* lays down that revenue and profits are not anticipated but should only be recorded when earning is reasonably certain. Expenses and liabilities should, however, be recorded when anticipated, as best estimates if no actual figures are available.

Loss in value of assets, whether realised or not, should be recorded when it arises, but a gain in value of an asset should not be recorded except via an unrealised reserve and only then if properly warranted.

An example of the application of the prudence concept is the requirement to value stock at the lower of cost and net realisable value.

3 LIMITATIONS OF HISTORICAL COST ACCOUNTING

The presentation of the financial affairs of a business in the form of a balance sheet and profit and loss account, using the 'historical cost convention' and generally accepted principles of accounting suffers from a number of fairly serious shortcomings at the best of times, but there are particular problems in times of inflation.

(a) The values disclosed in the financial statements are expressed in terms of an unstable measuring unit, ie sterling. Because of the continuing erosion of the purchasing power of money, historical cost values of assets bear no relation to current values. In other words, comparisons of the current trading results of a business with its results, of say, ten years ago might indicate that in money terms the business has had a satisfactory growth in profits and assets. However, when the effects of inflation have been taken into account and the money values are restated as real values it is very possible that the business is worse off now compared with its position ten years ago. The use of an unstable measuring unit is the greatest drawback of financial statements for interpretation purposes. Consider the comparison of the balance sheets of two companies, A and B.

BALANCE SHEET AS AT 31 DECEMBER 19X0 (EXTRACT)

	Company A	*Company B*
	£	£
Fixed assets		
Factory buildings at cost	200,000	100,000

It would appear from the balance sheets that company A owns a factory building either twice as large or twice as valuable as the building owned by company B. In fact, the building owned by B is exactly the same as that owned by A, but was built five years earlier, when it cost half as much to build. To be able to compare the assets owned by company A and company B, the historical cost convention must be abandoned, and the assets stated in terms of current market value, or replacement cost.

(b) The return on capital employed in historical cost accounts gives a misleading comparison of results over a period of years. If profits are the same each year, they are really declining in value because of inflation. This means that whereas ROCE might be constant, or even rising, year by year in the historical cost accounts, the real position might be getting worse.

(c) After paying taxation, interest and some (necessary) dividends, most companies have insufficient internally-generated funds to survive in the long term, without an improvement in real profits. (Shortages of cash are essentially the problem, which historical cost accounts do not reveal because they do not disclose the cost of replacing the assets of the business.)

(d) Accounting profits are an inadequate guide to the amount which may safely be distributed as dividend. This is because at least a part of the profit shown by the historical cost account must be ploughed back into the business just to maintain its previous operating capacity.

(e) There are difficulties in measuring profits. In historical cost accounts, holding gains on stocks are included in the gross profit figure. Such gains merely represent the amount the business would have to spend to maintain its existing level of stocks. Conversely profits or losses on holdings of monetary items are not shown.

4 ESTIMATION/DEPRECIATION

Depreciation is defined, in statement of standard accounting practice 12 as 'the measure of the wearing out, consumption, or other reduction in the useful economic life of a fixed asset whether arising from the use, effluxion (ie passage) of time or obsolescence through technological or market changes.'

The main concepts relating to depreciation are the *accruals* concept and the *prudence* concept.

A fixed asset is acquired for continuing use in an organisation. According to the *accruals* concept, costs should be applied over the periods to which they relate. A fixed asset is used over a number of years, and so depreciation comprises the cost of that asset allocated over its years in use.

On the other hand, under the *prudence* concept, any expense or liability must be recognised as soon as it arises. If an asset suddenly ceases to work, or have any use to the business, it might be prudent not to value it in the balance sheet, and to write it off.

As the cost of the asset is spread over the periods of its use, the profit for a period therefore takes into account all the costs associated with that period. Even though an asset might have a higher market value than its cost or net book value, especially in times of inflation, then depreciation should still be provided, as the asset is being used up.

Current cost accounting seeks to take inflation into account in the preparation of financial statements. Its aim is to ensure, amongst other things, that assets are realistically valued, and that reported increases in profits are not caused by inflation. Fixed assets are valued at replacement cost, and depreciation is charged on this current cost. This is to reflect 'wearing out' of the asset in terms of current prices.

Estimation is a practical necessity in the calculation of the depreciation charge. When an asset is purchased, its useful economic life is estimated in advance. Similarly, in current cost accounting estimates are used to determine the replacement cost of particular assets. This can be achieved by taking the current market price. If the asset is one which is no longer made, and for which there is no obvious equivalent, the estimate might have to be based on general or industry price indices, or on some other way of estimating the asset's economic value to the business.

5 RESEARCH AND DEVELOPMENT EXPENDITURE

(a) SSAP 13 describes the three categories of research as follows.

(i) *Pure or basic research*: experimental or theoretical work undertaken primarily to acquire new scientific or technical knowledge for its own sake rather than directed towards any specific aim or application.

(ii) *Applied research*: original or critical investigation undertaken in order to gain new scientific or technical knowledge and directed towards a specific practical aim or objective.

(iii) *Development*: use of scientific or technical knowledge in order to produce new or substantially improved materials, devices, products, or services, to install new processes or systems prior to the commencement of commercial production or commercial applications, or to improving substantially those already produced and installed.

(b) The accounting treatment of research and development expenditure highlights an issue where two of the fundamental concepts of accounting are in conflict, namely the *accruals* concept and the *prudence* concept.

Under the accruals concept, revenue and costs are matched with one another and dealt with in the profit and loss account of the period to which they relate. Following the concept of prudence, on the other hand, requires that revenue and profits are only included in the profit and loss account only when realisation is assessed with certainty. Provision is made in the profit and loss account for all known expenses or losses whether known for certain or merely estimated.

Research and development expenditure is expenditure incurred now with some future benefit in mind. Therefore, under the accruals concept, research and development expenditure incurred now should not be charged to the profit and loss account until some time in the future when the cost can be matched against the revenue generated by the product or service for which the research and development expenditure was made. However, these future benefits are not known with certainty, whereas the costs incurred to date most definitely are, and so under the prudence concept research and development expenditure should be written off to the profit and loss account in the period in which it was incurred.

SSAP 13 recommends that of the three categories of research and development expenditure only development costs ((a)(iii) above) can be carried forward, and even then this treatment is not compulsory. The benefits from pure and applied research are too *indirect* to carry forward to future periods.

6 FINANCIAL REPORTING

(a) Shareholders require information on a company and its performance to make investment decisions, and to assist in voting at general meetings. This information should be provided in sufficient detail to allow informed decision-making but without obscuring the important issues.

The shareholders' primary interest lies in the earnings and dividend trends revealed by the profit and loss account, as these are traditionally the main factors in share valuation. Further information on future projects and dividend policy will make it easier to establish trends. Comparison with other companies is facilitated by presentation of information in a similar format by all companies.

Additionally, shareholders in large public companies will wish to check the stewardship of the directors to whom they have delegated the company's management. Where shareholders are in close touch with management (or comprise the management), this is not as important.

Finally, many investors nowadays wish to avoid investment in companies whose ecological, social and political activities are at odds with their own attitudes. The corporate report should therefore give full details of all investments, products, overseas locations, charitable and political donations and initiatives etc.

(b) In times of high inflation, growth in dividends and earnings can be insufficient to keep ahead of rising prices. Under the historical cost basis of accounting, this is not obvious from the accounts because they are not stated in 'real' terms, ie adjusted to show what the results would have been if there had no been no inflation in the period.

The two most common alternatives to historical cost accounting are *current cost accounting (CCA)* and *current purchasing power accounting (CPP)*.

Under CCA, assets are valued at replacement cost. Various adjustments to profit are made so that the current cost profit 'represents the surplus arising from the ordinary activities of the company in the period after allowing for the impact of price changes on the net assets needed to maintain its operating capital' (ASC Handbook *Accounting for the effects of changing prices).*

CCA's aim is to make it easier to assess how well the company is maintaining its operating capacity. By contrast, under CPP the aim is to measure how well the equity investors' capital has been maintained in the period. All non-monetary assets are restated after adjustment for changes in the retail price index since acquisition. An adjustment to profit is made to reflect the reduction in value in real terms of long-term debt when inflation rises and the loss of value when non-monetary items (eg stock) are turned into monetary items (eg debtors).

The application of general price indices means that for businesses affected by non-standard levels of inflation, the adjusted accounts have little relevance to the company's operating capacity. However, the investor needs to know how the investment has performed in terms of increasing his purchasing power.

A disadvantage of both CCA and CPP is that neither has gained general acceptance in the UK and neither is straightforward to interpret, even for the more financially sophisticated investor, especially as no consistent application has been made mandatory. Accounts prepared to allow for inflation are therefore not directly comparable with most similar enterprises' accounts.

A more important point for most investors is to examine the company's liquidity, which is stretched in times of inflation because of the constant increases in the replacement costs of materials and in labour costs. This can be gauged from the balance sheet, flow of funds statement and notes. The investor needs to know whether sufficient funds are being generated to cover dividend payments as well as other liabilities and new investment plans and to maintain current levels of operation. More fundamentally, the company must remain solvent if the investment of shareholders is to remain secure.

To this end, companies need to disclose future commitments under leases and other financing agreements, together with contingent liabilities and guarantees.

7 INFORMATION USER GROUPS

1 *Owners*. In the case of a limited company these are the shareholders; in the case of a partnership, the partners; in the case of a public sector organisation, the government or a local authority. Where owners do not themselves exercise management control, they need to assess how well management is looking after the organisation, and if it is a profit making organisation how much profit has been made, will be made, and how much is to be distributed.

2 *Management* needs information of an organisation's current financial circumstances to run it efficiently, and to take decisions relating to its future. Financial information is a very important component of management's information requirements.

3 *Employees* need information about their organisation as their careers and salaries are directly affected. Moreover, it means that employee representatives are as well informed as management in the context of any discussion of wage claims, productivity improvements or other changes in working practices.

4 *Bankers* who lend money to an organisation have an interest in ensuring that the money can be returned. Accounting information is used to establish an organisation's creditworthiness.

5 *Suppliers* wish to know about an organisation's ability to pay its debts, and also any other commercial developments which might affect them.

6 *Customers* need to know that the organisation is a going concern and is a secure source of supply.

7 *The Inland Revenue, Customs and Excise, and other government departments* need accounting information to assess the amount that an organisation should contribute, in the form of taxation, to social welfare.

8 *Various organisations* for example pressure groups such as the Consumers Association, Friends of the Earth etc use accounting information as material to further their campaigns.

9 *Financial analysts, journalists, credit reference agencies, investment advisors* use accounting information for the benefit of their clients (eg to alert them to new investment opportunities).

10 *Competitors* use financial information to gain commercial advantage if there is any to be gained from it.

(*Tutorial note*: only six user groups were required)

8 INFORMATION NEEDS OF CREDITORS

A creditor is a person (or institution) owed money by an organisation, and, as such, is a liability of the organisation. However, there are many different types of creditor.

A business purchases its supplies from trade creditors, whether for production or for administration. Trade creditors need information to see if the business is a going concern, has sufficient resources to pay them, and will place more orders.

An overdraft is a liability to a bank, maintained on a continuing basis. The bank needs information to ensure that there is enough cash flow coming into the business to finance the overdraft. Bank overdrafts are often unsecured, and so the bank must be satisfied with the long term prospects of the business.

Some bank loans (especially long term bank loans) are secured. This means that if the loan is not repaid, then the bank has the right to an asset, or some or all of the assets of the business (similar to a mortgage institution repossessing a house). The secured creditor not only needs to know whether the loan and any interest will be paid back in the normal course of business, but also the value of the security. If the security is land and buildings then the value of these will be of use to them in assessing the value of the security.

Audited published financial statements go some way towards meeting these information requirements. A source and application of funds statement gives an indication of the liquidity of the company. This shows the changes in the liquid resources (cash, or assets and liabilities of a business.) Moreover, it is a relatively simple exercise for creditors, and other users of financial statements to calculate liquidity ratios and so forth.

Long term and secured creditors need reassurance that the organisation is a going concern, and that there is no threat to the security of the assets. A limited company must provide details of securities over its assets. However, a bank with a secured loan will take other steps to ensure that its security is not jeopardised.

9 CAPITAL AND REVENUE

(a) Capital items are assets and liabilities which appear on a company's balance sheet. Many assets represent capitalised expenditure which provides an enduring benefit, either inherently, in the form of fixed assets, for example, or because they generate cash or other funds required to operate the business, in the form of investments, for example.

Revenue items are items of income and expense which are usually recurrent; eg sales of goods or services, purchases of components and payment of professional fees. Revenue income derives from the exploitation of assets. This may be directly, as in the case of interest earned from bank deposits, or indirectly, as when salesmen are given company cars to enable them to perform their duties.

Revenue items are allocated to the accounting periods in which they arise and are charged or credited to that period's profit and loss account. When income has been received or an expense paid after the end of the accounting period, an asset or liability, as appropriate, should be created to defer recognition of the item until the proper period (ie deferred income, accruals and prepayments).

An example of the distinction is the difference in accounting treatment between buying an asset, for example a taxi cab, and renting it. Because an outright purchase results in an enduring benefit to the owner, the expenditure would be capitalised, as would enhancement expenditure of a permanent nature (eg a new engine). However, routine maintenance and refurbishment would not be capitalised but written off to the profit and loss account as incurred because this expenditure merely puts the owner in a better position to exploit the asset in the short term.

Similarly, because rental of an asset confers only the right to use the asset for a specified period, the expense incurred in respect of a given accounting period would be written off against the revenue earned in that period. For the same reason, depreciation is charged in respect of assets with a limited economic life, to recognise their contribution towards the revenue generated in the period.

(b) The distinction between capital and revenue items is sometimes difficult to make; for example, repairs may be considered capital or revenue items depending on the nature of the expenditure. To facilitate comparison between accounting periods and between companies, it is important to establish a policy and keep to it consistently.

This is particularly important where inconsistency would result in a large difference to profits, for example, if a surplus on revaluation of a property were to be recorded in the profit and loss account rather than a revaluation reserve.

10 ENGINEERING

(a) SSAP9 requires that stock 'shall be valued at cost or net realisable value, whichever is the lower'. By 'cost' is meant all costs incurred to get the goods into a selling condition; thus in a retail business the 'cost' is taken as the purchase price. The 'net' realisable value is the amount at which it is expected that items of stocks and work in progress can be disposed of less selling expenses and expenses incurred in bringing work in progress to a saleable condition without creating either profit or loss in the year of sale. The accounting choice of the lower value is dictated by the doctrine of prudence, and the attachment to historical cost by a desire to remain objective.

(b) The historic cost of the electric circuits has been determined on a LIFO basis which is not normally acceptable (for both tax and practical reasons) for valuation purposes. Revaluing that item on a FIFO basis, therefore, would produce the following value for closing stock.

	£	£
Purchases during year		
250 at £30		7,500
300 at £35		10,500
200 at £40		8,000
		26,000
Issues		
200 at £30	6,000	
50 at £30	1,500	
110 at £35	3,850	
		11,350
Value of closing stock (FIFO)		14,650

Retabulating the values we therefore have the following.

	Historical cost	*Replacement cost*	*Net realisable value*
	£	£	£
Sheet steel	8,000	9,500	8,600
Iron bars	7,600	6,750	7,000
Electrical circuits	14,650	16,000	13,100
	30,250	32,250	28,700

The lowest aggregate value is £28,700 but the dictum of 'lower of cost and net realisable value' should be applied to separate groups of items, and hence, the value to be placed on closing stock should be as follows.

	£
Sheet steel	8,000
Iron bars	7,000
Electrical circuits	13,100
	28,100

(Note that the replacement cost values are a 'red herring', as they represent neither historical cost nor net realisable values and are not, therefore, used in calculating the 'lower of cost and net realisable value'.)

11 CLOSING STOCK

	£
Original valuation of stock at 30 April 19X2	187,033
Adjustments	
(i)	-
(ii)	(140)
(iii)	8,010
(iv)	(6,480)
(v)	1,200
(vi)	-
(vii)	(152)
Amended valuation at 30 April 19X2	189,471

Reasons

(i) Original cost still remains below net realisable value and so no adjustment necessary.

(ii) Net realisable value = £6,321 - £804 = £5,517 which is £140 lower than original cost.

(iii) Arithmetical error under-valuing stock by £8,010 (£9,105 - £1,095).

(iv) Arithmetical error over-valuing stock by £6,480 (480 x £13.50).

(v) Goods belong to Cranfleet Commodities and should be included in stock at cost (100/125 x £1,500) = £1,200.

(vi) Ownership of the goods belong to Cranfleet Commodities, even though payment has not been made, and so they should be included in stock - no adjustment necessary.

(vii) Whilst free samples belong to Cranfleet the cost was zero and no value should be included.

12 BASIC REVISION QUESTION: RBD

Tutorial note: there are two possible methods of recording the £1,043 discounts received from creditors, each of which leads to the same figure for purchases. In the suggested solution below the simpler method is used: £1,043 is debited to creditors control account and credited to discounts received. The only entries in the provision for discounts receivable account are the balances b/f and c/f and the transfer of the difference to P & L account.

Alternatively, the credit entry could be taken to the provision account. The net transfer from that account to P & L account would then be £1,031.

RENT RECEIVABLE

	£		£
Rent received in advance c/f	517	Rent received in advance b/f	463
∴ P & L account	4,004	Bank - rents rec'd	4,058
	4,521		4,521

RENT AND RATES PAYABLE

	£		£
Prepayment b/f	1,246	Accrual b/f	315
Bank - rent paid	7,491		
Bank - rates paid	2,805	∴ P & L account	10,100
Accrual c/f	382	Prepayment c/f	1,509
	11,924		11,924

CREDITORS

	£		£
Bank - payments	75,181	Balance b/f	5,258
Discounts received	1,043	∴ Purchases	75,686
Balance c/f	4,720		
	80,944		80,944

PROVISION FOR DISCOUNTS RECEIVABLE

	£		£
Balance b/f	106	Balance c/f	94
		∴ P & L account	12
	106		106

13 AB THE SOLE TRADER

Tutorial note: the question clearly asks for more than one account so do not try to prepare a single account for both types of expense, otherwise you are likely to confuse both yourself and the examiner!

There are no accruals or prepayments brought forward because AB has just commenced trading. In each account the transfer to the profit and loss account is deduced as a balancing figure.

TELEPHONE ACCOUNT

19X0		£	*19X0*		£
1 January	Bank	15	31 October	Profit and loss *	677
1 April	Bank (159 + 15)	174	31 October	Balance c/d (working 1)	10
1 July	Bank (211 + 15)	226			
1 October	Bank (183 + 15)	198			
31 October	Balance c/d	74			
		687			687
1 November	Balance b/d	10	1 November	Balance b/d	74

* Balancing figure

RENT ACCOUNT

19X0		£	*19X0*		£
1 January	Bank	600	31 October	Profit and loss *	2,350
1 April	Bank	750	31 October	Balance c/d (working 2)	500
1 July	Bank	750			
1 October	Bank	750			
		2,850			2,850
1 November	Balance b/d	500			

* Balancing figure

Workings

1. Telephone rental paid in advance = 2/3 x October payment
 = 2/3 x £15
 = £10

2. Rent paid in advance = 2/3 x October payment
 = 2/3 x £750
 = £500

(b) The accruals concept is also described as the matching concept. Revenue and expenditure are matched under this concept and are recorded in the accounts when they are earned or incurred rather than when the associated cash movement takes place.

For example the proportion of the telephone rental which has been paid in advance is carried forward to be matched against the revenue of the following period. Conversely, not all of the telephone calls have been paid for at the end of October. The charge to the profit and loss account is therefore increased to take account of the amount which is still owing. A credit balance is carried forward on the telephone account to be offset against the call charges when they are paid next period.

Adjusting for accruals and prepayments in this way ensures that costs are correctly matched against revenues for the period and that profits are not under or over stated.

14 PLANT AND MACHINERY

Tutorial note: for this type of question, the best approach is to set out a table showing all the workings for the various figures, from which the specific answers required by the question can be extracted.

Date	Cost	*Cumulative dep'n to 31.10.X4*	*NBV 31.10.X4*	*Additions*	*19X5 dep'n*	*NBV 31.10.X5*
	£	£	£	£	£	£
31.10.W4	30,000	30,000	-	-	-	-
31.10.W4	10,000	10,000	-	-	-	- *
30. 4.W5	20,000	19,000	1,000	-	1,000	-
30. 4.W5	10,000	9,500	500	-	250	- *
31.10.W9	10,000	5,000	5,000	-	1,000	4,000
31.10.W9	5,000	2,500	2,500	-	375	- *
31. 7.X2	20,000	4,500	15,500	-	2,000	13,500
31. 1.X3	5,000	875	4,125	-	500	3,625
30. 4.X4	10,000	500	9,500	-	1,000	8,500
	120,000	81,875	38,125	-	6,125	29,625
30. 4.X5				8,000	400	7,600
					6,525	37,225

* These items shown as nil net book values as they were scrapped or sold during the year. The net book values of the three items which were scrapped or sold are set against the proceeds of those items to determine whether there has been a profit or loss on disposal.

	Net book value	*Disposal Proceeds*
	£	£
£10,000 plant bought on 30 April 19W5	250	400
£5,000 plant bought on 31 October 19W9	2,125	-
£10,000 plant bought on 31 October 19W4	-	
	2,375	400

Net loss on disposal = £2,375 - £400 = £1,975.

(a)

PLANT AND MACHINERY ACCOUNT

		£			£
31.10.W4	Balance b/d	38,125	31.1.X5	Sales	400
30.4.X5	Purchases	8,000	31.10.X5	Profit and loss account (19X5 depreciation)	6,525
			31.10.X5	Profit and loss account (net loss on disposals)	1,975
			31.10.X5	Balance c/d	37,225
		46,125			46,125
31.10.X5	Balance b/d	37,225			

(b)

BALANCE SHEET (EXTRACT) AS AT 31 OCTOBER 19X5

Fixed assets
Plant and machinery

		£
Cost:	as at 1 November 19X4	120,000
	additions	8,000
	disposals	(25,000)
	as at 31 October 19X5	103,000
Depreciation:	as at 1 November 19X4	81,875
	charge for year	6,525
	disposals	(22,625)
	as at 31 October 19X5	65,775
Net book value at 1 November 19X4		38,125
Net book value at 31 October 19X5		37,225

15 BRAMWELL FACTORS

		Debit £	*Credit* £
(a)	Provision for discounts allowed to debtors	72.13	
	Profit and loss		72.13
	Being release of provision no longer required		
(b)	Profit and loss (bad debts)	43.36	
	Debtors		43.36
	Being bad debt written off (£64.80) less recovery of £21.44 previously written off as a bad debt		
(c)	Debtors	3.20	
	Profit and loss (discount allowed)		3.20
	Being correction of amount of discount allowed to credit customer		
(d)	Prepayments	22.45	
	Profit and loss (electricity)	36.71	
	Accruals		36.71
	Profit and loss (insurance)		22.45
	Being electricity accrued and insurance prepaid at this date		
(e)	Bank	126.55	
	Creditors (unclaimed wages)		126.55
	Being unclaimed wage arrears banked		

		Debit £	Credit £
(f)	Profit and loss (wages)	464.12	
	Profit and loss (salaries)	301.70	
	Creditors (wages and salaries)		765.82
	Being amounts earned by employees at this date due for payment in January 19X3		
(g)	Profit and loss (repairs and renewals)	5,000.00	
	Provision for depreciation	100.00	
	Profit and loss (depreciation)		100.00
	Premises		5,000.00
	Being correction for repairs capitalised in error and for the resultant overcharge for depreciation		
(h)	Creditors (Conbrec Limited)	163.04	
	Debtors (Conbrec Limited)		163.04
	Being settlement in contra		

16 JOURNAL ENTRIES

	Date	*Narrative*	*Debit* £	*Credit* £
(a)	27.1.X6	N Limited	20,000	
		Sales		20,000
		Being sale of goods on credit		
(b)	31.1.X6	Bills receivable	20,000	
		N Limited		20,000
		Being three month bill of exchange accepted by N Limited		
(c)	1.2.X6	Bank	19,250	
		Discounting charge	750	
		Bills receivable		20,000
		Being bill discounted with bank		
(d)	5.2.X6	Purchases	10,000	
		P Limited		10,000
		Being goods purchased on credit		
(e)	6.2.X6	P Limited	10,000	
		Bills payable		10,000
		Being three month bill of exchange accepted from P Limited		
(g)	30.4.X6	N Limited	20,000	
		Bank		20,000
		Being N Limited's bill dishonoured by non-payment		

			Debit £	Credit £
(h)	6.5.X6	Bills payable	10,000	
		Bank		10,000
		Being payment of bill drawn by P Limited		
(j)	23.9.X6	Bank	6,000	
		Bad debts	14,000	
		N Limited		20,000
		Being first and final dividend arising from liquidation of N Limited (30p in £)		

Note that neither (f) nor (i) are relevant as far as M Limited's journal is concerned.

17 XYZ LIMITED

Tutorial note: since 80 hours of the overtime were worked at the specific request of a customer the overtime premium on those hours is a direct cost of that job. The premium for the overtime that cannot be traced to a specific job is treated as an indirect cost.

Suggested solution

Initial workings

		£
1.	Gross wages bill:	
	net wages	34,000
	PAYE	16,500
	employees national insurance	2,900
		53,400
	Basic wage cost for 10,500 hours = 10,500 x £5	52,500
	Overtime premium paid	900
	÷ £2.50 per hour =	360 hours of overtime

		£
2.	*Analysis of production overhead*	
	Overtime premium (360-80)hrs x £2.50	700
	Employers national insurance	3,300
	Non productive hours (940 x £5)	4,700
		8,700

		£
3.	*Analysis of direct wages*	
	Hours worked on customers' jobs = 8,260 x £5	41,300
	Overtime premium incurred for customer = 80 x £2.50	200
	Total direct wages	41,500

(a)

	Debit £	Credit £
Work in progress control (direct wages)	41,500	
Production overhead control	8,700	
Capital expenditure control (1,300 x £5)	6,500	
PAYE creditor		16,500
National insurance creditor		6,200
Bank (net wages paid)		34,000

Being wages for the week ending 27 October 19X0

(b) Costs incurred on the company's capital expenditure are treated in the same way as any other capital expenditure. This means that the relevant wages, materials and any related overhead expenditures are not charged against revenue in the period in which they are incurred. Instead they are included with fixed assets on the balance sheet and a proportion of the expenditure is written off as depreciation each year, according to the company's depreciation policy.

Reported profit for the current year will be higher than if the expenditure is treated as revenue expenditure, but profits in future years will be lower as the expenditure is depreciated over the useful life of the relevant fixed asset.

18 LEDGER ACCOUNTS WITH CONTROL ACCOUNTS

DEBTORS LEDGER CONTROL

	£		£
Balance b/d	63,158	Sales returns	6,000
Sales	550,000	Cash	514,268
Provision for bad debts		Provision for discounts allowable	12,790
(bad debt recovered)	542	Provision for bad debts	4,100
		Cash	542
		Creditors ledger control	4,000
		Balance c/d	72,000
	613,700		613,700
Balance b/d	72,000		

CREDITORS LEDGER CONTROL

	£		£
Purchases returns	4,000	Balance b/d	32,000
Cash	258,100	Purchases	276,000
Provision for discount received	5,900		
Debtors ledger control	4,000		
Balance c/d	36,000		
	308,000		308,000
		Balance b/d	36,000

PROVISION FOR BAD DEBTS

	£		£
Debtors ledger control		Balance b/d	3,158
bad debts written off	4,100	Debtors ledger control	
Balance c/d (5% of £72,000)	3,600	bad debt recovered	542
		P & L account	4,000
	7,700		7,700
		Balance b/d	3,600

PROVISION FOR DISCOUNTS RECEIVABLE

	£		£
Balance b/d	800	Creditors ledger control	5,900
P & L account	6,000	Balance c/d (2½% of £36,000)	900
	6,800		6,800
Balance b/d	900		

PROVISION FOR DISCOUNTS ALLOWABLE

	£		£
Debtors ledger control	12,790	Balance b/d	1,500
Balance c/d (2½% of (72,000-3,600))	1,710	P & L account	13,000
	14,500		14,500
		Balance b/d	1,710

19 NOSTLA PRODUCTS LIMITED

(a)

PURCHASES LEDGER CONTROL
YEAR ENDED 30 NOVEMBER 19X9

		£			£
19X8			*19X8*		
30 Nov	Balance b/d	1,242	1 Dec	Balance b/d	24,647
19X9			*19X9*		
30 Nov	Purchases returns	15,113	30 Nov	Purchases	176,410
30 Nov	Bank	159,400	30 Nov	Balance c/d	1,350
30 Nov	Discounts receivable	3,900			
30 Nov	Sales ledger control: J Dyke	1,268			
30 Nov	Balance c/d	21,484			
		202,407			202,407
1 Dec	Balance b/d	1,350	1 Dec	Balance b/d	21,484

SALES LEDGER CONTROL

		£			£
19X8			*19X8*		
1 Dec	Balance b/d	39,650	1 Dec	Balance b/d	941
19X9			*19X9*		
30 Nov	Sales	310,690	30 Nov	Sales returns	6,764
30 Nov	Balance c/d	813	30 Nov	Bank	306,540
			30 Nov	Discounts allowable	1,070
			30 Nov	Purchases ledger control: J Dyke	1,268
			30 Nov	Bad debts written off	970
			30 Nov	Balance c/d	33,600
		351,153			351,153
1 Dec	Balance b/d	33,600	1 Dec	Balance b/d	813

(b) (i) JOURNAL

		Debit £	Credit £
19X9			
30 Nov	Profit and loss account	840	
	Provision for doubtful debts		840

Being creation of provision for doubtful debts 2½% of total amount due from customers at 30 November 19X9 (£33,600).

(ii) The creation of a provision for doubtful debts does not affect the present indebtedness to the company. Consequently no adjustment or entry in the sales ledger control account is necessary.

20 C LIMITED

(a) SALES LEDGER CONTROL

	Dr £			Cr £
Per question	54,358.37		Per question	1,194.26
			Sales day book	500.00
			Sales returns book	10.00
Balance c/d	1,867.72	(W1)	Balance c/d	54,521.83
	56,226.09			56,226.09

(*Note:* the net balance is £54,521.83 - £1,867.72 = £52,654.11)

Reconciliation

			£	£
Individual customer balances:	debits			55,136.65
	credits			(1,194.26)
				53,942.39
Bad debts written off				(474.16)
Debt collection fee				108.81
Dishonoured cheque	correction		601.75	
	reposting		607.15	
				1,208.90
Contra	correction		(378.82)	
	reposting		(378.82)	
				(757.64)
Transposition error	correction		(374.85)	
	reposting		347.58	
				(27.27)
Credit balance as debit	correction		(673.46)	
	reposting		(673.46)	
				(1,346.92)
Control account balance (net)				52,654.11

Working

1. | | |
|---|---|
| 1,194.26 | |
| 673.46 | adjustment |
| 1,867.72 | |

Although the error comes from the listing of balances, the control account needs to be adjusted as the credit balances on the listing of balances were assumed to be correct on the control account.

(b) A control account is a total account. It is used for the following purposes.

(i) To provide a check on the accuracy of entries made in the memorandum accounts, by comparing the total balance on the sales ledger control account with the total of individual balances on the personal accounts in the sales ledger.

(ii) To provide a balance more quickly for trial balance preparation.

(iii) To summarise the transactions of ledger accounts.

21 BASIC REVISION QUESTION: REX LIMITED

(a) BANK RECONCILIATION AT 30 JUNE 19X5

	£	£
Balance as per cash book		(380)
Adjustments and corrections		
Standing order paid, not recorded	(40)	
Cheques for advertising, payment in cash book overstated	18	
Payments with cash discount; receipt in cash book overstated	(6)	
		(28)
Corrected balance in cash book (overdraft)		(408)
Cheques paid out but not yet presented	1,037	
Cheques paid in but not yet cleared by bank	(1,680)	
		(643)
Balance as per bank statement - account overdrawn		(1,051)

(b) Profit and cash are not synonymous for the following reasons.

(i) Profit is measured by matching revenue and expenses, the cash balance by matching receipts and payments.

(ii) The company might have prepaid a large amount of expenses.

(iii) Assets with long lives acquired for cash in one period are not treated as an expense of that period, but expenses (depreciated) over time.

(iv) Certain disbursements of cash are treated as appropriations of profit rather than as a reduction of profit. For example in the case of a limited company the major disbursements are dividends and taxation.

22 JC LIMITED

Tutorial note: a systematic approach is needed to work through this fairly involved reconciliation. One approach is to mark the items in the reports which match and then pick up those items which do not match and include them in the reconciliation statement. Remember to check that the unpresented cheques from last month have now been presented. If they have not then they must be included in the reconciliation statement. One last point to help you on your way is that the receipts which are debited in the computerised accounting system are grouped together as 'counter credits' in the bank statement. For example J Smith & Sons (£1,405) and White Brothers (£697) together make up the £2,102 counter credit on 6 March.

(a) RECONCILIATION STATEMENT AS AT 31 MARCH 19X0

	£	£
Balance as per bank statement		5,467
Items not recorded by computerised system		
Bank charges	195	
Brown & Co cheque dishonoured	234	
Standing order: rates	4,029	
		4,458
		9,925
Less cheques not yet presented		
Cheque no: 543984	(1,512)	
543987	(279)	
543993	(2,305)	
543994	(5,242)	
		(9,338)
		587
Differences requiring investigation		
Difference on cheque 543989	(10,790)	
Difference on counter credit 14 March	(100)	
Difference on cheque 543991	(490)	
Difference on counter credit 23 March *	(2,086)	
		(13,466)
Balance per computerised accounting system		(12,879)

* £5,332 in bank statement - £(2,569 + 34 + 643)

(b) Three reasons why bank reconciliation statements should be prepared regularly are as follows.

(i) To update the company's records for items such as bank charges and dishonoured cheques so that managers are not working with an incorrect figure for the bank balance.

(ii) To identify and correct any errors as soon as possible, whether they are made by the company or by the bank.

(iii) To check on the time delay between cheques being written and their presentation for payment, and to check the time taken for cheques and cash paid in to be credited to the account. A better understanding of such timing differences will help managers to improve their cash planning.

23 BASIC REVISION QUESTION: TIMBER PRODUCTS

(a) DIFFERENCE ON TRIAL BALANCE SUSPENSE ACCOUNT

	£		£
Balance per trial balance	2,513	Wages	2,963
Discounts received	324	J Winters	198
Discounts allowed	324		
	3,161		3,161

(b) CORRECTED NET PROFIT

	£	£
Net profit per draft accounts		24,760
Add: discounts allowed transferred to discounts received	648	
stationery stock	1,500	
		2,148
Subtract: wages	2,963	
remittance from D North	3,000	
		(5,963)
Adjusted net profit		20,945

Workings

		£
J Winters:	posted	143
	paid	341
	difference	198

Stationery purchase	£2,000
stock £2,000 x $\frac{3}{4}$ =	£1,500

(c) *Principal uses of trial balances*

(i) They can provide an indication of accounting errors, with the exception of misposting or compensating errors.

(ii) They provide a start point for the preparation of annual accounts.

(iii) In small organisations, they can form the principal control mechanism.

24 RST

Tutorial note: the main difficulty here is deciding which items affect the suspense account. The only ones which do are those which affect the balancing of the trial balance. Any items which are normally entered as adjustments on the trial balance *after* the balances have been extracted from the books will not be passed through suspense account. This applies, for example, to the following items.

(a) Adjustments to provisions, for example for doubtful debts or discounts allowed.

(b) Valuation of closing stock.

(c) Calculation of closing accruals and prepayments.

For convenience, the suggested solution sets out the journal entries required in respect of those items which do not affect the suspense account.

(a)

STATEMENT OF ADJUSTMENTS TO PROFIT

	£	£
Draft net profit after tax		78,263
Add: reduction in provision for doubtful debts £1,300 - 2% x £(55,210 - 610)	208	
equipment incorrectly debited to purchases	9,800	
closing stock omitted	2,171	
prepayment omitted	162	
miscast of wages account	100	
	12,441	
Less: bad debts	610	
provision for discounts allowed 2% x £(55,210 - 610)	1,092	
opening rates prepayment omitted	491	
loss on disposal of vehicle £((8,100 - 5,280) - 1,350)	1,470	
disposal proceeds wrongly credited to sales	1,350	
depreciation on equipment originally debited to purchases (20% x £9,800)	1,960	
accrual omitted	543	
	7,516	
Net increase in profit		4,925
Revised net profit after tax		83,188

(b)

SUSPENSE ACCOUNT

	£		£
Supplier's account transposition error	90	Rates - opening prepayment omitted	491
Wages - miscast	100		
∴ Original balance	301		
	491		491

JOURNAL ENTRIES
(Other than those affecting the suspense account)

		Debit £	Credit £
(a) (i)	Bad and doubtful debts (P & L a/c)	610	
	Debtors		610
(ii)	Provision for doubtful debts	208	
	Bad & doubtful debts (P & L a/c)		208
(iii)	Discounts allowed (P & L a/c)	1,092	
	Provision for discounts allowed		1,092

(b) See suspense account

		Debit £	Credit £
(c)	Sales	1,350	
	Accumulated depreciation	5,280	
	Loss on disposal (P & L a/c)	1,470	
	Fixed assets at cost		8,100
(d)	See suspense account		
(e)	Equipment at cost	9,800	
	Purchases		9,800
	Depreciation (P & L a/c)	1,960	
	Accumulated depreciation		1,960
(f)	Closing stock (balance sheet)	2,171	
	Closing stock (trading account)		2,171
(g)	Electricity charges (P & L a/c)	543	
	Accrued expenses (balance sheet)		543
	Prepaid expenses (balance sheet)	162	
	Insurance (P & L a/c)		162
(h)	See suspense account		

25 IN SUSPENSE

Tutorial note: this question required you to analyse carefully a number of accounting errors. Some are errors in memorandum accounts only. Not all relate to the double entry.

(a) SUSPENSE ACCOUNT

	£		£
Sales ledger control	1,248	Difference on trial balance	2,045
Bank charges	66	Telephone	9
Disposal	740		
	2,054		2,054

(b)

		£
Balance per sales ledger control account		327,762
Discounts allowed		(1,248)
Contra: correction of error	(731)	
reposting	(731)	
		(1,462)
SEC Limited: adjust for sale		857
Adjusted control account balance		325,909
SEC Limited - not entered in sales day book or sales ledger		857
Balance per sales ledger		325,052

(c) *Adjusted net profit*

	£	£
Per draft accounts		412,967
Add: sale to SEC		857
		413,824
Less: telephone	9	
purchase day book (£11,629 - 11,269)	360	
loss on disposal of fixed asset £(800 - 740)	60	
		429
Adjusted net profit		413,395

26 BASIC REVISION QUESTION: HERBERT HOWELL

Tutorial note: although this question is not based on incomplete records it is important that you work through it before attempting the rest of the questions in this section. It is designed to help you to ensure that you know how to prepare a basic profit and loss account and balance sheet. There is no point in attempting to prepare accounts from incomplete information without first checking that you know how to prepare them when the information is complete!

HERBERT HOWELL
TRADING AND PROFIT AND LOSS ACCOUNT
FOR THE YEAR ENDED 31 MAY 19X9

	£	£
Sales		405,000
Cost of sales		
Opening stock	27,400	
Purchases (£259,600 - £1,040)	258,560	
	285,960	
Closing stock	25,900	
		260,060
Gross profit		144,940
Other income		
Discounts received		4,420
		149,360
Expenses		
Discounts allowed	3,370	
Loan interest	1,560	
Bad and doubtful debts (W1)	1,671	
Carriage out	5,310	
Wages and salaries	52,500	
Depreciation (W2)	9,525	
Other operating expenses (W3)	38,500	
		112,436
Net profit		36,924

HERBERT HOWELL
BALANCE SHEET AS AT 31 MAY 19X9

	Cost	*Dep'n*	*Net book value*
	£	£	£
Fixed assets			
Property (W4)	90,000	13,400	76,600
Equipment (W4)	57,500	41,125	16,375
	147,500	54,525	92,975
Current assets			
Stock		25,900	
Trade debtors	46,200		
Less provision for doubtful debts (W1)	231		
		45,969	
Prepayment		500	
Cash on hand		151	
		72,520	
Current liabilities			
Bank overdraft		14,500	
Trade creditors		33,600	
Accruals (140 + 200)		340	
		48,440	
Net current assets			24,080
Total assets less current liabilities			117,055
Long-term liabilities			
13% loan			12,000
			105,055
Capital			
Balance at 1 June 19X8			98,101
Net profit for the year			36,924
Drawings (£28,930 + £1,040)			(29,970)
Balance at 31 May 19X9			105,055

Workings

1. *Bad debts*

	£
Provision required: 0.5% x £46,200	231
Provision b/f	280
Decrease required	(49)
Add bad debts	1,720
Bad and doubtful expense for the year	1,671

2. *Depreciation*

	£
Property: 1% x £90,000	900
Equipment: 15% x £57,500	8,625
	9,525

		£
3.	*Other operating expenses*	£
	As trial balance	38,800
	Less prepayment	(500)
	Add accrual	200
		38,500

		Property	*Equipment*
4.	*Provision for depreciation*	£	£
	Balance b/f	12,500	32,500
	Charge for the year (W2)	900	8,625
	Balance c/f	13,400	41,125

27 MISS TEEK

Tutorial note: the opening balance sheet is given and so need not be reconstructed: Miss Teek's capital at 31 March 19X8 is £3,795. Accounts should be opened for the trading account, debtors, creditors and cash. Since some payments are in cash from cash takings, a two column cash book should distinguish between cash transactions and bank transactions.

MISS TEEK
TRADING AND PROFIT AND LOSS ACCOUNT
FOR THE YEAR ENDED 31 MARCH 19X9

	Working	£	£
Sales: cash	1		10,850
credit	2		1,650
			12,500
Opening stock		500	
Purchases	3	7,600	
		8,100	
Closing stock	4	(600)	
Cost of sales			7,500
Gross profit			5,000
Expenses			
Rent		970	
Repairs to canopy		201	
Van running expenses (520 + 80 + 323)		923	
Depreciation		1,000	
Sundry expenses (24 + 31)		55	
Bank interest		47	
Accounting fees		75	
Bad debts		29	
			3,300
			1,700
Profit on disposal of van			1,300
			3,000

MISS TEEK
BALANCE SHEET AS AT 31 MARCH 19X9

	Working	£	£	£
Fixed assets				
Motor van: cost	5			5,000
depreciation	5			1,000
net book value				4,000
Current assets				
Stock	4		600	
Debtors	2		320	
Cash in hand	1		39	
			959	
Current liabilities				
Bank overdraft	1	474		
Bank interest (presumably not paid until 1 April)		27		
Creditors	3	233		
			734	
Net current assets				225
				4,225
Proprietor's capital				
Balance at 31 March 19X8				3,795
Profit for the year			3,000	
Less drawings			2,570	
Retained profit for the year				430
Balance at 31 March 19X9				4,225

Workings

1.

CASH BOOK

	Cash £	Bank £		Cash £	Bank £
Balance b/d	55	2,800	Drawings (52 x £50)	2,600	
Cash takings banked (contra entry)		7,521	Petrol (52 x £10)	520	
Cheques banked		1,500	Sundry expenses	24	
Dividend income: drawings a/c		210	Repairs to canopy	201	
Cash takings (balancing figure)	10,850		Takings banked (contra entry)	7,521	
			Purchase of van		3,200
			Road fund licence		80
			Insurance on van		323
			Creditors		7,777
			Rent		970
			Sundry		31
			Accounting work		75
			Bank interest		20
			Returned cheque: bad debt		29
Balance c/d (overdraft)		474	Balance c/d	39	
	10,905	12,505		10,905	12,505
Balance b/d	39		Balance b/d		474

2.

DEBTORS

	£		£
Balance b/d	170	Cash	1,500
Credit sales - balancing figure	1,650	Balance c/d	320
	1,820		1,820

3.

CREDITORS

	£		£
Bank	7,777	Balance b/d	230
Balance c/d	233	Purchases (balancing figure)	7,780
	8,010		8,010

Goods taken as drawings

		£
Selling price	(100%)	300
Gross profit	(40%)	120
Cost	(60%)	180

Therefore, purchases taken to the trading account = £7,780 - £180 = £7,600.

4. *Closing stock*

		£
Sales (10,850 + 1,650)	(100%)	12,500
Gross profit	(40%)	5,000
Cost of goods sold	(60%)	7,500
Opening stock		500
Purchases (W3)		7,600
		8,100
Cost of goods sold		7,500
Closing stock (balancing figure)		600

5. *New van*

The bank statement shows that the cash paid for the new van was £3,200. Since there was a part exchange of £1,800 on the old van, the cost of the new van must be £5,000 with first year depreciation (20%) £1,000.

6. *Disposal of van*

	£		£
Van at cost	3,000	Provision for depreciation at date of sale	2,500
Profit on disposal	1,300	Asset account (trade in value for new van)	1,800
	4,300		4,300

7. *Drawings*

	£		£
Cash	2,600	Dividend income	210
Stock	180	Capital account (balance)	2,570
	2,780		2,780

Since there are no investments in the business balance sheet, the dividend income must be separate from the business. However, since it is paid into the business bank account, it should be accounted for, in effect, as a reduction in drawings.

28 BYRD

The first stage in a solution is to establish the opening balance sheet.

BYRD
BALANCE SHEET AS AT 1 JANUARY 19X0

	£
Fixtures and fittings, net book value	500
Stock	2,700
Debtors	430
Prepayments	30
Cash in bank and hand	2,170
	5,830
Trade creditors and accrual	1,690
	4,140
Proprietor's capital as at 1 January 19X0	4,140

Tutorial note: the next stage is to open up a trading account, a trade creditors account, a debtors account and a cash book. However, in this problem, you might have noticed that the bank statements do not make a distinction between cash banked and cheques banked. This means the following.

(a) A two column cash book cannot be prepared, since the distinction between cash in hand and cash in the bank cannot be made fully.

(b) The value of sales for the period, both cash sales and credit sales, must be calculated in a 'debtors' account.

The insurance premium paid for cover against theft relates to Byrd's business, but the life insurance premium does not. This should be accounted for as a drawing. On the other hand, the investment income is also unrelated to the business and should be credited to the drawings account.

TRADING ACCOUNT

	£		£
Opening stock	2,700	Sales (notes 1 and 2)	25,000
Purchases	20,500		
	23,200		
Stock stolen (note 4)	3,200		
	20,000		
Closing stock (all stolen)	0		
Cost of goods sold (note 3)	20,000		
Gross profit c/d (note 3)	5,000		
	25,000		25,000
		Gross profit b/d	5,000

TRADE CREDITORS

	£		£
Cash	17,850	Opening balance b/f	1,650
Cash	2,400	Purchases (balancing figure)	20,500
Closing balance c/f	1,900		
	22,150		22,150

CASH SALES AND DEBTORS (MEMORANDUM)

	£		£
Opening balance - debtors	430	Cash - banking of cash and credit sales income	20,060
Cash sales and credit sales (balancing figure)	25,000	Cash income from cash sales (subsequently paid out before banking)	5,100
		Closing balance - debtors	270
	25,430		25,430

CASH

	£		£
Opening balance in bank	2,140	Trade creditors	17,850
Opening balance in till	30	Rent	1,200
Debtors (cash and credit sales income banked)	20,060	Electricity	155
		Insurance - theft	45
Investment income (drawings a/c)	182	Life insurance (drawings a/c)	107
Debtors account (recording cash sales for cash income subsequently paid out before banking (2,400 + 2,655 + (75 - 30) - note 2)	5,100	Telephone	83
		Trade creditors	2,400
		Drawings (9 x £295)	2,655
		Till float stolen	75
		Cheque for telephone bill	52
		Balance in bank c/f	2,890
	27,512		27,512

Notes

1. See cash sales and debtors account (memorandum).
2. The cash sales and credit sales are perhaps more simply calculated as follows.

	£	£
Income from sales banked		20,060
Plus cash income from sales not banked		
Paid to trade creditors	2,400	
Taken in drawings	2,655	
Stolen from till	75	
	5,130	
Less cash in till at start of period	30	
		5,100
		25,160
Adjust for opening and closing debtors		
Less opening debtors (ie cash receipts from sales in a previous period)	(430)	
Plus closing debtors (ie sales this period for which no cash yet received)	270	
		(160)
Sales for current period		25,000

3. The gross profit margin is 20% - presumably 20% of the sales price.

		£
Sales	(100%)	25,000
Gross profit	(20%)	5,000
Cost of goods sold	(80%)	20,000

4.

	£
Opening stocks plus purchases less closing stock	23,200
Cost of goods sold (note 3)	20,000
Cost of goods stolen (balancing figure)	3,200

Since the goods are all insured, the theft of the goods is not reported in the P & L account.

5. DRAWINGS

	£		£
Life insurance	107	Investment income	182
Cash	2,655	Balance - P & L account	2,580
	2,762		2,762

6. *Other expenses for P & L account*

(i) RATES

	£		£
Prepayment b/f (presumably to 1 April)	30	P & L account	105
Accrual c/f	75		
	105		105

(ii) RENT

	£		£
Cash	1,200	P & L account (9 months)	900
		Prepayment c/f (3 months)	300
	1,200		1,200

(iii) ELECTRICITY

	£		£
Cash	155	Accrual b/f	40
		P & L account	115
	155		155

(iv) *Depreciation:* the charge for depreciation of the fixtures and fittings should be sufficient to bring their net book value down to their current worth - ie £(500 - 200) = £300.

(v) There is no cost in the P & L account for the theft of either stock or cash, since both are presumably covered in full by the insurance policy.

7. *Balance sheet item: insurance claim*
The insurance claim is for stock and cash stolen: ie £3,200 + £75 = £3,275.

BYRD
TRADING AND PROFIT AND LOSS ACCOUNT
FOR THE NINE MONTHS TO 30 SEPTEMBER 19X0

	£	£
Sales		25,000
Less cost of sales		
Opening stock	2,700	
Purchases	20,500	
	23,200	
Less closing stock (all stolen)	3,200	
		20,000
Gross profit		5,000
Less expenses		
Rent	900	
Rates	105	
Depreciation	300	
Telephone (83 + 52)	135	
Electricity	115	
Insurance (theft)	45	
		1,600
Net profit for the period		3,400

BYRD
BALANCE SHEET AS AT 30 SEPTEMBER 19X0

	£	£
Fixed assets		
Fixtures and fittings		
Cost		900
Accumulated depreciation		700
Net book value		200
Current assets		
Debtors	270	
Prepayments of rent	300	
Insurance claim	3,275	
Cash at bank	2,890	
	6,735	
Less current liabilities		
Creditors	(1,900)	
Accrued rates	(75)	
		4,760
Net current assets		4,960
Opening capital		4,140
Profit for the period	3,400	
Less drawings	2,580	
		820
Proprietor's interest		4,960

29 JB

Tutorial note: a lot of information is given here. You should read each note in the question carefully and check the relationship between notes 1 and 2. This is a straightforward question, for which a methodical approach is needed. Draw up a proforma profit and loss acount and balance sheet, so that you can note down any accruals, provisions and prepayments and so on as you calculate them.

PROFIT AND LOSS ACCOUNT
FOR THE PERIOD ENDED 31 DECEMBER 19X8

	£	£	£
Sales (21,250 + 1,955 + 431)			23,636
Cost of sales - purchases (2,160 + 7,315 + 749)		10,224	
less closing stock		1,425	
			8,799
Gross profit			14,837
Other expenses			
Postage and stationery		474	
Motor expenses		919	
Bank interest		450	
Rent and rates (1,850 - $\frac{3}{12}$ 1,200)		1,550	
Light and heat (923 + $\frac{2}{3}$ 114)		999	
Depreciation: van (1,100 x $\frac{9}{12}$)		825	
equipment ($\frac{1,280}{5}$ x 15/12)		320	
Loss on sale of van			
Sale proceeds	850		
Value introduced	1,500		
		650	
			6,187
Net profit			8,650

BALANCE SHEET AS AT 31 DECEMBER 19X8

Fixed assets	*Cost*	*Depreciation*	
	£	£	£
Equipment	1,280	320	960
Van	4,000	825	3,175
			4,135
Current assets			
Stock		1,425	
Debtors (431 - 189)		242	
Prepayments (1,200 x 3/12)		300	
Cash at bank (6,877 + 160)		7,037	
Cash in hand		697	
			9,701
Current liabilities			
Creditors (749 - 189)		560	
Accruals (2/3 114)		76	
Bank loan		4,500	
Interest on £4,500 at 10%		450	
			(5,586)
			8,250

	£
Proprietor's capital	5,000
Profit	8,650
	13,650
Less drawings	5,400
	8,250

Notes

1. It is assumed that the bank loan is repayable on demand, in the absence of information to the contrary.

2. Cash paid to the bank = £21,350 which is £160 more than the amounts indicated as received by the bank. It is assumed that these lodgements have not yet been credited.

30 ABC LIMITED

ABC LIMITED
PROFIT AND LOSS ACCOUNT
FOR THE YEAR ENDED 31 OCTOBER 19X7

	Working	£'000	£'000
Sales	1		14,000
Cost of goods sold	2		9,000
Gross profit			5,000
Expenses			
Administration			
Rent	6	24	
Rates	7	20	
Fire insurance	8	2	
Administration costs (bank + 3 from debtors)		1,909	
Depreciation	9	45	
		2,000	
Selling			
Rent	6	6	
Rates	7	5	
Fire insurance	8	1	
Selling and distribution costs		1,403	
Bad debts	10	40	
Depreciation	9	45	
		1,500	
			3,500
Profit before tax			1,500
Tax	11		620
Profit after tax			880
Dividends			640
Retained profit for the year			240
Retained profit brought forward			2,760
Retained profit carried forward			3,000

BALANCE SHEET AS AT 31 OCTOBER 19X7

	£'000	£'000	£'000
Fixed assets at cost		5,000	
Accumulated depreciation		2,000	
			3,000
Current assets			
Material stock		1,700	
Work in progress		300	
Finished goods		3,000	
Debtors	1,200		
Less bad debt provision	60		
		1,140	
Prepayments: rates	45		
fire insurance	6		
		51	
Cash in hand		1	
		6,192	
Current liabilities			
Bank overdraft		467	
Creditors		460	
Accruals: rent	20		
wages	5		
		25	
Corporation tax (working 11)		600	
Dividends		640	
		2,192	
Net currrent assets			4,000
			7,000
Financed by			
Share capital			4,000
Retained profit			3,000
			7,000

Workings

1. *Sales*

CASH IN HAND

	£'000		£'000
Opening balance	2	Bank	13,768
Debtors (balancing figure)	13,770	Admin. expenses	3
		Closing balance	1
	13,772		13,772

DEBTORS

	£'000		£'000
Opening balance	1,000	Bank	13,770
P & L (sales - balancing figure)	14,000	Bad debts provision	30
		Closing balance	1,200
	15,000		15,000

2. *Cost of goods sold*

	£'000
Opening stock of finished goods	2,500
Cost of finished goods produced (working 3)	9,500
	12,000
Closing stock of finished goods	3,000
Cost of goods sold	9,000

3. *Cost of finished goods produced*

ABC LIMITED
MANUFACTURING ACCOUNT

	Working	£'000	£'000
Materials			
Opening stock		1,400	
Purchases	4	5,300	
		6,700	
Closing stock		1,700	
			5,000
Wages	5		1,400
Prime cost			6,400
Production overheads			
Rent	6	90	
Rates	7	75	
Fire insurance	8	17	
Manufacturing overheads		2,458	
Depreciation	9	360	
			3,000
			9,400
Work in progress			
At 1 November 19X6		400	
At 31 October 19X7		300	
			100
Cost of finished goods sold			9,500

4. *Purchases*

CREDITORS

	£'000		£'000
Bank statement	5,328	Opening balance	490
Adjustment for unpresented cheques	2	Purchases (balancing figure)	5,300
Closing balance	460		
	5,790		5,790

5. WAGES

	£'000		£'000
Bank	1,418	Opening balance	23
Closing balance	5	Manufacturing a/c (balancing figure)	1,400
	1,423		1,423

6. RENT

	£'000		£'000
Bank	110	Opening balance	10
Closing balance *	20	Manufacturing a/c (balancing figure)	120 **
	130		130

* Need to accrue for two months rent at £110 ÷ 11 = £10 per month

** Apportioned:

manufacturing	90
administration	24
selling	6
	120

7. RATES

	£'000		£'000
Opening balance	37	Manufacturing a/c (balancing figure) **	100
Bank	108	Closing balance *	45
	145		145

* Prepayment for five months (5/12 x £108)

** Apportionment:

manufacturing	75
administration	20
selling	5
	100

8. FIRE INSURANCE

	£'000		£'000
Opening balance	2	Manufacturing a/c (balancing figure) **	20
Bank	24	Closing balance *	6
	26		26

* Prepayment for three months (3/12 x 24)

** Apportionment:	manufacturing	17
	administration	2
	selling	1
		20

9. *Fixed assets and depreciation*

		£'000	£'000
Fixed assets at cost 1 November 19X7			4,000
Additions			1,000
Fixed assets at cost 31 October 19X7			5,000
Accumulated depreciation 31 October 19X7			1,550
Depreciation for year	(10% x 1,000 x ½)	50	
	(10% x 4,000)	400	
			450 *
Accumulated depreciation 31 October 19X7			2,000

* Apportionment:	manufacturing	360
	administration	45
	selling	45
		450

10. BAD DEBTS

	£'000		£'000
Debtors	30	Opening balance	50
Closing balance	60	P & L a/c (balancing figure)	40
	90		90

11. CORPORATION TAX

	£'000		£'000
Bank	500	Opening balance	480
Closing balance	600	P & L a/c (balancing figure)	620
	1,100		1,100

31 BASIC REVISION QUESTION: PROFIT FORECAST

Tutorial note: before you have a go at some of the questions on company accounts, this question will help you to revise a few of the basic rules.

(1) *Not feasible.* The gross amount of debenture interest, that is the actual net amount paid as well as the income tax deducted is charged in arriving at the final profit figure. Withholding the income tax will in no way affect the profit figure and could make the company liable to a legal action from the collector of taxes.

(2) *Not feasible.* Repainting the exterior of the company's premises does not improve or enhance the original value of the premises and therefore cannot be treated as capital expenditure.

(3) *Not feasible.* Proceeds from the sale of plant and machinery is a capital receipt, and cannot directly be credited to the profit and loss account, but must firstly be compared to the underlying net book value and only the profit or loss as compared to this value can be credited or debited to the profit and loss account.

(4) *Not feasible.* The general reserve account represents an accumulation of transfers from profits earned in the past. Whilst it is technically possible to transfer amounts back from general reserve to the profit and loss account, such a transfer would not have an effect on the current operating profit.

(5) *Not feasible.* The market value of the company's issued share capital is not reflected anywhere in the books or accounts. No entries are made by the company to record movements in the price at which shares are changing hands between investors. This is because such prices are a matter for the investors concerned and provide no benefit to the company. The only transaction which benefits the company is the original issue of the shares.

(6) *Not feasible.* The premises were bought as a permanent asset and not with the intention of resale. The increase in value does not represent a realised profit and as the premise is a fixed asset, if any increase in its value is to be shown in the accounts, then it should be reflected through an undistributable reserve.

32 HB TENNIS CLUB

Tutorial note: a common mistake in this question would be to forget that you are preparing the accounts for six months. Try to keep this in mind all the time so that you do not include the figures for the whole year by mistake.

(a) HB TENNIS CLUB
INCOME AND EXPENDITURE ACCOUNT
FOR THE SIX MONTHS ENDED 30 SEPTEMBER 19X0

	£	£
Income		
Subscriptions (working 1)		7,050
Net income from tournaments £(465 - 132)		333
Bank interest received		43
Net income from sale of club ties (working 2)		103
Life membership fees (working 3)		210
		7,739
Expenditure		
Depreciation of equipment (working 4)	403	
Groundsman's wages (4,520 + 40)	4,560	
Rent and business rates (636 - 68)	568	
Heating and lighting (674 + 53)	727	
Postage and stationery (41 + 12)	53	
Court maintenance	1,000	
		7,311
Surplus transferred to accumulated fund		428

Workings

1. *Subscriptions income*

	£
Subscriptions received for full year	12,600
∴ subscriptions for six months	6,300
Plus subscriptions outstanding (5 x £150)	750
	7,050

2. *Sale of club ties*

	£	£
Sales income		373
Purchases of ties	450	
less closing stock (40/100 x £450)	180	
		270
Net income from sale of club ties		103

3. *Life membership fees*

	£
Fees received (4 x £1,050)	4,200
One years' instalment (÷ 10)	420
∴ income for six months	210

4. *Depreciation of equipment*

	£
Purchase cost of equipment	4,080
Estimated scrap value	50
	4,030
Annual depreciation (÷ 5 assuming straight line depreciation)	806
Charge for six months	403

HB TENNIS CLUB
BALANCE SHEET AS AT 30 SEPTEMBER 19X0

	£	£	£
Fixed assets			
Equipment at cost			4,080
Depreciation to date			403
			3,677
Current assets			
Stock of ties (working 2)		180	
Subscriptions owing (working 1)		750	
Prepaid business rates		68	
Bank		6,148	
		7,146	
Current liabilities			
Subscriptions in advance (working 1)	6,300		
Accrued expenses	105		
		6,405	
Net current assets			741
			4,418
Financed by			
Accumulated fund			428
Life membership fund £(4,200 - 210)			3,990
			4,418

33 GD SPORTS

(a)

BAR TRADING ACCOUNT
FOR THE YEAR ENDED 31 MARCH 19X8

	£	£
Sales (W1)		10,137
Opening stock	840	
Purchases (W2)	7,295	
	8,135	
Closing stock	(920)	
Cost of sales		(7,215)
Profit (taken to income and expenditure account)		2,922

(b)

INCOME AND EXPENDITURE ACCOUNT
FOR THE YEAR ENDED 31 MARCH 19X8

	£	£
Income		
Contributions (W3)	490	
Net income from bar trading	2,922	
Building society interest	350	
		3,762
Expenses		
Rent	1,000	
Heat and light (W4)	269	
Repairs to snooker tables	176	
Trophies etc	424	
Referees' fees and expenses	675	
Refreshments	235	
Depreciation (W5)	410	
		3,189
Surplus transferred to accumulated fund		573

(c)

BALANCE SHEET AS AT 31 MARCH 19X8

	£	£
Fixed assets		
Equipment at net book value (W5)		3,690
Current assets		
Bar stocks	920	
Building society account	5,200	
	6,120	
Current liabilities		
Bar creditors	470	
Heat/light creditors	41	
	511	
Net current assets		5,609
		9,299
Accumulated fund		
Balance at 1 April 19X7 (W7)		8,726
Surplus for the year		573
Balance at 31 March 19X7		9,299

Workings

1. *Cash*

	£		£
Subscription income (W2)	440	Deposit to building society a/c	250
Bar sales (balancing figure)	10,137	Purchase of dartboards	100
		Heat/light	262
		Repairs	176
		Bar creditors	7,455
		Rent	1,000
		Referees	675
		Trophies	424
		Refreshments	235
	10,577		10,577

2. *Bar creditors*

	£		£
Cash	7,455	Balance b/f	630
Balance c/f	470	Purchases (balancing figure)	7,295
	7,925		7,925

3. *Subscription income*

	£		£
Income and expenditure a/c	490	Advance payments b/f (10 x £5)	50
		Received in year (88 x £5)	440
	490		490

4. *Heat/light*

	£		£
Cash	262	Accrual b/f	34
Accrual c/f	41	Income and expenditure account (balancing figure)	269
	303		303

5. *Equipment*

	£		£
Balance b/f	4,000	Depreciation	410
Dartboards	100	NBV c/f	3,690
	4,100		4,100

6. *Building society account*

	£		£
Balance b/f	4,600	Balance c/f	5,200
Cash	250		
Interest	350		
	5,200		5,200

7. *Accumulated fund at 31 March 19X7*

	£
Equipment	4,000
Bar stock	840
Building society account	4,600
Bar creditors	(630)
Accrual	(34)
Advance subscriptions (W3)	(50)
	8,726

34 TALLIS LIMITED

(a)

TALLIS LIMITED
TRADING PROFIT AND LOSS AND APPROPRIATION ACCOUNT
FOR THE YEAR ENDING 30 JUNE 19X5

	£'000	£'000	£'000
Sales			3,400
Less cost of sales			
Opening stock		149	
Purchases (£2,785 + £30) - working 1		2,815	
		2,964	
Less closing stock - working 4		176	
			2,788
Gross profit			612
Decrease in provision for doubtful debts - working 5			9
			621
Less expenses			
Wages and salaries		214	
Light and heat - working 7		35	
Rates and insurance - working 7		41	
Printing, postage and stationery		53	
Legal and audit fees (16 + 15 accrued)		31	
Sundry expenses		18	
Loss on sale of equipment - working 2		1	
Depreciation: freehold buildings - working 3		2	
plant and equipment - working 2		80	
Discounts allowed		9	
Bank overdraft charges		11	
Debenture interest (12% x 200)		24	
			519
Net profit for the year			102
Appropriations			
Dividends: preference (paid 8% of 100)	8		
ordinary (proposed) - working 8	46		
		54	
Transfer to general reserve		30	
			84
Retained profit for the year			18
Retained profits brought forward			52
Retained profits carried forward			70

(b)

TALLIS LIMITED
BALANCE SHEET AS AT 30 JUNE 19X5

	Cost/ valuation £'000	*Accum dep'n* £'000	*NBV* £'000
Fixed assets			
Goodwill - working 1	30	-	30
Freehold property	500	-	500
Plant and equipment - working 2	320	170	150
	850	170	680
Current assets			
Stock - working 4		176	
Debtors	280		
Less provision - working 5	14		
		266	
Prepayment - working 7		24	
Cash in hand		3	
		469	
Creditors: amounts falling due within one year			
Bank overdraft	14		
Accruals (15 + 8) - working 7	23		
Proposed dividend - working 8	46		
Sundry creditors - working 6	166		
		249	
Net current assets			220
			900
Creditors: amounts falling due in more than one year			
12% debentures			(200)
			700
Financed by			
Share capital			
25p ordinary shares (fully paid) (920,000 shares - working 8)		230	
8% £1 preference shares (fully paid)		100	
			330
Reserves			
Share premium - working 9		20	
Land revaluation - working 3		210	
Retained profits		70	
General (40 + 30 transferred from P & L)		70	
			370
Shareholders funds			700

Workings

1. *Goodwill on purchase of H Purcell & Co*

	£'000
Consideration	140
Less assets acquired (80 + 30)	110
Goodwill	30

The stock acquired should be added to purchases.

2.

Plant and equipment (at cost)

	£'000		£'000
Balance b/f	275	Disposals	35
H Purcell	80	Balance c/f	320
	355		355

Depreciation on plant and equipment

	£'000		£'000
Disposals (35 - 4)	31	Balance b/f	121
Balance c/f	170	Charge for the year	
		(25% x £320)	80
	201		201

Disposal of equipment

	£'000		£'000
Plant and equipment	35	Provision for depreciation, plant and equipment	31
		Suspense a/c - proceeds	3
		Loss on sale - P & L a/c	1
	35		35

3. *Freehold premises*

			£'000
Cost			300
Less:	depreciation b/f	8	
	charge for year 100/50	2	
			10
Net book value after current year's depreciation			290
Revaluation			500
Surplus on revaluation - credit revaluation reserve			210

4. *Stock*

	£
10,000 midgets at £6 (cost)	60,000
20,000 fidgets at £4 (cost)	80,000
9,000 didgets at £4 (net realisable value £7 - £3)	36,000
	176,000

5. *Provision for doubtful debtors*

5% of 280 = 14

Current provision, per trial balance = 23. Reduction in provision (credit P & L) = 9

6. *Sundry creditors*

	£
Per trial balance	154,000
Debenture interest payable	
(12% of 200,000, less £12,000 already paid, per trial balance)	12,000
	166,000

7. *Accruals and prepayments*

There is an accrual of £15,000 for audit fees and £8,000 for electricity (therefore light and heat charges are 27 + 8 = 35) and a prepayment for rates and insurance of £24,000, making the P & L account expense 65 - 24 = 41.

8. *Final ordinary dividend*

	£
Number of shares at start of year (210 x 4)	840,000
Issued during year	80,000
	920,000

Dividend 5p each = £46,000 in total

9. *Shares issued*

	£'000
Nominal value 80,000 x 25p	20
Proceeds	40
Share premium	20

35 STU LIMITED

Workings

1. *Sales*

	£
Sales	164,751
Returns in	(921)
	163,830

2. *Purchases*

	£
Purchases	73,501
Returns out	(434)
	73,067

3. *Stock valuation*

Stock code	*Quantity at 31 January 19X8*	*Unit price (lower of cost & NRV)* £	£
101	50 + 24 = 74	12.00	888
102	62 - 15 = 47	8.00	376
103	34	6.00	204
501	1,200 - 200 = 1,000	1.50	1,500
502	1,600	2.50	4,000
503	2,250 + 220 = 2,470	2.50	6,175
			13,143

4. *Bad debt provision*

(Assuming that the £68 written off was previously provided for.)

	£
Trade debtors net of bad debt = £15,748 - £68 = 15,680	
Provision required at 25% = £392	
Provision brought forward	889
Less bad debt written off, previously provided for	(68)
	821
Less provision carried forward	(392)
Decrease in provision	429

5. *Selling and distribution costs*

	£
As trial balance	4,515
Less prepayment	(559)
	3,956

6. *Administration expenses*

	£
As trial balance	7,233
Add accruals	741
	7,974

7. *Debenture interest*

	£
Profit and loss account charge £20,000 at 10%	2,000
Paid in year to date	(1,000)
Accrual required	1,000

8. *Depreciation*

	£
Buildings: 2% x £48,000	960
Fixtures: 10% x £23,110	2,311
Motor vehicles	
Net book value b/f = £40,100 - £24,060 = £16,040	
Net book value c/f = £16,040 - £3,072 + £1,300 = £14,268	
Depreciation = 20% x £14,268	2,854
	6,125

9. *Profit/(loss) on disposal of motor vehicle*

	£
Net book value at January 31 19X7 = £6,000 x 0.8^3	3,072
(assuming no depreciation charged in year of disposal)	
Less proceeds	(1,300)
Loss	1,772

10. *Final dividend*

£0.04 x 40,000	£1,600

(a) TRADING AND PROFIT AND LOSS ACCOUNT FOR THE YEAR ENDED JANUARY 31 19X9

	Working	£	£
Sales (W1)	1		163,830
Cost of sales			
Opening stock		9,906	
Purchases (W2)	2	73,067	
Carriage in		3,810	
Less: closing stock (W3)	3	(13,143)	
			73,640
Gross profit			90,190
Discount received			2,027
			92,217
Expenses			
Selling and distribution costs	5	3,956	
Administration expenses	6	7,974	
Wages and salaries		18,891	
Debenture interest	7	2,000	
Directors' fees		10,100	
Depreciation	8	6,125	
Loss on disposal	9	1,772	
Discount allowed		1,528	
Decrease in bad debt provision		(429)	
			51,917
Net profit before taxation			40,300
Corporation tax at 30%			12,090
Profit after taxation			28,210
Dividends			
Interim, paid		2,540	
Final, proposed	10	1,600	
			4,140
Retained profit for the year			24,070
Retained profit brought forward			16,852
Retained profit carried forward			40,922

(b) The *going concern* concept allows a business to value its assets and liabilities on the basis that it will continue to operate for the foreseeable future.

This means that special stock or equipment whose value on a forced sale would be lower than book value can be recorded at book value in the accounts if they are still useful to the business in generating profits. (However, any permanent diminution in value must be recorded immediately, even under the going concern concept).

Additionally, bad debt provisions would be higher if a business was not a going concern and many long term liabilities would have to be shown as current, thus possibly rendering the company insolvent.

Finally, the separable constituents of a business will rarely be worth as much in aggregate as the valuation of a business as a going concern, as non-purchased goodwill is not recorded in the accounts because of the difficulties in valuing it.

(c) Day to day accounting transactions include the following.

(i) Recording of cash receipts and payments.

(ii) Sales invoicing and issue of credit notes.

(iii) Recording purchase invoices and credit notes received.

(iv) Payroll.

(v) Maintenance of fixed asset register, sales ledger and purchases ledger.

(vi) Journals for period end adjustments and corrections.

Each of these would be entered into the microcomputer via a different module in a suite of accounting software, probably fully integrated, so that updating the sales, purchase or stock ledger will also update the nominal ledger. Each module will make use of standing data, eg customer account code, so that the minimum of keying in is necessary to record the transaction in full.

A validation check will usually be made on the data to pick up wrong codes, customer accounts exceeding credit limits, credit balances on sales ledger accounts and so on. Management reports can also be produced immediately summarising the data on file. This allows users of information to concentrate on the important areas (summaries and exceptions), not the detail.

Data entry will be facilitated by the design of the display on screen, usually including a summary of available options. Often such systems are menu driven, which means that at each stage the user can easily move backwards and forwards through the system from the general to the specific. As well as computerising the daybooks, many systems allow for the creation of source documents like invoices, cheques and payslips.

36 BASIC REVISION QUESTION: COST BEHAVIOUR

Tutorial note: this question tests your knowledge of the behaviour of costs and also illustrates the links between cost accounting, financial accounting and economics. When drawing the sketch diagrams you will gain extra marks if you label the axes clearly. In (a)(i) we have shown two diagrams. The question requests only one and either would be acceptable in an examination.

(a) (i) CURVILINEAR VARIABLE COST

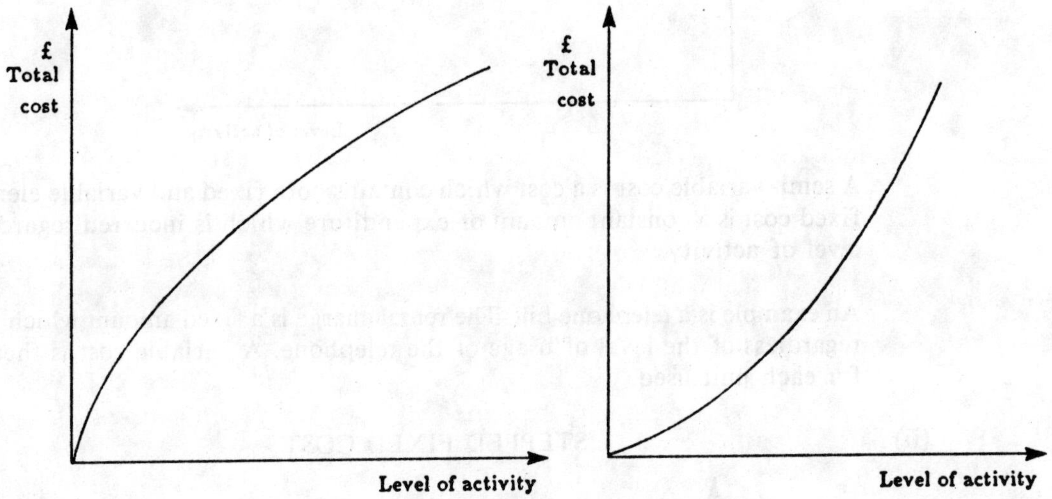

(ii) LINEAR VARIABLE COST

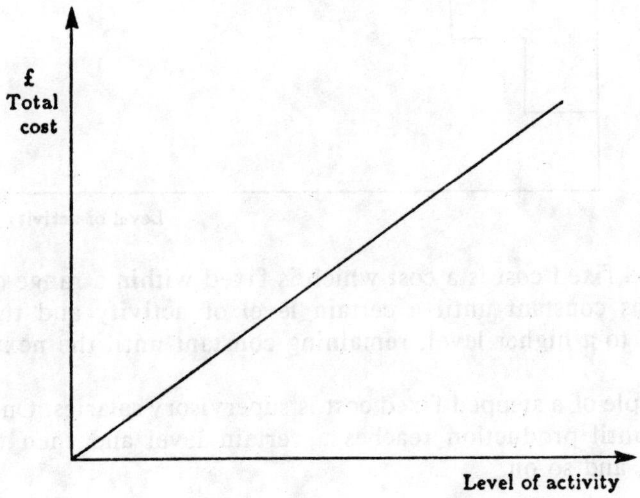

(b) (i) SEMI-VARIABLE COST

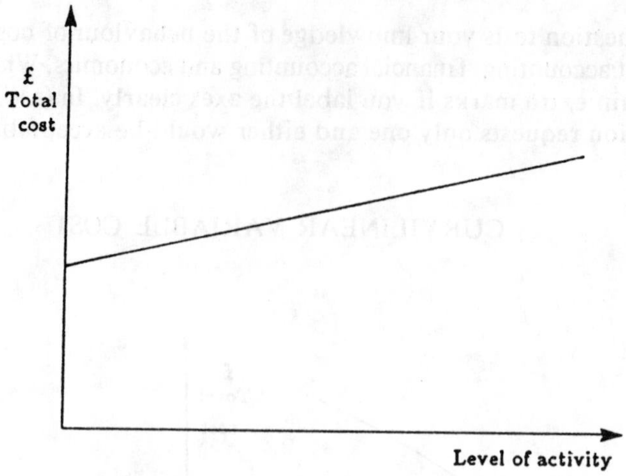

A semi-variable cost is a cost which contains both fixed and variable elements. The fixed cost is a constant amount of expenditure which is incurred regardless of the level of activity.

An example is a telephone bill. The rental charge is a fixed amount which is incurred regardless of the level of usage of the telephone. A variable cost is then incurred for each unit used.

(ii) STEPPED FIXED COST

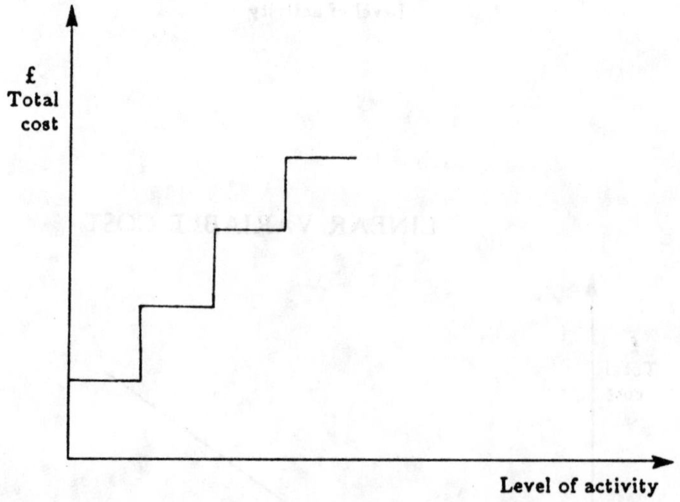

A stepped fixed cost is a cost which is fixed within a range of levels of activity. It remains constant until a certain level of activity and then the expenditure increases to a higher level, remaining constant until the next step is reached.

An example of a stepped fixed cost is supervisory salaries. One supervisor may be needed until production reaches a certain level and then two supervisors are required, and so on.

37 DIRECT/INDIRECT

(a) (i) Direct costs are those costs which can be separately identified in a specific product or service. Direct materials costs, for example, are those costs relating to the actual material from which a product is made. Direct labour costs are those incurred in the form of wages for those workers directly involved in the production process.

(ii) Indirect costs are costs which are not charged directly to a product or service, or cannot be separately identified in it. The *CIMA Official Terminology* gives the costs of coolants, cleaning materials, supervision of labour, water rates as examples of indirect costs.

(b) (i) *Collection of indirect costs*

Different indirect costs are captured in different ways.

Indirect materials costs, such as coolants, lubricants, cleaning materials and so forth can be readily identified according to the department which uses them. At a detailed level, the cost of these items may be allocated over each product.

Indirect labour costs can be incurred:

- in a department not involved directly with production;
- in the production department, but in the form of wages or salaries for non-production personnel.

In the former case, some estimate of the labour expended on work relating to production departments should be made, and the costs allocated to those departments. If workers keep time sheets, these can be used as records for cost allocation.

In the production department, indirect labour can be absorbed into the cost of production like indirect materials. The actual cost may be spread over production units, with each item deemed to have cost a certain amount of indirect labour.

Indirect expenses, such as rates, buildings and so forth, are collected by purely administrative departments. These will be allocated in some way to other departments, by a means appropriate to the costs. For example, rates may be allocated according to floor space.

(ii) *Ascertainment of stock and work in progress cost*

Stocks are valued at lower of cost or net realisable value.

Stocks of finshed goods are valued at all those costs required to bring them to their current location and condition. This includes raw materials, direct labour costs and a proportion of production overheads as well. These costs are ascertained in different ways. Raw materials costs can be gleaned from invoices; direct labour costs can be picked up from timesheets and/or departmental cost centres and can be allocated over cost units. Indirect costs are also allocated to cost units. Some overheads can only be ascertained centrally.

38 BASIC REVISION QUESTION: ROSEBOWL HOTEL

Tutorial note: a clear layout to your answer will help both you and the examiner.

Working

The closing stock on October 9 can be analysed as follows.

Quantity	*Value*	£
100	1.50	150
300	1.52	456
200	1.55	310
600		916

Weighted average price = $\frac{£916}{600}$ = £1.5267

FIFO

	Issues			*Closing stock balance*		
	Quantity	*Value*	£	*Quantity*	*Value*	£
October 11	100	1.50	150	150	1.52	228
	150	1.52	228	200	1.55	310
	250		378	350		538
October 12	150	1.52	228	200	1.55	310

LIFO

October 11	200	1.55	310	100	1.50	150
	50	1.52	76	250	1.52	380
	250		386	350		530
October 12	150	1.52	228	100	1.50	150
				100	1.52	152
				200		302

Weighted average

October 11	250	1.5267	382	350	1.5267	534
October 12	150	1.5267	229	200	1.5267	305

The FIFO method will show the highest profit figure in time of inflation. This is because the lower prices paid for other stock will be charged against cost of sales for the period, and the more recent higher prices will be carried forward in stock to the next period. The lower cost of sales will result in a higher profit figure.

39 RECEIPTS AND ISSUES

Tutorial note: a very straightforward question examining the different methods of stock valuation using a simple example.

(a) LIFO

	Date	Receipts	Issues	Balance	Value £
b/f					Nil
	3/9	200 x £1		200 x £1	200
	7/9		180 x £1	20 x £1	20
	8/9	240 x £1.50		20 x £1	20
				240 x £1.50	360
				260	380
	14/9			20 x £1	20
			170 x £1.50	70 x £1.50	105
				90	125
	15/9	230 x £2		20 x £1	20
				70 x £1.50	105
				230 x £2	460
				320	585
	21/9			20 x £1	20
				70 x £1.50	105
			150 x £2	80 x £2	160
				170	285

Weighted average

	Date	Receipts	Issues	Balance	Value £
b/f					Nil
	3/9	200 x £1		200 x £1	200.00
	7/9		180 x £1	20 x £1	20.00
	8/9	240 x £1.50		260 x £1.46(W1)	379.60
	14/9		170 x £1.46	90 x £1.46	131.40
	15/9	230 x £2		320 x £1.85(W2)	592.00
	21/9		150 x £1.85	170 x £1.85	314.50

Workings

			£
1.	240 x £1.50	=	360
	20 x £1		20
	260		380

£380 ÷ 260 = £1.4615, rounded to two decimal places = £1.46.

2. £460 x £131.40 = £591.40

$$\frac{£591.40}{90 + 230} = 1.848 \text{ or } £1.85 \text{ rounded to two decimal places}$$

(b) The effect of valuing stock at LIFO *reduces* profits in a period of rising prices, because stock is always valued at its lowest historic purchase price in any period. That means that cost of sales are higher, hence profits are lower, because more expensive stock has been charged to production.

Under the weighted average method, stock valuation is higher because the latest and most expensive stock (assuming prices are rising) is not charged to production first as it is with LIFO.

40 MATERIALS CONTROL

(a) *Material flows*

1 Purchase requisition made out and sent to purchase office.

2 Buyer selects a supplier and raises a purchase order.

3 Purchase order authorised and sent to supplier.

4 Supplier forwards goods and invoice.

5 Goods received noted on a GRN.

6 Goods inspected and note made of any faults.

7 Goods passed into store and details recorded on a stores record card.

8 Supplier's invoice checked to GRN and passed for payment.

9 Materials requisition made out for the material stating job details for which it is required.

10 Materials passed from stores and requisition retained by storekeeper.

11 Details entered on stores record card. Pricing may occur here or in the cost office.

12 Requisition passed to cost office.

13 Details entered on materials analysis.

14 Materials analysis figure posted to the job card.

(b) *Continuous stocktaking*

1 Items reviewed and a decision made as to the number of times each item will be checked per year.

2 A schedule is prepared of items to be checked each week (or other period) of the year.

3 A batch of blank standard forms is prepared for the purpose to show full item details and any discrepancies and comments.

4 Form pre-prepared each week showing which items to be checked.

5 Stock-taker given the appropriate form to work through.

6 Discrepancies are examined and any comments made, taking care to allow for requisitions and receipts not recorded on a stores record card.

7 Shortages are signed for by a responsible official to be subsequently written off in the stores account.

8 Corrections made to record cards indicating that a check has been made.

9 An element of surprise is to be maintained each week by keeping the items to be checked a secret before the checks are carried out.

41 COMPONENT X

(a)

Date	*Received* Units	*Issued* Units	*Balance* Units	*Total stock* £	*Unit cost* £	*Price of issue* £
1.1.X7	Opening stock		200	10,000	50	
8.1.X7	600			34,800	58	
			800	44,800	56	
16.1.X7		400		22,400		56
			400	22,400	56	
3.2.X7	400			25,600	64	
			800	48,000	60	
12.2.X7		600		36,000		60
			200	12,000	60	
11.3.X7	600			43,200	72	
			800	55,200	69	
23.3.X7		200		13,800		69
			600	41,400	69	
3.4.X7	200			14,600	73	
	Closing stock		800	56,000	70	

(b) Two other methods of pricing material issues from stock are FIFO and LIFO.

(i) FIFO (first in, first out) assumes that materials are issued out of stock in the order in which they were delivered into stock, ie issues are priced at the cost of the earliest delivery remaining in stock. The method is based on common sense, since it is reasonable to issue old stock before new (otherwise the old stock might deteriorate or become obsolete). FIFO is the method which should be used in preparing *financial* accounts (according to SSAP 9).

(ii) LIFO (last in, first out) assumes that materials are issued out of stock in the reverse order to which they were delivered, ie most recent deliveries are issued before earlier ones, and are priced accordingly. At first sight this might seem an odd way to value stock, but if you consider the problems of a *liquid* stock which is topped up from time-to-time, you can see that it might occasionally be relevant. However, LIFO is discouraged (by SSAP9) as far as stock valuation for financial accounts is concerned.

(iii) Suppose component X was valued using the FIFO method. Then the balance of 800 units would be valued as follows.

	£
200 units (purchased 3 April 19X7)	14,600
600 units (purchased 11 March 19X7)	43,200
	57,800

So the FIFO method values closing stock at £1,800 higher than the weighted average method. Closing stock is a deduction cost of sales, so the FIFO method leads to a lower cost of sales, which in turn leads to a higher reported profit figure. The FIFO method would therefore show profit as being £1,800 higher than the weighted average method.

42 BASIC REVISION QUESTION: JOB COSTING

(a) Job costing is the costing method which is used when every cost unit is separately identifiable. Each job is usually given a number against which the job costs are collected.

Batch costing is the costing method which is used when similar articles are made in batches. The cost per unit manufactured in a batch is the total batch cost divided by the number of units per batch.

Batch costing is similar to job costing in that each batch of similar articles is separately identifiable.

(b)

		Job 4321 £	£
Direct materials:	department A	4,000	
	B	1,000	
	C	1,500	
			6,500
Direct labour:	department A	900	
	B	800	
	C	2,000	
			3,700
Fixed production overhead:	900 hrs x £5		4,500
Total production cost			14,700
Fixed administration overhead:	80% x £14,700		11,760
Total cost			26,460
Profit	20/80 x £26,460		6,615
Selling price			33,075

43 SP

(a) *Statement of apportionment of service function costs*

	North west £'000	*West* £'000	*South* £'000	*Total* £'000
Personnel and staff training costs (1)	16.9	14.3	25.8	57
Window display, sales promotion and advertising costs (2)	69.0	58.0	103.0	230
Warehousing and distribution costs (3)	86.6	73.3	125.1	285
	172.5	145.6	253.9	572

1. Apportioned by reference to divisional wage costs
2. Apportioned by reference to divisional sales
3. Apportioned by reference to divisional cost of sales

(b) To: ....
From: ....
Subject: Basis of apportioning service function costs
Date: ....

The apportionment of service function costs is to some extent an arbitrary procedure. There is no simple formula to determine what proportion of each service department's costs arise from the activities of each production or selling department. A process of estimation is the best that can be achieved. To arrive at a realistic result it is necessary to take into account the factors which are peculiar to the company concerned so as to derive a meaningful basis of apportionment for each service department.

In the present case, apportionment has been carried out as follows.

(i) Personnel and staff training costs have been apportioned by reference to divisional wages. Such costs depend principally on the number of employees involved, and ideally apportionment could have been made by reference to staff numbers in each division. This information, however, is not available and the nearest approximation to numbers employed is the amounts spent on wages.

(ii) Window display, sales promotion and advertising costs are incurred in the hope of generating sales. Presumably the amounts expended on these activities bear some relation to the level of sales achieved, even though it would be over-simplifying to say that the relationship was identical in all three regions. The level of sales achieved by each division is therefore the most sensible basis for apportioning these costs.

(iii) Warehousing and distribution costs have been apportioned by reference to divisional cost of sales. These costs are a function of the volume of goods purchased, stored and distributed to shops. The volume of goods purchased by each division is presumably reflected in the figures for cost of sales.

With additional information, a more accurate apportionment would have been possible. For example, distribution costs depend only partly on the volume of goods purchased; an additional factor would be the distance of each division (and each shop) from the central warehouse.

44 APPORTIONMENT

Tutorial note: in part (a) of the question, the aim is to apportion all overheads to the two production cost centres (process A and process B). We begin by allocating overheads over all four cost centres (ie including the two service departments, stores and canteen). The totals allocated to each service department are then re-apportioned to the production departments.

(a) PRODUCTION OVERHEAD ANALYSIS AND APPORTIONMENT SHEET

	Production dept's		*Service dept's*		
	Process A	*Process B*	*Stores*	*Canteen*	*Total*
	£	£	£	£	£
Directly allocated o'heads					
Indirect wages	25,000	40,000	20,000	10,000	95,000
Indirect materials	51,510	58,505	1,310	8,425	119,750
Apportionment of other o'heads					
Rent and rates (1)	150,000	75,000	150,000	75,000	450,000
Depreciation of P & M (2)	100,000	20,000	15,000	5,000	140,000
Power (3)	40,000	10,000	-	-	50,000
Insurance: fire (1)	1,250	625	1,250	625	3,750
compensation (4)	6,100	5,300	400	200	12,000
Heat and light (1)	1,500	750	1,500	750	4,500
	375,360	210,180	189,460	100,000	875,000
Canteen (5)	50,000	37,500	12,500	(100,000)	
	425,360	247,680	201,960	-	
Stores (6)	134,640	67,320	(201,960)		
	560,000	315,000	-	-	875,000

Bases of apportionment
(1) Floor area
(2) Book value of plant and machinery
(3) Horsepower of machinery
(4) 2% of wages (see working below)
(5) Number of employees
(6) Number of stores issue notes.

(b) An overhead recovery rate can be calculated based on the number of direct hours worked in each process (see workings 1 for details).

$$\text{Process A rate} = \frac{£560,000}{70,000\text{hrs}} = £8 \text{ per hour}$$

$$\text{Process B rate} = \frac{£315,000}{45,000 \text{ hrs}} = £7 \text{ per hour}$$

(c) and (d)

	Product X		*Product Y*	
	£	£	£	£
Unit cost of production				
Material P	37		93	
Material Q	2		48	
Material R	4		15	
		43		156
Process A labour	8		16	
Process B labour	5		15	
		13		31
Production overheads				
Process A	16		32	
Process B	7		21	
		23		53
Salesmen's commission		5		15
Packing		1		4
Transport		2		5
Royalties		1		-
Advertising (workings 2)		2		6
Total costs per unit		90		270
Selling price per unit		100		300
Profit per unit		10		30

Workings

1. *Wages incurred in year*

		£	£
Process A:	product X (15,000 x 2 x £4)	120,000	
	product Y (10,000 x 4 x £4)	160,000	
	indirect	25,000	
			305,000
Process B:	product X (15,000 x 1 x £5)	75,000	
	product Y (10,000 x 3 x £5)	150,000	
	indirect	40,000	
			265,000
Stores			20,000
Canteen			10,000
			600,000

2. *Allocation of advertising costs*
Allocated in proportion to sales revenue

	£
Revenue from product X	1,500,000
Revenue from product Y	3,000,000
	4,500,000

Allocated to product X: £90,000 x 15/45	=	£30,000
	=	£2 per unit
Allocated to product Y: £90,000 x 30/45	=	£60,000
	=	£6 per unit

45 ABACUS LIMITED

Tutorial note: you must remember to highlight the contribution in your marginal costing statement before deducting all of the fixed overhead incurred in the month.

Suggested solution

(a) Abacus Limited

(i) *Profit statement for October 19X0 using absorption costing*

	£	£
Sales (8,400 x £23)		193,200
Cost of goods sold		
Opening stock (250 x £19)	4,750	
Variable production costs (9,200 x £13.75)	126,500	
Fixed overhead (9,200 x £5.25)	48,300	
	179,550	
Closing stock (1,050 x £19)	19,950	
		159,600
Profit		33,600

(ii) *Profit statement for October 19X0 using marginal costing*

	£	£
Sales (8,400 x £23)		193,200
Cost of goods sold		
Opening stock (250 x £13.75)	3,437.50	
Variable production costs (9,200 x £13.75)	126,500.00	
	129,937.50	
Closing stock (1,050 x £13.75)	14,437.50	
		115,500
Contribution		77,700
Fixed overhead (9,200 x £5.25)		48,300
Profit		29,400

(b) The difference in profits arises because of the different treatment of fixed production overhead. Marginal costing values stock at variable cost only and charges all fixed overhead to the period, whereas absorption costing includes some fixed production overhead in stock.

Absorption costing therefore carries some fixed overhead forward to be matched against the sales of future periods. This means that profit will be higher with absorption costing when stocks are increasing, as they are in this example.

The absorption costing profit is £4,200 higher than the marginal costing profit and the difference can be analysed as follows.

Increase in stock	=	800 units
Fixed production overhead per unit	=	£5.25
∴ Fixed overhead carried forward in stock with absorption costing (£5.25 x 800)	=	£4,200

(c) *Tutorial note:* don't be misled by the monthly production figure of 10,000 units. We are given this so that we can calculate the total expected *fixed* overhead expenditure, which should not reduce when only 9,200 units are produced. On the other hand the expected *variable* costs should be based on the lower output of 9,200 units because they should change with the volume of production.

(i) *Direct materials*

		£
Standard cost	9,200 x £4.40	40,480
Actual cost	9,200 x £4.50	41,400
Total variance		920 Adverse

(ii) *Direct labour*

		£
Standard cost	9,200 x £5.85	53,820
Actual cost	9,200 x £6.00	55,200
Total variance		1,380 Adverse

(iii)

		£	£
Overhead			
Variable			
Standard cost	9,200 x £3.35	30,820	
Actual cost	9,200 x £3.25	29,900	
			920 Favourable
Fixed			
Standard cost	10,000 x £5.40	54,000	
Actual cost	9,200 x £5.25	48,300	
			5,700 Favourable
Total variance			6,620 Favourable

46 PROFIT DIFFERENCES/COSTING METHODS

(a) (i) *Absorption costing*

	Six months to 30 June £	*Six months to 31 Dec* £	*Year* £
Sales	1,326,000	1,512,000	2,838,000
Opening stock	130,500	170,500	130,500
Direct labour	374,400	374,400	748,800
Direct material	420,000	420,000	840,000
Direct expenses	85,600	85,600	171,200
Fixed overhead	360,000	360,000	720,000
Less closing stock	170,500	108,500	108,500
Cost of sales	1,200,000	1,302,000	2,502,000
Gross profit	126,000	210,000	336,000

(ii) *Marginal costing*

	Six months to 30 June £	*Six months to 31 Dec* £	*Year* £
Sales	1,326,000	1,512,000	2,838,000
Opening stock	94,500	121,000	94,500
Direct labour	374,400	374,400	748,800
Direct material	420,000	420,000	840,000
Direct expenses	85,600	85,600	171,200
Less closing stock	121,000	77,000	77,000
Cost of sales	853,500	924,000	1,777,500
Fixed costs	360,000	360,000	720,000
Gross profit	112,500	228,000	340,500

Workings

1.

Cost item	*Current cost* £	*Increase* %	*Next year's cost* £
Direct labour (two hours)	9	4%	9.36
Direct material	10	5%	10.50
Direct expenses	2	7%	2.14
Fixed overhead	8	12.5%	9.00
Total	29		31.00

2. *Stock units*	*Six months to 30 June*	*Six months to 31 Dec*
Opening	4,500	5,500
Produced in period	40,000	40,000
Sold units	39,000	42,000
Closing stock	5,500	3,500

The difference in profits of £4,500 (£340,500 - £336,000) is caused by the different methods of treating fixed overheads. Under a marginal costing regime, all fixed overheads are treated as period costs: ie they are charged to the profit and loss account in the period in which they arise.

Under absorption costing, cost of sales invludes some filed overhead from a previous period, in opening stock. Opening stock of 4,500 units has fixed overheads absorbed from the previous period of £8 per unit, and thus is valued at £36,000. Closing stock of 3,500 units includes fixed overheads absorbed, at a rate of £9 per unit, of £31,500. The difference is £4,500.

When unit sales exceed unit production, a higher profit results under marginal costing than absorption costing. In the six months to 31 December the profit under marginal costing was higher, because no extra fixed overhead was charged. In the first half of the year, when unit production exceeded sales, fixed overheads are carried over to the next period.

(b) (i) *Under/over absorption of fixed overhead cost*

An organisation involved in the production of a good or service incurs direct costs (for example materials, directly related to production) and indirect costs. Indirect costs are called overheads, and are split into variable overheads (for example power usage) which vary with the level of production, and fixed overheads (for example rent of premises) which do not, at least in the short run.

It is easy to relate direct costs and variable overheads to units of production. Fixed overheads are more difficult. Rent is a cost of the business, but you cannot add a dollop of rent-stuff to every unit produced. For stock valuation purposes, therefore, an amount of fixed overhead is deemed to *be absorbed* by each unit produced. This amount is based on the estimated level of production, and the estimated level of fixed overheads. If more units are produced than estimated, then the total amount of overhead absorbed in production units at the preset rate will work out greater than the actual overhead cost incurred. Fixed overhead is said to be over absorbed. (Similarly, fixed overhead will also be over absorbed if the actual overhead expenditure is less than anticipated.)

Under absorption of overhead is the opposite: the total overhead absorbed in the units produced is less than the actual overhead expenditure incurred.

(ii) Over absorption of fixed overhead will occur if production levels are higher than anticipated or fixed overhead expenditure is less than anticipated. Under absorption occurs when production levels are less than anticipated or where fixed overhead expenditure is more than anticipated.

(iii) Fixed overhead absorption rates have to be set in advance of the period in which they will be used. The future is impossible to predict: not all fixed costs (eg rates) are subject to management control. Output, also, is not always predictable. There might be production difficulties, or demand for the product may exceed or fall below the estimates at the beginning of the period.

(c) Cost classification is defined in the *CIMA Management Accounting - Official Terminology* as 'the arrangement of items in logical groups having regard to their nature (subjective classification) or the purpose to be fulfilled (objective classification).'

Cost information is used to fulfil a number of purposes. Examples are as follows.

(i) Budgeting.
(ii) Preparation of financial accounts for publication.
(iii) Management control.
(iv) Decision making.

Financial accounting is designed in large part for external reporting, and expenses are classified by type (for example interest payable, distribution costs, administrative expenses, cost of sales). The law does not require details of how these types of expenditure are related to cost centres, or cost units.

The definition of integrated accounts in the *CIMA Management Accounting - Official Terminology* is 'a set of accounting records which provides financial and cost accounts using a common input of data for all accounting purposes.'

There are times when these requirements conflict. For example the stock valuation used for financial accounting purposes might be different form the method used for internal management reporting. It is clear that adjustments have to be made to data produced from a set of integrated accounts to fulfil the different purposes outlined.

47 LMN LIMITED

(a) *Machining*

$$\frac{£175,500}{30,000} = £5.85 \text{ per machine hour}$$

This is the obvious choice for a machining department because of the likely significance of depreciation, maintenance, insurance and so on.

Assembly

$$\frac{£56,450}{14,000} = £4.03 \text{ per labour hour}$$

Labour hours are chosen because this is a labour intensive operation, involving a much smaller proportion of machine hours than labour hours.

Finishing

$$\frac{£98,750}{26,000} = £3.80 \text{ per labour hour}$$

There is no requirement for machine time and so labour hours are the obvious choice.

A proviso for both assembly and finishing is that no information is given on grades of labour and so total figures have to be used.

(b) *Job 123*

	£	£
Material cost		
Machining	1,369	
Assembly	124	
Finishing	93	
		1,586
Labour cost		
Machining	608	
Assembly	90	
Finishing	251	
		949
Overhead absorbed		
Machining : 147 x £5.85	860	
Assembly : 30 x £4.03	121	
Finishing : 70 x £3.80	266	
		1,247
Total cost		3,782
Profit : £3,782 x $\frac{40}{60}$		2,521
Sales price		6,303

(c) Stock valued at marginal cost includes only variable costs, for example direct labour and materials, and no element of overheads incurred. Stock valued at absorption cost includes an element of fixed overheads allocated according to a predetermined absorption rate, calculated using budgeted costs and activity levels.

For decision making purposes, especially in respect of pricing and production, it is more useful to use marginal costing. Fixed overheads, by their nature, do not change with the level of production, and so decisions on how many units to produce and at what price are most usefully made by looking at contribution and using breakeven analysis. This means using marginal costing.

However, the use of absorption costing for stock valuation conforms to SSAP9, which requires that stock valuation should include all relevant costs incurred to bring stock to its present location and condition. This includes a suitable proportion of overheads, where appropriate in the particular circumstances of the business. It can, therefore, be convenient to use absorption costing for management accounting because no adjustment is required when preparing financial accounts.

When production exceeds sales, under absorption costing, a proportion of fixed overhead incurred in the period will be deferred by inclusion in closing stock and so profits will be higher than under marginal costing.

However, when sales exceeds production, use of marginal costing will result in a higher profit than absorption costing, because the fixed overhead element in stock brought forward valued at absorption cost will be charged to profit and loss. In marginal costing, this would already have been charged in an earlier period.

In the long run, of course, total profits are the same under both systems.

48 FIXED OVERHEADS

(a) Marginal costing matches variable costs of production with sales revenue to establish the *contribution* per unit towards covering fixed costs. Stocks are valued at marginal production cost and fixed costs are allocated to the periods in which they are incurred.

Absorption costing regards both fixed and variable costs as operational costs. An *overhead absorption rate* is used so that fixed costs are allocated to units of production and included in stock valuation. This means that fixed costs are only charged to the profit and loss account in the period of sale of the units produced in the period when the fixed costs were incurred.

In a period where production exceeds sales, the inclusion of fixed costs in closing stock will result in a higher profit under absorption costing than under marginal costing. However, when sales exceed production, and therefore under absorption costing fixed costs go through the profit and loss account, marginal costing will produce higher profits.

Profits in the long run are the same under both systems.

Example

Brutus Limited sells the Caesar for £100 each. Variable cost per unit is £60 and fixed production costs are £22,500. Other fixed costs are £10,000. Sales are budgeted at 2,000 units and production at 2,250 units. There is no opening stock.

Marginal costing

	£
Sale price per unit	100
Variable cost per unit	60
Contribution per unit	40
Contribution for period £40 x 2,000	80,000
Fixed costs	32,500
Net profit	47,500
Stock: 250 x £60	15,000

Absorption costing

	£
Variable cost per unit	60
Production overhead per unit (£22,500 for 2,250 units)	10
Full production cost per unit	70
Sales	200,000
Production cost of sales	140,000
Gross profit	60,000
Overheads	10,000
Net profit	50,000
Stock 250 x £70	17,500

(b) Predetermined rates are used to absorb overhead costs into product costs because this is easier and quicker and, although it does not reflect the likely fluctuation of fixed costs over a period, differences will even out overall.

The first step in calculating the rate is to allocate and apportion fixed costs to cost centres using appropriate criteria, for example floor space for rates, number of staff for personnel costs.

Where fixed costs have been allocated and apportioned to a cost centre which is itself an overhead (for example stores, maintenance) these costs must be apportioned between the ultimate cost centres, the production departments; for example, a maintenance department's costs might be reapportioned on the basis of hours worked for each production department.

Finally, the estimated overhead is divided by the budgeted activity level to give the absorption rate. The activity level chosen is usually direct labour hours or machine hours, because these are time-based methods. Since most overhead costs tend to increase with time it is fairer to absorb overheads into the cost of a unit according to how long it takes to produce. The predetermined rate is then applied to actual labour hours or actual machine hours in each period.

A rate per unit is also commonly used but unless all units produced are homogeneous this may result in disparities. It is, however, possibly easier to gather the required data.

Example

As above, the budgeted factory overhead was divided by budgeted production to give an absorption rate of £10 per unit. If actual production was 2,500, therefore, £25,000 would be absorbed, giving rise to an over absorption of £2,500 to be credited to the profit and loss account.

Over and under absorption will also arise because actual overheads are unlikely to be the same as the budgeted figures.

49 BASIC REVISION QUESTION: ABCOLL LIMITED

Tutorial note: use this question to practice preparing a complete manufacturing, trading and profit and loss account before you proceed to the more advanced questions in this section.

MANUFACTURING ACCOUNT FOR THE YEAR ENDED 31 DECEMBER 19X5

	£	£
Raw materials		
Stock on hand 1 January 19X5	25,000	
Purchases	80,000	
	105,000	
Less stock on hand at 31 December 19X5	24,000	
		81,000
Direct wages accrued (33,300 + 700)		34,000
Prime cost		115,000
Work in progress		
Balance at 1 January 19X5 at prime cost	5,800	
Less balance at 31 December 19X5 at prime cost	5,000	
		800
Indirect factory expenses		
Manufacturing expenses	61,900	
Depreciation 7/10 x £(39,000 + 30,000 - 60,000) (note 1)	6,300	
		68,200
Factory cost of finished goods produced (transferred to trading account)		184,000

TRADING AND PROFIT AND LOSS ACCOUNT
FOR THE YEAR ENDED 31 DECEMBER 19X5

	£	£	£
Sales			243,000
Less cost of sales			
Finished goods stock at 1 January 19X5		51,000	
Factory cost of finished goods produced		184,000	
		235,000	
Less finished goods stock at 31 December 19X5		52,000	
			183,000
Gross profit			60,000
Less selling and distribution expenses			
Sundry (16,800 - 1,200 prepayments)	15,600		
Depreciation (1/10 x £9,000) - see note 1)	900		
Discount allowed	5,400		
Bad debts	1,100		
		23,000	
Administration expenses			
Sundry (16,200 + 600 prepayments b/f + 1,100 accrued c/f)	17,900		
Depreciation (2/10 x £9,000) - see note 1	1,800		
		19,700	
		42,700	
Less discount received		1,700	
			41,000
Net profit for the year			19,000
Retained profit at the beginning of the year			1,000
Retained profit at the end of the year			20,000

Note 1	*Fixed assets at cost*	*Net book value*	*Accumulated depreciation*
	£	£	£
At 31 December 19X4	60,000	39,000	21,000
At 31 December 19X5	90,000	60,000	30,000
Depreciation charge for the year			9,000
Manufacturing share 70%			6,300

50 MANUFACTURING LIMITED

Tutorial note: for clarity, the suggested solution includes a budgeted manufacturing account although this is not required by the question. In the examination itself time could be saved by proceeding directly to the profit and loss account.

(a)

FORECAST MANUFACTURING TRADING AND
PROFIT AND LOSS ACCOUNTS
FOR THE MONTHS OF JUNE AND JULY 19X6

	June		*July*	
	£'000	£'000	£'000	£'000
Raw materials				
Opening stock	560		500	
Purchases (Working 3)	220		180	
	780		680	
Less closing stock	500		400	
		280		280
Direct labour (14,000 x £16)		224		224
		504		504
Production overheads				
Variable costs (14,000 x £5)		70		70
Fixed costs		170		170
Depreciation (Working 4)		20		20
Factory cost of goods produced		764		764
Sales		1,100		900
Cost of sales				
Opening stock of finished goods (Working 2)	720		900	
Factory cost of goods produced	764		764	
	1,484		1,664	
Closing stock of finished goods (Working 2)	900		1,200	
		584		464
Gross profit		516		436
Administration costs				
Fixed*	197.5		197.5	
Depreciation (Working 4)	2.5		2.5	
		(200)		(200)
Distribution costs				
Fixed	97.5		97.5	
Variable	55		45	
Depreciation	2.5		2.5	
		(155)		(145)
Profit before taxation		161		91
Taxation (at 50%)		80.5		45.5
Profit after tax		80.5		45.5

* After adjusting for accruals and prepayments.

(b)

FORECAST BALANCE SHEETS

	30 June 19X6		31 July 19X6	
	£'000	£'000	£'000	£'000
Fixed assets				
Cost	3,000		3,000	
Depreciation	1,275		1,300	
Net		1,725		1,700
Current assets				
Stock				
Materials	500		400	
Work in progress	10		10	
Finished products	900		1,200	
Debtors				
May sales	1,000		-	
June sales	1,100		1,100	
July sales	-		900	
Prepayment	16		17	
Cash at bank (Working 5)	176		3	
	3,702		3,630	
Current liabilities				
Creditors for materials				
June purchases	220		-	
July purchases	-		180	
Accrued expenses	22		24	
Taxation	80.5		126	
Proposed dividend	150		-	
	472.5		330	
		3,229.5		3,300
		4,954.5		5,000
Capital and reserves				
Ordinary shares of 25p each fully paid		3,000		3,000
Retained profits		1,954.5		2,000
		4,954.5		5,000

Workings

1 *Valuation of finished goods (per unit)*

	£
Materials (2 lb at £10 per lb)	20
Direct labour (4 hrs at £4 per hour)	16
Variable manufacturing costs	5
Total variable cost	41
Fixed manufacturing costs	19
Total standard cost	60

2 *Finished goods production*

Stocks of finished goods are to be increased from 12,000 units at 31 May to 20,000 units at 31 July, an increase of 8,000 units. The budgeted sales target to be met is 11,000 + 9,000 = 20,000 units. Total production over the two months must therefore be 8,000 + 20,000 = 28,000 units, ie 14,000 units per month.

Stocks of finished goods will increase as follows.

	June units	July units
Opening stock	12,000	15,000
Production	14,000	14,000
	26,000	29,000
Less sales	11,000	9,000
Closing stock	15,000	20,000
at unit cost of £60	900,000	1,200,000

(*Note:* work in progress may be ignored because its level is said to be constant.)

3 Materials budget

	June units	July units
Required for production	28,000	28,000
Required closing stock	50,000	40,000
	78,000	68,000
Less opening stock	56,000	50,000
∴ Purchases	22,000	18,000

4 Depreciation

Cost of fixed assets £(2,900,000 + 100,000) = £3,000,000

Depreciation at 10% pa = £300,000

Monthly depreciation = £300,000/12
= £25,000

Allocated as follows.

Manufacturing (8/10)	£20,000
Administration (1/10)	£ 2,500
Distribution (1/10)	£ 2,500

5 *Cash at bank*

In the examination, it would be advisable to enter a balancing figure in the balance sheet for cash at bank. The working below gives a proof of the balancing figure.

CASH BUDGET	June £'000	July £'000
Expenditure		
Creditors for materials	160	220
Direct labour	224	224
Variable production overheads	70	70
Fixed production overheads	170	170
Fixed administration overheads	196.5	196.5
Fixed distribution overheads	97.5	97.5
Variable distribution overheads	55	45
Purchase of fixed assets	100	-
Payment of dividend	-	150
Payment of taxation	250	-
	1,323	1,173
Receipts from debtors	800	1,000
Reduction in cash balance	523	173
Opening balance	699	176
Closing balance	176	3

51 STUART LIMITED

Tutorial note: the key to completing this question successfully is to work logically through the information given, first writing out the proformas and slotting in the known figures and then preparing workings for the others. It is important to grasp that a *flexed* budget will use the *actual* production to establish the cost allowances for the year, but that *budgeted* production is used to calculate the standard costs to be used for valuing stock.

To derive the actual costs you should calculate the budget cost allowances based on actual production and then add the adverse variances and subtract the favourable variances to derive the actual cost.

Do not be put off by the necessity to calculate balancing figures for the balance sheet; the aim of the question is to test how well you understand the principles of accounts preparation and therefore whether you can work out what is missing.

(a)

STUART LIMITED
MANUFACTURING ACCOUNT
FOR THE YEAR ENDED 30 SEPTEMBER 19X8

	Working	£	£
Direct materials			
Opening stock		3,000	
Purchases	1	70,420	
		73,420	
Less closing stock	2	3,000	
			70,420
Direct labour	3		102,840
Prime cost			173,260
Manufacturing overhead	4a		87,300
Manufacturing cost of finished goods produced			260,560

TRADING AND PROFIT AND LOSS ACCOUNT
FOR THE YEAR ENDED 30 SEPTEMBER 19X8

	Working	£	£
Sales			512,400
Cost of sales			
Opening stock of finished goods		5,482	
Manufacturing cost of finished goods purchased		260,560	
		266,042	
Less closing stock of finished goods	5	22,695	
			243,347
Gross profit			269,053
Overheads			
Administration	4b	31,600	
Selling	4c	22,545	
			54,145
Net profit before tax			214,908
Taxation charge			64,500
Profit after taxation			150,408
Retained profit brought forward (balancing figure)			32,923
Retained profit carried forward (from balance sheet)			128,331

STUART LIMITED, BALANCE SHEET AS AT 30 SEPTEMBER 19X8

	Working	£	£
Fixed assets			327,000
Current assets			
Stock of raw materials	2	3,000	
Stock of finished goods	5	22,695	
Debtors	6	63,000	
Cash at bank and in hand	9	96,680	
		185,375	
Current liabilities			
Trade creditors	7	11,544	
Proposed dividend	8	33,000	
Corporation tax		64,500	
		109,044	
Net current assets			76,331
			403,331
Share capital and reserves			
Share capital	8		275,000
Profit and loss account (balancing figure)			128,331
			403,331

Workings

1 *Direct materials*

	£
Budgeted (flexed) cost: £6 x 11,000	66,000
Add adverse variance	4,420
Actual cost	70,420

2 *Stock of raw materials*

Valuation at standard cost: £6 x 500 = £3,000

[Cost, for management accounts purposes with a standard costing system, means standard cost, not actual.]

3 *Direct labour*

	£
Budgeted cost (flexed): £9 x 11,000	99,000
Add adverse variance	3,840
Actual cost	102,840

4 *Overheads*

(a) *Manufacturing*
The unit cost for manufacturing overhead changes as production increases, therefore it must include a fixed element.

(i) Variable cost per unit

	£
10,000 x £7.50	75,000
12,000 x £7.40	88,800
	13,800

∴ Variable cost per unit = £13,800/(12,000 - 10,000) = £6.90

(ii) Proof:

	10,000 units	*12,000 units*
Total variable cost at £6.90 per unit	69,000	82,800
Fixed costs (balancing figure)	6,000	6,000
Total budgeted overhead	75,000	88,800

(iii) Budgeted overhead for production of 11,000 units is as follows.

	£
Variable costs (11,000 x £6.90)	75,900
Fixed costs	6,000
	81,900
Add: adverse variance	5,400
Actual cost	87,300

(b) *Administration*

(i) Variable cost per unit

	£
10,000 x £4.00	40,000
12,000 x £3.90	46,800
	6,800

£6,800/2,000 = £3.40

∴ Fixed costs = £40,000 - (10,000 x £3.40) = £6,000

(ii) Budgeted overhead for production of 10,250 units is as follows.

	£
Variable costs (10,250 x £3.40)	34,850
Fixed costs	6,000
	40,850
Favourable variance	(9,250)
Actual cost	31,600

(c) *Selling*

(i) Variable cost per unit

	£
10,000 x £2.50	25,000
12,000 x £2.48	29,760
	4,760

£4,760/2,000 = £2.38

∴ Fixed costs = £25,000 - (10,000 x £2.38) =£1,200

(ii) Budgeted overhead for production of 10,250 units is as follows.

	£
Variable costs (10,250 x £2.38)	24,395
Fixed costs	1,200
	25,595
Less: favourable variance	(3,050)
Actual cost	22,545

5 *Stock of finished goods*

	Units
Balance at 1 October 19X7	260
Production in year	11,000
Sales in year	10,250
Balance at 30 September 19X8	1,010

Standard cost per unit	£
Direct materials	6.00
Direct labour	9.00
Manufacturing overhead:	
variable (W4a)	6.90
fixed $\frac{£6,000}{10,500}$ (based on budgeted production)	0.57
	22.47

Total stock valuation: 1,010 x £22.47 = £22,695.

6 *Debtors*

Year end debtors = 45 days sales out of a total of 366 days

$= \frac{45}{366} \times £512,400$

= £63,000

7 Year end creditors = 60 days purchases out of a total of 366 days

$= \frac{60}{366} \times £70,420$

= £11,544

8 *Share capital and final dividend*

A dividend of two pence per share totalled £22,000

∴ number of shares $= \frac{22,000}{£0.02} = 1,100,000$

∴ nominal value of shares at 25 pence each

= 1,100,000 x £0.25

= £275,000

Final dividend = three pence per share

= £0.03 x 1,100,000

= £33,000

9 *Current assets*

Current assets:current liabilities = 1.7:1

	£
Total current assets = £109,044 x 1.7 =	185,375
Less:	
stock of raw materials	(3,000)
stock of finished goods	(22,695)
debtors	(63,000)
Cash at bank and in hand (balancing figure)	96,680

(b) (i) *Standard marginal cost*

	£
Direct materials	6.00
Direct labour	9.00
Manufacturing overhead - variable element	6.90
	21.90

Total stock valuation: 1,010 x £21.90 = £22,119

(ii) *Average actual cost*

	£
Direct materials: £70,420/11,000	6.40
Direct labour: £102,840/11,000	9.35
Manufacturing overhead: £87,300/11,000	7.94
	23.69

Total stock valuation: 1,010 x £23.69 = £23,927.

(c) Standard costs should only be used when the company expects no marked variance from standard cost because of inflation, scarcity of materials and so on. Additionally, they should be reviewed regularly because the use of out of date standards will produce misleading management information.

However, use of standard costs is easy and administratively convenient. Standard costs can also be used as an efficient way to monitor performance, since discrepancies from standard costs will show up as variances, thus allowing management by exception.

Financial accounts cannot, however, be prepared using standard costs, and so stock will have to be valued at actual cost as well as standard cost if standard costing is in use for internal purposes. This could be time consuming and expensive but with a good computer system this problem can be minimised.

52 DICK TURNIP

HIGHWAYMAN STORES
DEPARTMENTAL TRADING, PROFIT AND LOSS ACCOUNT
FOR THE YEAR ENDED 31 MARCH 19X9

	Stationery		*Confectionery*		*Total*	
	£	£	£	£	£	£
Sales (workings 1 and 2)		30,000		36,000		66,000
Opening stock	0		0		0	
Purchases	26,000		29,250		55,250	
	26,000		29,250		55,250	
Closing stock (working 1)	2,000		2,250		4,250	
Cost of goods sold (working 1)		24,000		27,000		51,000
Gross profit (working 2)		6,000		9,000		15,000
Expenses						
Staff wages	2,200		1,540		3,740	
Depreciation of fixtures and fittings (working 3)	260		150		410	
Rent (working 4)	800		400		1,200	
Rates	380		190		570	
Electricity (working 5)	360		120		480	
Advertising (working 6)	500		600		1,100	
		4,500		3,000		7,500
Net profit		1,500		6,000		7,500

Workings

1. Since there was no opening stock, purchases during the year must be sufficient to provide stocks for:

   (a) sales during the year (12 months) and
   (b) closing stocks (1 month).

	Stationery	*Confectionery*
	£	£
Purchases	26,000	29,250
Cost of goods sold (12 months)	24,000	27,000
Closing stock (1 month)	2,000	2,250
	26,000	29,250

2. Cost of goods sold	(80%)	24,000	(75%)	27,000
Gross profit	(20%)	6,000	(25%)	9,000
Sales	(100%)	30,000	(100%)	36,000

3. Depreciation		
10% of £2,600	£260	
10% of £1,500		£150

4.

RENT ACCOUNT

	£		£	£
Cash	1,300	P & L account (12 months)		
		Stationery (2/3)	800	
		Confectionery (1/3)	400	
				1,200
		Prepayment c/d (1 month)		100
	1,300			1,300
Prepayment b/d	100			

5.

ELECTRICITY

	£		£
Cash	370	Stationery (¾) - P & L a/c	360
Accrual c/d	110	Confectionery (¼) - P & L a/c	120
	480		480
		Accrual b/d	110

6. Advertising

Stationery: $\frac{30,000}{66,000} \times £1,100 = £500$

Confectionery: $\frac{36,000}{66,000} \times £1,100 = £600$

7.

CASH

	£		£
Opening balance	3,000	Fixtures and fittings	4,100
Cash sales and debtors (30,000 + 36,000 - 9,000 drs)	57,000	Wages	3,740
		Rent	1,300
		Rates	570
Capital - Dick Turnip legacy	5,000	Electricity	370
Loan - Mrs Green legacy	4,000	Advertising	1,100
Balance c/d	730	Creditors	53,550
		Drawings	5,000
	69,730		69,730
		Balance b/d	730

CREDITORS

	£		£
Cash	53,550	Purchases (26,000 + 29,250 + 500 drawings)	55,750
Balance c/d	2,200		
	55,750		55,750
		Balance b/d	2,200

HIGHWAYMAN STORES
BALANCE SHEET AS AT 31 MARCH 19X9

	£	£	£
Fixed assets			
Fixtures and fittings at cost			4,100
Less provision for depreciation			410
Net book value			3,690
Current assets			
Stock		4,250	
Debtors		9,000	
Prepayment (rent - working 4)		100	
		13,350	
Creditors: amounts falling due within one year			
Bank overdraft (working 7)	730		
Creditors (working 7)	2,200		
Accrual (electricity - working 5)	110		
		3,040	
Net current assets			10,310
			14,000
Loan - Mrs Green			4,000
			10,000
Proprietor's capital			
Capital as at 1 April 19X8			3,000
Capital introduced			5,000
			8,000
Net profit for the year		7,500	
Less drawings (5,000 cash + 500 stock)		5,500	
Retained profit			2,000
Capital as at 31 March 19X9			10,000

53 SMITH PLC

Tutorial note: part (a) of the question only asks for a profit and loss account. But in order to calculate many of the figures to be shown in the P & L account, it makes sense to start off the question by preparing a manufacturing account. Obviously the P & L account statement is the actual answer to the question, and is therefore shown first in the solution below. The manufacturing account is given as *working 1*.

(a)

SMITH PLC
PROFIT AND LOSS ACCOUNT
FOR YEAR ENDED 31 DECEMBER 19X7

	Working	*Product X*	*Product Y*	*Total*
		£'000	£'000	£'000
Sales		24,000	16,000	40,000
Cost of sales	1	15,000	12,000	27,000
Gross profit		9,000	4,000	13,000
Less: distribution costs	2	3,000	1,000	4,000
administrative expenses	3	3,840	960	4,800
		6,840	1,960	8,800
Net profit before tax		2,160	2,040	4,200
Corporation tax				1,680
Net profit after tax				2,520
Proposed dividends at 0.15p per share				1,500
Retained profit				1,020

Working 1

SMITH PLC
MANUFACTURING ACCOUNT
FOR YEAR ENDED 31 DECEMBER 19X7

	Note	*Product X*		*Product Y*		*Total*	
		£'000	£'000	£'000	£'000	£'000	£'000
Materials usage	1		6,410		4,785		11,195
Factory wages	2		3,205		1,595		4,800
Prime cost			9,615		6,380		15,995
Factory overhead							
Production overhead expenses	3	5,342		2,658		8,000	
Depreciation		1,068		532		1,600	
			6,410		3,190		9,600
			16,025		9,570		25,595
Work in progress							
Opening stocks		25		60		85	
Closing stocks		(50)		(30)		(80)	
(Increase)/decrease in WIP			(25)		30		5
Cost of finished goods produced			16,000		9,600		25,600

Calculation of cost of goods sold

	Product X	*Product Y*	*Total*
	£'000	£'000	£'000
Opening stock of finished goods	875	3,900	4,775
Cost of finished goods produced	16,000	9,600	25,600
	16,875	13,500	30,375
Closing stock of finished goods	1,875	1,500	3,375
Cost of goods sold	15,000	12,000	27,000

Notes

1. The 'indirect' materials of £105,000 are included in production overhead expenses, so that they can be apportioned between products X and Y.

2. Factory wages for each product = wages in trial balance - prepayments + accruals.

3.

	£'000
Production overhead expenses (trial balance figure)	7,674
Accrual	190
Indirect material	105
Stock loss on stocktake	31
Depreciation (production)	1,600
	9,600

Apportionment to product X
$£9,600,000 \times \frac{3,205}{4,800}$ 6,410

Apportionment to product Y
$£9,600,000 \times \frac{1,595}{4,800}$ 3,190

Working 2

	£'000
Distribution costs in trial balance	3,715
Accrual	90
Allocated depreciation	200
Allocated decrease in bad debt provision *	(5)
	4,000

Apportionment to product X
$£4,000,000 \times \frac{600,000}{800,000}$ 3,000

Apportionment to product Y
$£4,000,000 \times \frac{200,000}{800,000}$ 1,000

* 5% x debtors = £250,000
Existing provision = £255,000

∴ £5,000 needs to be written back - ie deducted from distribution expenses.

Working 3

	£'000
Administration costs in trial balance	4,520
Depreciation allocated	200
Accrual	80
	4,800
Apportionment to product X	
£4,800,000 x 640,000 / 800,000	3,840
Apportionment to product Y	
£4,800,000 x 160,000 / 800,000	960

(b) Two methods which may be used to calculate profit (other than using historical costs) are CPP (current purchasing power) and CCA (current cost accounting).

(i) CPP accounting is a method of accounting for *general* (not specific) inflation. It does so by expressing asset values in a stable monetary unit, the £c or £ of current purchasing power. Under this method, capital is maintained if the current purchasing power of equity is at least as great at the end of the period as it was at the beginning. As always, any excess over this is regarded as profit.

In the CPP balance sheet, monetary items are stated at their face value. Non-monetary items are stated at their current purchasing power as at the balance sheet date.

(ii) CCA is an alternative to the historical cost convention which attempts to overcome the problems of accounting for *specific* price inflation. Unlike CPP accounting, it does not attempt to cope with *general* inflation.

CCA is based on a *physical* concept of capital maintenance. Profit is recognised after the operating capability of the business has been maintained.

This capital maintenance concept is applied by stating assets in the current cost balance sheet at their deprival value, which in most cases is their net replacement cost. Adjustments are made to the historic cost profit and loss account so as to remove any holding gains on stock or fixed assets. To recognise holding gains as part of current cost profit would conflict with the principle of maintaining operating capability.

The current cost profit and loss account is constructed by taking historical cost profit before interest and taxation as a starting point. Current cost operating adjustments in respect of cost of sales, monetary working capital and depreciation are made so as to arrive at current cost operating profit. A gearing adjustment is then necessary to arrive at a figure of current cost profit attributable to shareholders.

54 BASIC REVISION QUESTION: HONECKER

Tutorial note: as well as some introductory budget practice this question contains material on marginal costing and variances which you should find useful.

(a)

	£'000	£'000
Sales £20 x 50,000		1,000
Cost of sales		
Production £15.20 (W1) x 60,000	912	
Less closing stock £15.20 (W1) x 10,000	(152)	
		760
		240
Fixed overhead under absorbed (W2)		6
Gross profit		234
Selling costs - variable (50,000 x £1)		(50)
Fixed selling costs		(10)
Net profit		174

Workings

1. Cost per unit

		£
Variable:	direct	10.00
	overhead	4.00
Fixed absorbed	$\frac{£72,000}{£60,000}$ =	1.20
		15.20

2.

Production overhead absorbed £60,000 x £1.20 =	72,000
Production overhead incurred	78,000
Underabsorbed fixed overhead	6,000

(b)

	£'000
Net profit under absorption costing	174
Less: fixed overheads absorbed in closing stock (10,000 x £1.20)	12
Net profit under marginal costing	162

Under marginal costing all fixed overheads are treated as *period* costs. None are carried forward to future periods in the closing stock valuation.

(c)

		£'000
Production cost variance		
£0.50 x 60,000	30	
Less £0.50 x 10,000 closing stock	5	
		25.0
Favourable selling expense variance £50,000 x £0.25		12.5
Effect on profit (reduction)		12.5

An adverse cost variance *reduces* profit. A favourable variance increases it.

(d) (i) Production budget

	Bricks '000
Required sales 19Y1	100
Closing stock required 19Y1	20
	120
Less opening stock 19Y1	(10)
Required production ('000 units)	110

(ii) *19Y1 Cash budget*

	£'000	£'000
Cash receipts		
19Y0 Sales 3/12 x £1,000,000	250	
19Y1 Sales 9/12 x 100,000 x £20	1,500	
		1,750
Cash payments		
Direct production costs £10 x 110,000	1,100	
Variable factory overhead £4 x ($\frac{3}{12}$ 60,000 + $\frac{9}{12}$ 110,000)	390	
Fixed overheads	80	
Variable selling expenses £1 x 100,000	100	
Fixed selling expenses	10	
		1,680
Net cash inflow 19Y1		70
Overdraft at end of 19Y0		(10)
Bank balance at end of 19Y1		60

Working

In 19Y0 total production was 60,000.

55 CASH BUDGETS

Workings

		Month 1	2	3	4	5	6
		£	£	£	£	£	£
1.	Sales		6,200	6,800	7,200	8,400	
2.	Receipts from debtors (2 months credit)				6,200	6,800	7,200
3.	Materials cost in sales (75% of sales)			5,100	5,400	6,300	
4.	Increase(decrease) in stocks			(100)	-	700	
5.	Materials purchased (item 3 + item 4)			5,000	5,400	7,000	
6.	Payments to creditors				5,000	5,400	7,000
7.	Wages: $\frac{3}{4}$ of current month				480	525	720
	$\frac{1}{4}$ of previous month				150	160	175
	Total wages paid				630	685	895
8.	Overhead expenses (presumably all cash expenses)						
	$\frac{1}{2}$ of current month				315	315	320
	$\frac{1}{2}$ of previous month				305	315	315
	Total paid				620	630	635

Note: if overhead expenses had included depreciation, which is not a cash expense, the amount of depreciation would have been subtracted from the total overheads to arrive at a figure for the cash expenses in overhead costs.

CASH BUDGET

	Month 4	Month 5	Month 6
	£	£	£
Balance b/f	540	(9,310)	(9,225)
Receipts			
Debtors	6,200	6,800	7,200
Issue of ordinary shares			35,000
Sale of plant	200	-	-
	6,940	(2,510)	32,975
Payments			
Creditors for materials	5,000	5,400	7,000
Wages paid	630	685	895
Overhead paid	620	630	635
Debenture interest paid			1,000
Taxation paid	10,000		
Dividends paid			500
Purchase of plant			1,945
Repayment of debentures			20,000
	16,250	6,715	31,975
Balance c/f	(9,310)	(9,225)	1,000
	6,940	(2,510)	32,975

There is a cash balance of £1,000 at the end of month 6, although there will be overdrafts in excess of £9,000 at the end of both month 4 and month 5.

56 FLEXIBLE BUDGET

(a) *Fixed* budgets are based on estimated volumes of production and sales but do not include any provision for the event that actual volumes may differ from the budget.

A *flexible* budget is designed to change so as to relate to actual volumes achieved. This has two advantages.

(i) At the planning stage, it may be helpful to know what the effects would be if the actual outcome differs from the prediction. This would enable contingency plans to be drawn up if necessary.

(ii) At the end of each month or year, actual results may be compared with the flexible budget as a control procedure.

(b) (i) FLEXIBLE BUDGET

	80%	*90%*	*100%*
Direct labour hours	48,000	54,000	60,000
	£	£	£
Variable costs			
Indirect labour (£0.75 per hour)	36,000	40,500	45,000
Consumable supplies (£0.375 per hour)	18,000	20,250	22,500
Canteen and other welfare services (see workings)	12,960	14,580	16,200
Semi-variable (£0.20 per hour - see workings)	9,600	10,800	12,000
	76,560	86,130	95,700
Fixed costs			
Depreciation	18,000	18,000	18,000
Maintenance	10,000	10,000	10,000
Insurance	4,000	4,000	4,000
Rates	15,000	15,000	15,000
Management salaries	25,000	25,000	25,000
Semi-variable (see workings)	8,000	8,000	8,000
	156,560	166,130	175,700

Workings

Canteen and other welfare services			
Direct labour (3.75 per hour)	180	202.5	225
Indirect labour (£0.75 per hour)	36	40.5	45
	216	243.0	270
Canteen costs (6%)	12.96	14.58	16.2

Semi-variable

Using data from 19X1 to 19X5, range of direct labour hours = 64,000 - 40,000 = 24,000 and range of semi-variable costs = £20,800 - £16,000 = £4,800.

∴ Variable costs = 64,000 x $\frac{£4,800}{24,000}$ = £12,800 out of a total of £20,800 costs.

∴ Fixed costs = £20,800 - £12,800 = £8,000
Variable costs = £12,800/64,000 = £0.20 per hour

(ii) *Budget cost allowance for 19X6*

	£
Fixed costs	80,000
Variable costs 57,000 hours x £1.595*	90,915
Budget cost allowance	170,915

* Standard variable cost per hour (using flexible budget in (b)(i)) = $\frac{£76,560}{48,000}$ = £1.595

57 SINGLE PRODUCT

(a)

BUDGETED PROFIT AND LOSS ACCOUNT FOR YEAR ENDED 31 DECEMBER 19X6

	£'000	£'000
Sales (£100 x 100,000)		10,000
Less		
Direct materials (10 x £3 x 100,000)	3,000	
Direct labour (5 x £4 x 100,000)	2,000	
Variable overheads (£10 x 100,000)	1,000	
Fixed overheads	2,000	
		8,000
Profit		2,000

(b)

ACTUAL PROFIT AND LOSS ACCOUNT FOR YEAR ENDED 31 DECEMBER 19X6

	£'000	£'000
Sales (£100 x 100,000)		10,000
Less		
Direct materials (£3 x 1,020,000)	3,060	
Direct labour (£4.20 x 500,000)	2,100	
Variable overheads	990	
Fixed overheads	2,030	
		8,180
Profit		1,820

(c)

RECONCILIATION STATEMENT BETWEEN ACTUAL AND BUDGETED PROFIT FOR YEAR ENDED 31 DECEMBER 19X6

	£'000	£'000
Standard (budgeted) profit		2,000
Cost variances (favourable/(adverse))		
Direct materials	(60)	
Direct labour	(100)	
Variable overhead	10	
Fixed overheads	(30)	
		(180)
Actual profit		1,820

(d) The figures for which both 19X5 and 19X6 results are available are as follows.

	19X5	*19X6*
Quantity of product manufactured and sold (units)	80,000	100,000
Direct material total cost variance	£1,000	£(60,000)
Direct labour total cost variance	£(90,000)	£(100,000)

The following conclusions can be drawn from these figures.

(i) Output has risen by 25%.

(ii) The direct materials cost variance has considerably worsened. Without more information, nothing can sensibly be said about the 19X5 variance. However, the poor variances in 19X6 cannot be blamed on increased prices, because the materials price of £3 per lb turned out to be exactly as budgeted. So the poor variances must be due to poor usage - perhaps wastage has increased, or perhaps the materials bought in are of a lower standard (bearing in mind the increased output, which may mean that the company has had to turn to new suppliers).

(iii) The direct labour cost variance has also worsened. Again, there is insufficient information for comment on the 19X5 variance. But the poor variance in 19X6 cannot be blamed on the time taken to do the work, because the direct labour of five hours per unit turned out exactly as budgeted. So the poor variance must be due to the rates of pay - the budget of £4/hour was too low. Bearing in mind the increased output, it is possible that the company has been obliged to pay overtime, or perhaps take on more experienced (better paid) staff.

58 BASIC REVISION QUESTION: MYCOST LIMITED

(a) *Standard cost*

A predetermined cost calculated in relation to a prescribed set of working conditions, correlating technical specifications and scientific measurements of materials and labour to the prices and wage rates expected to apply during the period to which the standard cost is intended to relate, with an addition of an appropriate share of budgeted overhead. Its main purposes are to provide bases of control through variance accounting for the valuation of stocks and work in progress and, in exceptional cases, for fixing selling prices.

(b) *The benefits of standard costing*

(i) Standard costs provide a consistent base whereby performance may be measured on the basis of what an item should cost or how much should have been produced, on the basis of the expected levels of activity.

(ii) It provides a method whereby labour and overheads can be consistently recovered and charged into stock.

(iii) It provides a basis of control of buying, of usage and of efficient work levels.

(iv) In setting up standards it enables management to reappraise activities to ascertain if they are being done in the most cost effective and efficient way.

(v) It creates an atmosphere of cost consciousness amongst all levels motivating staff and workers to see if there is a better way of performing a particular task.

(vi) By creating a realistic target it motivates staff and operatives to achieve or better the standard laid down.

(vii) It is a recognisable method of performance monitoring through variance analysis, motivating investigations into causes of shortfall and improving methods and procedures for the future.

(viii) It provides a recognisable basis for budgeting, forecasting and planning.

(ix) Where firms are in similar industries and are willing to compare a meaningful basis for comparison might be established.

(c) *Problems of standard costing*

(i) If a standard is too easy to attain or impossible to attain it becomes a disincentive and operatives go at their own pace.

(ii) Operatives will be suspicious of standards and will be reluctant to super-achieve in case the standard is changed. Also when standards are being set, the operatives will contrive to make the standard easy to beat by working slowly. The inevitable result will be a subjective standard.

(iii) Standards of material prices (which are largely uncontrollable) are at best opinions of what is likely to happen. Standards of labour cost should be set as a result of union negotiations. Consequently standards no longer measure buying powers but ability to predict accurately and to negotiate hard bargains with the unions.

(iv) The setting of standards and the reporting through variance accounting is now a complicated, laborious, time consuming and costly business. The savings arising from cost control are often eroded by the high reporting cost and any time lapse means that the detailed information is too late in presentation to be of real use.

(v) Standards are considered coercive and as such management and staff may find them a 'big stick' which may be dysfunctional. This may make management liable to 'passing the buck' to keep within standard or to be unadventurous for similar reasons.

(vi) Standards inevitably produce variances. For reasons outlined in (iii) above, many costs are now a 'fait accompli'. The non-recognition of this fact may give rise to there being a substantial amount of time wasting over uncontrollable variances.

59 AR LIMITED

Tutorial note: when you first look at this question it can seem like a mass of confusing data. However bear in mind that you have about an hour to answer both parts so there is plenty of time to sort out all the information. A good way to start is to set up the skeleton for the profit statement and then begin to decide which figures you require. When you reach a point where the figure is not available and you need to do some workings, head up a separate sheet 'workings' and do the necessary calculations.

It is important that you follow the instructions in the question when preparing your statement. The examiner asks for a columnar marginal costing format so you will lose easy marks if you do not show a separate column for each activity and highlight the contribution from each.

There are some more notes to guide you in the workings to this solution.

Suggested solution

AR LIMITED

PROFIT STATEMENT FOR THE YEAR ENDED 31 MARCH 19X1

	Flight services	*Cafeteria services*	*Souvenir services*	*Total*
	£'000	£'000	£'000	£'000
Sales (W1)	2,392.0	480	72	2,944.0
Opening stock		16	3	19.0
Purchases		233	44	277.0
		249	47	296.0
Less closing stock		15	5	20.0
Cost of sales		234	42	276.0
Variable flight services costs (W2)				
Direct wages of pilot and crew	126.0			126.0
Indirect labour costs	19.8			19.8
Fuel cost	899.0			899.0
In-flight catering	80.0			80.0
Indirect material cost	36.2			36.2
Ground services cost	83.4			83.4
Total variable cost	1,244.4	234	42	1,520.4
Contribution	1,147.6	246	30	1,423.6
Fixed ground services cost	182.0			182.0
Profit	965.6	246	30	1,241.6

Workings

1. Calculation of sales revenue from flight services

   The amount for flight ticket receipts must be adjusted for payments received in advance.

	£'000
Receipts during year	2,400
Plus receipts last year which related to this year	97
	2,497
Less receipts in advance this year	(105)
Revenue from sales this year	2,392

2. *Calculation of flight services costs*

   The actual costs of flight services are calculated as follows.

   (i) Multiply the standard cost per flight by 1,900 to determine the total standard cost.
   (ii) Add adverse variances and subtract favourable variances to determine the actual costs.

	Standard cost per flight £	*x 1,900 = total standard cost* £'000	*Total variance* £'000	*Total actual cost* £'000
Variable costs				
Direct wages of pilot and crew	60.00	114.0	12A	126.0
Indirect labour costs	12.00	22.8	3F	19.8
Fuel cost	440.00	836.0	63A	899.0
In-flight catering	50.00	95.0	15F	80.0
Indirect material cost	18.00	34.2	2A	36.2
Ground services costs (W3)	36.00	68.4	15A	83.4
Total variable costs	616.00	1,170.4	74A	1,244.4
Fixed ground services costs (W3)		168.0	14A	182.0

3. *Ground services costs*

Variable ground services cost = 60% x £60 = £36 per flight
Fixed ground services cost = 140% x £60 = £84 per flight, for 2,000 flights

The total amount of *fixed* cost would not be expected to reduce when only 1,900 flights were made. The total standard fixed cost for 1,900 flights is therefore the same as for 2,000 flights = £84 x 2,000 = £168,000.

(b) *Tutorial note:* nearly a third of the available marks are awarded for this part of the question so you need to write more than a couple of lines.

Suggested solution

A standard cost is a pre-determined calculation of what costs should be for a particular item of product or service. It is used as a basis for the control of actual costs by comparison with the standard.

Although standard costing techniques are more easily applied in a manufacturing environment, they can be used in any environment where there is a standard repetitive activity which can be measured. The technique has been applied to AR Limited to control the costs of a flight from London to Manchester, an activity which is repeated and for which the costs can be ascertained. This is a demonstration of standard costing being applied successfully in a non-manufacturing environment.

A number of benefits arise from the use of a standard costing system.

(i) Standard costs provide a yardstick for comparison with actual costs so that control action can be taken to correct any variances which arise.

(ii) The setting of standard costs provides a target of efficiency and may help to motivate employees and stimulate cost consciousness.

(iii) The principle of *management by exception* can be operated whereby management attention is directed to where it is most needed, to correct the variances which exceed acceptable tolerance limits.

(iv) If standards are analysed between fixed and variable costs (as in this example) then the total expected cost can be adjusted up or down to allow for changes in the level of activity (expected 2,000 flights reduced to actual 1,900 flights). A realistic target for total cost can therefore be established, which is more useful for control and motivation purposes.

(v) Standard costs may provide the basis for decisions such as determining selling prices, although some caution needs to be exercised when using standard costs in decision making.

60 PQR LIMITED

(a) (i) Standard costs for quarter ended 31 March 19X8.

Direct materials:

$$\frac{£48,000}{8,000} = £6 \text{ per unit}$$

Direct labour:

$$\frac{£28,000}{8,000} = £3.50 \text{ per unit}$$

Variable indirect overheads:

Power $\frac{£8,000}{8,000}$ = £1 per unit

Heat/light $\frac{£6,000}{8,000}$ = £0.75 per unit

Total variable indirect overheads £1.75 per unit

Fixed costs budgeted as follows.

	£	
Supervisor's salary	11,500	
Power	7,500	
Heat/light	1,000	
Factory rates	40,000	
	60,000	per annum

(ii) *Variances*

Tutorial note: assuming no seasonal variation was anticipated, it can be taken that production of 2,000 units per quarter was budgeted; the *total* variance would therefore be expected to include the effect of the shortfall in production as well as the price difference. However, your syllabus only requires you to understand total variances at this stage, and so the variances shown below ignore budgeted production.

(1) Direct materials:

	£	
Standard costs: 1,875 x £6	11,250	
Actual costs	11,400	
Variance	150	(A)

(2) Direct labour:

	£	
Standard costs: 1,875 x £3.50	6,562.50	
Actual	6,540.00	
Variance	22.50	(F)

(3) Indirect overheads:

	£	
Variable costs: 1,875 x £1.75	3,281.25	
Fixed	15,000.00	
	18,281.25	
Actual costs	18,381.00	
Variance	99.75	(A)

(b) Factors to consider when setting material cost standards include the following.

(i) Expected availability of bulk discounts, if worthwhile taking up.
(ii) Economic factors likely to affect prices in the period, such as inflation, exchange and interest rate movements.
(iii) Which grade to set as the standard where a choice exists, balancing technical considerations against cost and possible scarcity.
(iv) Setting an expected, rather an ideal standard, but building in a target for reducing wastage and shrinkage, where possible.
(v) Efficiency of machinery; if deteriorating through age, wastage may increase.
(vi) Ancillary costs should be included (for example carriage, insurance, freight, duty).

61 BUDGETS FROM VARIANCES

Tutorial note: this is a very lengthy question, but the mark allocation suggests that you can afford to take about an hour completing part (a).

(a) (i) *Production budget*

	Quarter ended 31 March 19X9
	units
Required sales (per question)	4,800
Required closing stock (1/3 × 1,500)	500
	5,300
Less opening stock (1/3 × 4,800)	1,600
Required production (units)	3,700

(ii) *Profit and loss account*

	Six months ended 31 March 19X9		Six months ended 30 September 19X9		Total	
	£	£	£	£	£	£
Sales		552,000		405,000		957,000
Opening stock (W2)		23,800		17,965 *		23,800
Production costs						
Materials (W3)	65,560		49,005		114,565	
Labour (W4)	117,533		89,994		207,527	
Expenses (W5)	26,465		19,592		46,057	
Variable overhead (W6)	29,195		21,613		50,808	
Fixed overhead (W7)	81,340		81,340		162,680	
		320,093		261,544		581,637
		343,893		279,509		605,437
Closing stock (W8)		17,965		34,493		34,493
Cost of sales		325,928		245,016		570,944

* Opening stock for second six months = closing stock for first six months.

	Six months ended 31 March 19X9	Six months ended 30 September 19X9	Total
	£	£	£
Gross profit	226,072	159,984	386,056
Bad debts (5% sales)	27,600	20,250	47,850
Net profit	198,472	139,734	338,206

(iii) *Cash budget for the quarter January to March 19X9*

	£
Overdrawn balance brought forward	(124,678)
Receipts	
Current quarter 4,800 x £80 x 50%	192,000
Previous quarter 2,100 x £80 x 45%	75,600
	267,600
Payments	
Materials (W9)	33,921
Wages (W4)	67,133
Direct expenses (prior quarter = £3.95 (W5) x 3,000 (W4))	11,850
Variable overhead (W10)	15,106
Fixed overhead (W11)	36,603
	164,613
Balance carried forward	(21,691)

Workings

(1) Production for six months

	to 31 March		*to 30 September*
Sales Oct to Dec 19X8	2,100	April to June 19X9	1,500
Jan to March 19X9	4,800	July to Sept 19X9	3,000
Closing stock	500		960
Opening stock	(700)		(500)
	6,700		4,960
		(Total 11,660 units)	

(2) Opening stock = 700 units x £34 = £23,800, as given in question.

(3) *Materials*

	£
19X8 production 9,800 units at standard £10 per unit =	98,000
Less favourable cost variance	(4,900)
19X8 total production cost	93,100

Standard cost = £93,100/9,800 units = £9.50 per unit

Six months to 31 March unit cost = £9.50 x 103% = £9.785
Six months to 30 September unit cost = £9.50 x 104% = £9.88

∴ Direct materials cost =
Six months to 31 March £9.785 x 6,700 (W1) = £65,560
30 September £9.88 x 4,960 (W2) = £49,005

(4) *Labour*

	£
19X8 production 9,800 units at standard £16 per unit =	156,800
Adverse variance	7,840
	164,640

Standard cost = £164,640/9,800 units = = £16.80 per unit

	Units
Units produced 1.10.X8 to 31.3.X9 (W1) =	6,700
Less produced 1.1.X9 to 31.3.X9 (part (i)) =	3,700
Produced 1.10.X8 to 31.12.X8	3,000

	£
∴ October to December 19X8	
3,000 units x £16.80	50,400
January to March 19X9	
3,700 units x £16.80 x 108%	67,133
	117,533

∴ April to September 19X9
4,960 units (W1) x £16.80 x 108% = £89,994

(5) *Direct expenses*

19X8 cost

		£
9,800 units x £4 per unit		39,200
Less favourable variance		490
Actual 19X8 cost		38,710
Unit cost = £38,710/9,800 units =		£3.95
Six months to 31 March 19X9	£3.95 x 6,700 (W1)	£26,465
Six months to 30 September 19X9	£3.95 x 4,960 (W1)	£19,592

(6) *Variable overhead*

20% of the production overhead is variable ∴ standard variable production overhead per unit in 19X8 is: £20 x 20% = £4

	£	
Standard variable overhead £4 x 9,800	39,200	
Fixed overhead £(20-4) x 10,000	160,000	(note)
Adverse variance	4,150	
	203,350	

(*Note:* Budgeted production is 10,000, and the fixed overhead expenditure is based on this.)

∴ Actual variable overhead (per question) = 20% x £203,350 = £40,670
÷ 9,800 units = £4.15 per unit

Six months to 31 March 19X9	6,700 units (W1) x £4.15 x 105%	= £29,195
Six months to 30 September 19X9	4,960 units (W1) x £4.15 x 105%	= £21,613

(7) *Fixed overhead*

This is assumed to be the same as 19X8 ie £203,350 x 80% = £162,680
This is also assumed to occur evenly over the period.

(8) *Closing stock*

Closing stock is valued at standard variable production cost based on the average expected cost for the year.

	£
Expected cost for year (from profit and loss account)	581,637
Less fixed overheads	(162,680)
Expected variable costs	418,957

Total production = 11,660 units (W1)

$$\therefore \text{Average cost} = \frac{£418{,}957}{11{,}660} = £35.93$$

∴ Closing stock

at 31 March 19X9 500 units x £35.93 = £17,965

at 30 September 19X9 960 units x £35.93 = £34,493

(9) *Materials: cash payments*

	£
2/3 x 3,700 units (W4) current quarter x £9.785	24,136
1/3 x 3,000 units (W4) previous quarter x £9.785	9,785
	33,921

(10) *Variable overhead: cash payments*

2/3 x 3,700 units (W4) x £4.15 x 105%	10,746
1/3 x 3,000 units (W4) x £4.15 x 105%	4,357
	15,106

(11) *Fixed overhead*

This is assumed to occur evenly $\frac{£162,680}{4}$ x 90% (exclude depreciation)

= £36,603 per quarter

(b) *Use of microcomputer spreadsheet package in budget production*

A spreadsheet is a software package that enables for the easy manipulation of financial data. It is structured like a piece of paper sectioned into columns or rows. A cell is where a column intersects with a row.

Cells can contain a various types of data: text, numerical information, and formulae. The use of formulae means that spreadsheets can be used for 'what-if?' analysis.

This means that if a number is altered, the whole spreadsheet is updated automatically, saving time consuming manual recalculation, and the reducing the risk of errors.

A budget proforma spreadsheet could be drawn up, and updated every month. Comparative data (for example percentages) can also be calculated. Some spreadsheets have functions that permit statistical analysis. Similarly, if ABC wanted to go into more detail, the budget could be created from several spreadsheets detailing inputs in more detail.

62 BASIC REVISION QUESTION: INTEGRATED ACCOUNTING SYSTEM

Tutorial note: examiners often comment that students do not read the question properly. A common error is to add narratives to journal entries when the question specifically states that this is not required. Even if you feel that narratives are essential to explain the transaction, you will not get any marks for including them so do not waste valuable examination time.

(a) An integrated accounting system is one in which the cost accounting function and the financial accounting function are combined in one system of ledger accounts, using a common set of data.

The advantages of an integrated system over alternative systems are as follows.

(i) It reduces the work involved in maintaining the accounts system and avoids duplication of effort.

(ii) It avoids the possible confusion arising from having two sets of accounts containing different figures.

(iii) It avoids the need for periodic reconciliation of the cost accounts with the financial accounts.

(iv) It is possible to have one person responsible for maintaining the complete accounting system.

(b)

	£	£
Raw materials stores	10,000	
Creditors		10,000
Work in progress	6,000	
Raw material stores		6,000
Production overhead control	1,000	
Raw materials stores		1,000
Production overhead control	2,000	
Cash		2,000
Production overhead control	4,000	
Provision for depreciation		4,000
Work in progress	7,000	
Production overhead control		7,000

63 INTEGRATED

Transaction number	*Code*	*Amount* £'000
1	50200	4,400
	50010	210
	50020	200
	50030	100
	30001	4,910
2	30000	5,100
	25001	4,975
	56021	125
3	51210	1,110
	51010	600
	51020	100
	51030	150
	51510	9
	25001	1,969
4	52010	300
	52020	880
	52030	250
	25001	1,430

Transaction number	*Code*	*Amount* £'000
5	53010	25
	53020	105
	53030	20
	25001	150
6	54030	900
	25001	900
7	55010	240
	55020	30
	55030	30
	15001	300
8	00210	4,440
	00010	300
	00020	60
	00030	55
	00201	4,847
	00501	8
9 (See working)	00210	1,665
	00520	10
	00011	1,675
10	00220	7,150
	00211	7,150
11	24000	10
	23001	10
12	58030	15
	24001	15
13	23000	10,000
	40401	10,000
14	00410	6,500
	00221	6,500
15	25000	9,555
	57020	245
	23001	9,800
16	00020	5
	00531	5
	00540	20
	00031	20
17	10000	250
	25001	250

Working

MANUFACTURING OVERHEAD ACCOUNT

Transaction no	£	*Transaction no*	£
1	210	9	1,675
3	600		
4	300		
5	25		
7	240		
8	300		
	1,675		1,675

64 INTERLOCKING LIMITED

Tutorial note: a straightforward question for practising interlocking accounts, but watch out for the following common pitfalls.

1 *Check* whether the opening bank balance is debit or credit by producing a rough trial balance from the figure given. Do not assume that it is a debit balance - it may be overdrawn.

2 *Do not* provide for depreciation for a whole year. The accounts are required for one month only.

Suggested solution

FINANCIAL LEDGER

CREDITORS CONTROL ACCOUNT

	£		£
Cash paid	1,600	Bal b/f	2,000
Discounts received	100	Purchases - cost control account	1,500
Balance b/f	1,800		
	3,500		3,500

DEBTORS CONTROL ACCOUNT

	£		£
Bal b/d	1,600	Cash received	2,750
Sales - cost control account	2,500	Discounts allowed	120
		Balance c/d	1,230
	4,100		4,100

BANK ACCOUNT

	£		£
Balance b/d	400	Creditors	1,600
Debtors	2,750	Wages - cost control account	1,000
Balance c/d	650	Operating expenses - cost control a/c	1,200
	3,800		3,800

FIXED ASSETS ACCOUNT

	£		£
Bal b/d	4,000	Depreciation - cost control account	45
Additions - production capitalised	500	Balance c/d	4,455
	4,500		4,500

CAPITAL ACCOUNT

	£		£
Balance c/d	10,000	Balance b/d	10,000

DISCOUNTS ALLOWED ACCOUNT

	£		£
Debtors	120	P & L a/c	120

DISCOUNTS RECEIVED ACCOUNT

	£		£
P & L a/c	100	Creditors	100

COST CONTROL ACCOUNT

	£		£
Bal b/d *	6,000		
Creditors	1,500	Debtors	2,500
Wages	1,000	Fixed assets	500
Operating expenses	1,200		
Depreciation	45	Bal c/d:* raw materials	500
Cost accounting profit	600	WIP	2,745
		finished goods	4,100
	10,345		10,345

* The balance on the cost control account consists of the stock balances for raw materials, work in progress and finished goods.

FINANCIAL PROFIT AND LOSS ACCOUNT

	£		£
Discounts allowed	120	Cost profit	600
Net profit	580	Discounts received	100
	700		700

COST LEDGER

FINANCIAL LEDGER CONTROL ACCOUNT (FLC)

	£		£
Sales - debtors	2,500	Balance b/d	6,000
Fixed assets	500	Raw materials - purchases	1,500
Balance c/d	7,345	Overhead control - operating expenses	1,200
		Wages to WIP	1,000
		Overhead control - depreciation	45
		Cost accounting profit	600
	10,345		10,345

RAW MATERIALS ACCOUNT

	£		£
Bal b/d	2,000	WIP	3,000
Purchases - FLC	1,500	Bal c/d	500
	3,500		3,500

OVERHEAD CONTROL ACCOUNT

	£		£
Operating expenses - FLC	1,200	WIP	1,345
Notional rent	100		
Depreciation - FLC	45		
	1,345		1,345

WORK IN PROGRESS ACCOUNT

	£		£
Bal b/d	2,100	Finished goods	4,200
Raw materials	3,000	Capital expenditure	500
Wages - FLC	1,000		
Overheads	1,345	Bal c/d	2,745
	7,445		7,445

NOTIONAL RENT ACCOUNT

	£		£
Profit and loss	100	Overheads	100

CAPITAL EXPENDITURE ACCOUNT

	£		£
WIP	500	Fixed assets - FLC	500

FINISHED GOODS ACCOUNT

	£		£
Bal b/d	1,900	Cost of sales	2,000
WIP	4,200	Bal c/d	4,100
	6,100		6,100

SALES ACCOUNT

	£		£
P & L	2,500	Debtors - FLC	2,500

COST PROFIT AND LOSS ACCOUNT

	£		£
Finished goods	2,000	Sales	2,500
Cost profit - FLC	600	Notional rent written back	100
	2,600		2,600

TRIAL BALANCE AT 31 JANUARY 19X3

	£	£
Capital		10,000
Fixed assets	4,455	
Debtors	1,230	
Materials	500	
Work in progress	2,745	
Finished goods	4,100	
Creditors		1,800
Bank		650
Profit and loss		580
	13,030	13,030

65 BASIC REVISION QUESTION: CHECKLIST

A checklist of points to consider when choosing a suitable package would be as follows.

1 Does the package fit the user's particular requirements?
   (a) Does it produce all the reports that are wanted?
   (b) Can it handle the anticipated volume of data on file?
   (c) What data validation routine does it contain, and are these adequate?
   (d) Does it exclude some processing that the user wants? (If so, are these omissions serious?)

2 Does the package come with useful 'add-on' facilities? (For example, a nominal ledger package might be sold with the add-on of a report generation facility, to interrogate key accounts on the nominal ledger file so that simple management accounts could be produced).

3 If the package requires substantial changes to the user's organisation, the package might be rejected as unacceptable. The package should ideally be suited to the user and the user might rightly object to having to adjust his organisation to the dictates of the software.

4 Are the processing times fast enough? If response times to enquiries, for example, are fairly slow, the user might consider the package unacceptable because of the time wastage.

5 Is there full and clear documentation for the user? User manuals can be full of jargon and hard for a non-technical person to understand. They shouldn't be.

6 Can the supplier/dealer demonstrate the package, perhaps in the offices of an existing user of the package.

7 Is the package easy to use? Is the software 'user friendly' with menus and clear on-screen prompts for the keyboard operator? Some microcomputer packages are more user friendly than others. If a system operates in 'command mode', for example, the operator must know which commands to key in, and when. A user-friendly package will provide prompts and will be menu-driven, giving the operator a clear choice of what to do next. Some packages also provide extensive on-screen 'help' facilities for when the operator runs into difficulties and doesn't know what to do next.

8 What controls are included in the package? (For example passwords, data validation checks, spelling checks, standard accounting controls and reconciliations, an audit trail facility and so on)?

9 How will the package be kept up to date? (For example what if a fault is discovered in the program by the software manufacturer? In an accounting package, what if the rate of VAT alters?)

10 Can the package be modified by the user, for example allowing the user to insert amendments to the format of reports or screen displays? Or will the software supplier agree to write a few tailor-made amendments to the software?

11 How many other users have bought the package, and how long has it been on the market? New packages might offer enhanced facilities, whereas well established (but regularly updated) packages are more likely to be error free.

12 Will the package run on the user's computer? With additional peripheral equipment have to be bought, for example does the package need a hard disk file, when the computer user only has floppy disk drives with his micro?

13 Is the package well documented, with easy to follow user manuals?

14 What support and 'maintenance' service will the software supplier provide, in the event that the user has difficulty with the package?

15 *Comparative* costs of different packages should be a low priority. Off-the-shelf packages are fairly cheap on the whole, and a company should really buy what it needs for efficient operations rather than the least cost package available. The savings in purchase price would not be worth the trouble caused by trying to use an unsuitable package for a business application.

16 However, the package must not cost 'so much' that the costs are greater than the benefits of having it.

66 MICROCOMPUTERS

Tutorial note: the examiner is not asking you to tell him how the computer works when operating accounting packages. He is asking about the practicalities of *using* packages on a microcomputer.

(a) Accounting packages are ready made programs written to perform the task of maintaining a business accounting system. The growing use of microcomputers means that even many small businesses are using such packages to process their accounting transactions.

In principle, computerised accounting is exactly the same as manual accounting. Accounting functions retain the same names in a computerised system and the familiar ideas of day books, ledger accounts, double entry and trial balance still apply. The principles of working with computerised sales, purchase and nominal ledgers are exactly what would be expected in the manual methods they replace. The only difference is that these various books of account are invisible. In a computerised system, ledgers are now computer files which are held in a computer-sensible form, ready to be called upon.

An accounting package will consist of several *modules* which may include the following.

(i) Invoicing.
(ii) Stock.
(iii) Sales ledger.
(iv) Purchase ledger, and so on.

When a user begins to work with an accounting package he will usually be asked to key in a password. Separate passwords can be used for different parts of the system, for example for different ledgers if required.

The user will be presented with a menu of options such as *entering new data* or *printing accounting reports*. By selecting and keying in the appropriate option number the user will then be guided through the actions needed to enter the data or generate the report.

The computer uses code numbers to identify different ledgers and the accounts within those ledgers. Code numbers also indicate to the computer which accounts to debit and which to credit. A transaction (for example debit a/c 121, credit a/c 140) will be given an identifying number for audit trail purposes.

Each module in the computer may be integrated with the others so that data in one module will be passed automatically or by simple user request through into any other module where the data is of some relevance. For example if the user inputs some data to the invoicing module authorising the despatch of an invoice to a customer, there might be automatic links to other modules such as the sales ledger to update the customers' account and the stock module to update the stock file.

Thus the user does not need to be an accounting specialist because the computer will enter the data correctly according to the code numbers used. In addition the system will not accept incomplete data entries and the user is prompted to provide complete information.

The system will print a variety of output reports, including transaction listings, account balances, sales analyses and so on.

(b) The advantages of accounting packages compared with a manual system are as follows.

(i) As mentioned in (a), the packages can be used by non-specialists.
(ii) A large amount of data can be processed very quickly.
(iii) Computerised systems are more accurate than manual systems.
(iv) A computer is capable of handling and processing large volumes of data.
(v) Once the data has been input, computerised systems can analyse data rapidly to present useful control information for managers such as a trial balance or a debtors schedule.

67 MATRIX FORM

(a) Computer programs specifically designed to use the matrix form are often called spreadsheets. A spreadsheet is a software application which allows you to define a problem logically (ie construct a *model*) in terms of text, data and formulae, and then lets the computer bear the brunt of complicated or tedious calculations. It can be used wherever the problem can be set out in logical stages (not just accounting).

The idea behind a spreadsheet is that the model builder should construct a model in rows and columns format as follows.

(i) Identify what data goes into each row and column and insert text, for example column headings and row identifications.

(ii) Specify how the numerical data in the model should be derived. Numerical data might be inserted into the model via keyboard input, or calculated from other data in the model by means of formulae specified within the model itself. The model builder must insert these formulae into the spreadsheet model when it is first constructed. Occasionally, data might be obtained from a disk file from another computer application program or module.

So a spreadsheet user will have to go through the three steps of *inserting text, inserting formulae and inputting data.*

Spreadsheets are versatile tools. Different spreadsheets will offer different facilities, but some of the more basic ones which should feature in all spreadsheet programs are as follows.

(i) *Print*: the user should be able to print the contents of the spreadsheet in total or in part, with or without the spreadsheet row and column labels.

(ii) *Save*: the user should be able to save the balance sheet data on your disk, either all of it, or just part of it. Obviously, the model user might want to use the data again, and so the facility to save data is an essential one.

(iii) *Edit*: the program should allow alteration of anything shown on the spreadsheet. This is particularly useful for 'what if' calculations. For instance, in a balance sheet example, you might want to know what net current assets would be if taxation was £1m instead of £0.8m. Using the edit command, you just have to change the taxation figure, then ask the computer to recalculate the entire spreadsheet on the basis of the new figures. This 'what if' manipulation of data is probably the most important facility in a spreadsheet package. But there are many other spreadsheet commands which involve some form of editing.

  (1) *Insert* a column or row at a desired spot. For example, you might wish to split 'debtors' into 'trade' and 'other'. The insert command facilitates this, and the formulae in the spreadsheet are adjusted automatically.

  (2) *Move or copy* a cell, row or column (or block of cells) elsewhere.

  (3) *Delete* a cell row or column.

(iv) *Sort*. A spreadsheet package will usually provide a facility for sorting data (alphabetically or numerically).

(v) *Replicate a formula* - ie ask the computer to perform the same formula along a line or column, to save keying it in over and over again.

(vi) *Construct bar charts or graphs*.

(vii) *Format*: this command controls the way in which headings and data are shown, for example by altering column widths, 'justifying' text and numbers (to indent or have a right-hand justification etc) changing the number of decimal places displayed and so on.

(b) Some of the more common accounting applications of spreadsheets are:

- (i) balance sheets;
- (ii) cash flow analysis/forecasting;
- (iii) general ledger;
- (iv) inventory records;
- (v) job cost estimates;
- (vi) market share analysis and planning;
- (vii) profit projections;
- (viii) profit statements;
- (ix) project budgeting and control;
- (x) sales projections and records;
- (xi) tax estimation.

What all these have in common is that they all involve data processing with:

- (i) numerical data;
- (ii) repetitive, time-consuming calculations;
- (iii) a logical processing structure.

Spreadsheets provide a basically simple format for modelling, which is why they are provided for microcomputers rather than more powerful mainframe computers. The great value of spreadsheets, however, derives from their simple format of rows and columns of data, and the ability of the data users to have direct access themselves to their spreadsheet model via their own personal microcomputer. For example, an accountant can construct a cash flow model with a spreadsheet package on the microcomputer in his or her office(s): he can create the model, input the data, manipulate the data and read or print the output direct. He or she will also have fairly instant access to the model whenever it is needed, in just the time it takes to load the model into his or her microcomputer. Spreadsheets therefore help to bring computerised data processing more within the everyday reach of data users.

A popular use of spreadsheets is the consideration of 'what if?' problems. One or two key figures are changed and then the computer automatically makes all the consequential changes to all the other figures throughout the spreadsheets (an example of which is described in (a) (iii) above).

68 SPREADSHEETS AND DATABASES

(a) Databases and spreadsheets are examples of applications software, which are often used on microcomputer.

A spreadsheet appears to the user like a flat piece of paper divided into columns and rows to resemble a sheet of accountant's analysis paper. The intersection of each column and row is referred to as a cell. A cell can contain text, numbers or formulae. Use of a formula means that the cell which contains the formula will display the results of a calculation based on data in other cells. If the numbers in those other cells change, the result displayed in the formula cell will also change accordingly. With this facility, a spreadsheet is used to create financial models.

A database, on the other hand, is a collection of information which can be used in a number of different ways. It is like a filing cabinet, in that it contains items of information which different users can access at will. Information relevant to a particular issue can be selected from the database. The order of items in the database does not depend on the enquiries made of it.

A spreadsheet then is used for the manipulation of data. A database is used for the purposes of data storage and retrieval.

(b) An organisation, especially a large one, may possess a large quantity of fixed assets. Before computerisation these would have been kept in a manual fixed asset register. A database enables this fixed asset register to be stored in an electronic form. A database file with fixed assets would contain the following categories of information.

(i) Code number to give the asset a unique identification in the database.

(ii) Type of asset (for example motor car, leasehold premises), for published accounts purposes.

(iii) More detailed description of the asset (for example car registration number, make).

(iv) Physical location of the asset (for example address).

(v) Organisational location of the asset (for example accounts department).

(vi) Person responsible for the asset (for example in the case of a company-owned car, the person who uses it).

(vii) Original cost of the asset.

(viii) Date of purchase.

(ix) Depreciation rate applied to the asset.

(x) Accumulated depreciation to date.

(xi) Net book value of the asset.

(xii) Estimated residual value.

(xiii) Date when the physical existence of the asset was last verified.

(xiv) Supplier.

Obviously, the details kept about the asset would depend on the type of asset it is. The code number would be the key in the database file.

(c) A spreadsheet would be an ideal tool for use in budget preparation, simply because it could be used to construct a financial model of the relationships between the different variables in a budget. For example the person preparing the budget could devise a labour budget based on units of production by taking the hours needed to produce a unit, with the labour rate per hour, and devising a formula to multiply the units produced by the number of hours per unit by the labour rate per hour to come up with an estimated total labour cost.

This data can be used by a formula elsewhere in the model. This could position the revenue and expense headings as rows, with the budgeted and comparative figures as columns. If the budgets are to be based on two or three different assumptions then a table of base data would be used, and the contents of these cells could be referred to in formulae in the main model.

OBJECTIVE TESTS

QUIZ 1

1 An item of stock has a cost of £4 and a net realisable value of £3. Which of the following concepts dictates the amount at which it should be stated in the balance sheet?

A Going concern
B Accruals
C Consistency
D Prudence

2 Which of the following does not form part of a limited company's equity capital?

A Ordinary share capital
B Revaluation reserve
C Preference share capital
D Debenture redemption reserve

3 A company has authorised share capital of 1,000,000 50p ordinary shares and an issued share capital of 800,000 50p ordinary shares. If an ordinary dividend of 5% is declared, the amount payable to shareholders is:

A £50,000
B £25,000
C £40,000
D £20,000

4 A trader's accounts showed a gross profit for the year of £27,200. After the accounts were prepared it was found that the opening stock had been overstated by £1,200 while closing stock had been understated by £1,700.

What is the corrected gross profit for the year?

A £24,300
B £26,700
C £27,700
D £30,100

5 A creditors control account contains the following entries.

	£
Bank	79,500
Credit purchases	83,200
Discounts received	3,750
Contra with debtors control account	4,000
Balance c/f at 31 December 19X8	12,920

There are no other entries in the account. What was the opening balance brought forward at 1 January 19X8?

A £8,870
B £8,970
C £16,970
D £24,370

6 A rates prepayment of £370 was treated as an accrual in preparing a trader's profit and loss account. As a result, his profit was:

A understated by £740
B overstated by £740
C understated by £370
D overstated by £370

7 On the last day of a company's accounting period goods costing £570 and invoiced to a customer for £780 were awaiting collection by the customer. They were erroneously counted as stock in the annual stock take. As a result, the company's profit for the year was:

A overstated by £570
B overstated by £780
C overstated by £210
D correctly stated

8 A company achieves a constant 20% gross profit margin. An amount of £2,400, taken from a proforma invoice relating to goods sent to a customer on a sale or return basis, has been credited to sales in the company's accounts. As a result, profit is overstated by:

A £400
B £480
C £2,000
D £2,400

9 Which one of the following occurrences might explain the existence of a debit balance on an individual creditor's account? The bookkeeper:

A failed to put through a contra entry with creditor's account in the debtor's ledger
B failed to make a posting from the returns outwards book to the creditors ledger
C posted a total of discounts received to creditors control accounts twice by mistake
D failed to post an invoice from the purchase day book to the creditors ledger

10 Mr Harmon does not keep full accounting records, but the following information is available in respect of his accounting year ended 31 December 19X9.

	£
Cash purchases in year	3,900
Cash paid for goods supplied on credit	27,850
Creditors at 1 January 19X9	970
Creditors at 31 December 19X9	720

In his trading account for 19X9, what will be Harmon's figure for purchases?

A £27,600
B £31,500
C £31,750
D £32,000

11 Company Z has 85 units of stock in hand at its year end. They originally cost £60 each and now can not be sold until they are modified at a cost of £15 each. The selling price of the modified units will then be £80 each. Z's selling costs are 15% of selling price. What is the balance sheet valuation of this stock?

A £4,505
B £5,100
C £5,355
D £6,375

12 **Which one of the following costs would be classified as revenue expenditure on the invoice for a new company car?**

A Delivery costs
B Number plates
C Road tax
D A stereo radio

13 A company keeps one account for rent and rates. Payments for 19X6 were as follows.

7 January 19X6	Rent £350
1 April 19X6	Rates £900 for six months to 30 September 19X6
10 April 19X6	Rent £350 for three months to 31 March 19X6
7 July 19X6	Rent £425 (including £75 for repairs to the boiler) for three months to 30 June 19X6
30 September 19X6	Rates £700 (including a £200 rebate for the year 19X5/X6) for the six months ending 31 March 19X7
10 October 19X6	Rent £350 for three months to 30 September 19X6
5 January 19X7	Rent £350 for three months to 31 December 19X6.

If the rates paid for the year to 31 March 19X6 were £1,700 and the rent is fixed at £1,400 pa. for seven years ending 31 December 19X9, what is the company's charge in the profit and loss account for rent and rates for the year ending 31 December 19X6?

A £2,975
B £3,050
C £3,075
D £2,550

14 Which of the following expenses does not normally vary with seasonal turnover?

A Salesmen's commission
B Discounts allowed
C Salesmen's salaries
D Bad debts

15 A trader gives a 5% trade discount to all his credit customers. In addition, he allows a cash discount at 5% of net sales price (after deducting trade discount) to customers who pay in the month of sale. The cash discount is reduced to 2½% of the net sales price for customers paying in the month after sale, and to nil for later payments. The trader estimates that 20% of his credit customers pay in month of sale, 50% a month later and 30% in the month after. Credit sales (before deducting any discounts) were £14,000 in January, £18,000 in February and £20,000 in March. The cash received from debtors in March will be:

A £14,392
B £15,150
C £15,936
D £16,775

QUIZ 2

1 What is cost apportionment?

A The charging of discrete identifiable items of cost to cost centres or cost units
B The collection of costs attributable to cost centres and cost units using the costing methods, principles and techniques prescribed for a particular business entity
C The process of establishing the costs of cost centres or cost units
D The division of costs amongst two or more cost centres in proportion to the estimated benefits received, using a proxy, eg square feet

2 Edison has the following data relating to overheads.

	Budget	*Actual*
Fixed overheads	£15,000	£14,000
Units of production	10,000	10,100
Direct labour hours	20,000	19,500

Overheads are absorbed on the basis of labour hours.

Which of the following statements is true? Overheads will be:

A underabsorbed by £1,000 due to the lower than expected expenditure
B overabsorbed by £1,150 due to the unexpected increase in production
C overabsorbed by £150 due to the difference in expenditure and production
D overabsorbed by £625 due to lower than expected expenditure and lower than expected labour hours.

3 What is the name given to a system of stocktaking, whereby a stock count is made each day of a number of items in store, and the count is checked against stock records, so that every item in store is checked at least once a year?

A Continuous stocktaking
B Perpetual inventory
C ABC inventory analysis
D Annual stock accounting

4 Gross wages incurred in department 1 in June were £54,000. The wages analysis shows the following summary breakdown of the gross pay.

	Paid to direct labour	*Paid to indirect labour*
	£	£
Ordinary time	25,185	11,900
Overtime: basic pay	5,440	3,500
premium	1,360	875
Shift allowance	2,700	1,360
Sick pay	1,380	300
	36,065	17,935

What is the direct wages cost for department 1 in June?

A £25,185
B £30,625
C £34,685
D £36,065

5 The following information relates to job 2468, which is being carried out by Soxon Feet Limited to meet a customer's order.

	Department A	*Department B*
Direct materials consumed	£5,000	£3,000
Direct labour hours	400 hours	200 hours
Direct labour rate per hour	£4	£5
Production overhead per direct labour hour	£4	£4
Administration and other overhead	20% of full production cost	
Profit margin	25% of sales price	

What is the selling price to the customer for job 2468?

A £16,250
B £17,333
C £19,500
D £20,800

6 Each unit of product Echo takes five direct labour hours to make. Quality standards are high, and 8% of units are rejected after completion as sub-standard. Next month's budgets are as follows.

Opening stocks of finished goods	3,000 units
Planned closing stocks of finished goods	7,600 units
Budgeted sales of Echo	36,800 units

All stocks of finished goods must have successfully passed the quality control check.

What is the direct labour hours budget for the month?

A 198,720 hours
B 200,000 hours
C 223,560 hours
D 225,000 hours

7 The following data relates to the stores ledger control account of Duckboard Limited, a manufacturing company, for the month of October 19X2.

	£
Opening stock	18,500
Closing stock	16,100
Deliveries from suppliers	142,000
Returns to suppliers	2,300
Cost of indirect materials issued	25,200

The issue of direct materials would have been recorded in the cost accounts as follows.

			£	£
A	*Debit*	Stores ledger control account	112,100	
	Credit	Work in progress control account		112,100
B	*Debit*	Work in progress control account	112,100	
	Credit	Stores ledger control account		112,100
C	*Debit*	Stores ledger control account	116,900	
	Credit	Work in progress control account		116,900
D	*Debit*	Work in progress control account	116,900	
	Credit	Stores ledger control account		116,900

8 G Ltd makes the following purchases and sales.

1 January	Purchases	4,000 units for £10,000
31 January	Purchases	1,000 units for £2,000
15 February	Sales	3,000 units for £13,000
28 February	Purchases	1,500 units for £3,750
14 March	Sales	500 units for £1,200

At 31 March which of the following valuation combinations is correct?

	FIFO	LIFO
A	£7,000	£7,000
B	£7,500	£7,000
C	£7,000	£7,500
D	£7,500	£7,500

9 The following is a graph of cost against level of activity.

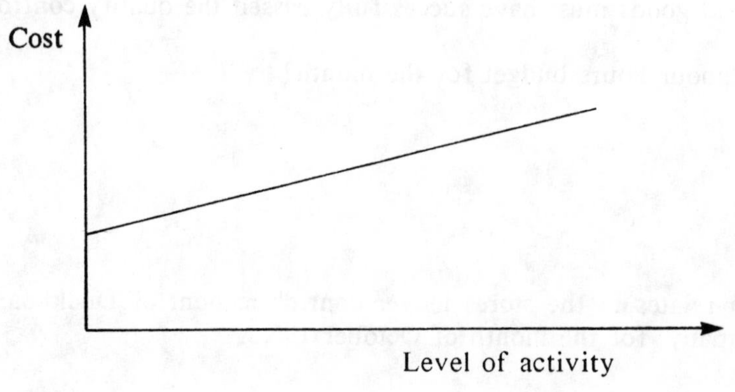

To which one of the following costs does the graph correspond?

A Electricity bills made up of a standing charge and a variable charge
B Bonus payment to employees when production reaches a certain level
C Salesman's commissions payable per unit up to a maximum amount of commission
D Bulk discounts on purchases, the discount being given on all units purchased

10

	Budget	Actual
Units of production	10,000	12,000
Overhead cost	£15,000	£21,000

Using the above figures the over/under absorption is:

A £3,000 under
B £6,000 over
C £3,000 over
D £6,000 under

The following information relates to questions 11 and 12.

Department A produces two products, Pinks and Perks. The budgeted production for period 6 is 5,550 Pinks and 3,760 Perks. In one standard hour a direct operative is expected to be able to produce either 30 Pinks or 40 Perks. During period 6, 266 direct labour hours were worked and actual production was 5,400 Pinks and 3,800 Perks.

11 What is the efficiency ratio for period 6?

A 97%
B 99%
C 101%
D 103%

12 What is the production volume ratio for period 6?

A 97%
B 99%
C 101%
D 103%

QUIZ 3

1 Which of the following statements are true?

(1) Bank reconciliations are necessary to keep control over cash balances.

(2) Depreciation provides a fund for future purchases of fixed assets.

(3) Employer's National Insurance Contributions are an added cost to the employer above salary costs.

(4) Crediting the wrong account will not cause a difference on the trial balance.

A (1), (2) and (3)
B (1) and (4)
C (1), (3) and (4)
D (2), (3) and (4)

2 The balance on a company's purchase ledger control account differs from the total of creditors' balances in the purchase ledger. Which of the following occurrences might account for the discrepancy?

A Incorrect calculation of a trade discount
B Failure to record in the books a cheque payment
C Error of addition in the bank control account
D Omission of returns outwards from Blogg's personal account

3 C Ltd has opening trade creditors of £10,748, and closing trade creditors of £15,407. If cash paid to trade creditors in the period was £94,275 after allowing for settlement discounts of £1,270, what were purchases on credit for the period?

A £90,886
B £97,664
C £98,934
D £100,204

4 Which one of the following items would *not* normally be classified as administration expenses in an analysed profit and loss account?

A Audit fees and expenses
B Finance director's salary
C Computer repairs and maintenance costs
D Legal fees for the purchase of a freehold warehouse

5 A sole trader who runs a newsagents business makes up his accounts each year to 31 May. His rent is payable quarterly in advance on 1 January, 1 April, 1 July and 1 October. Rates are paid each year in two equal instalments on 1 April and 1 October.

His annual rental for the calendar years 19X6 and 19X7 was £4,800 and £5,400 respectively but on 1 January 19X8 this was increased to £6,000 per annum. Local authority business rate for the last three years has been as follows.

	£
Year commencing 1 April 19X6	3,600
Year commencing 1 April 19X7	3,900
Year commencing 1 April 19X8	4,200

In preparing his accounts for the year ended 31 May 19X8 what would be the charge to profit and loss account from his rent and rates account?

A £6,100
B £7,070
C £8,750
D £9,600

6 Mrs Rayne, a sole trader, achieves a constant gross margin of 20% on sales.

During the coming year she anticipates purchases of £75,000 will be required in order that she can increase her stock level by £5,600. What sales revenue is she expecting?

A £83,280
B £86,750
C £88,150
D £93,750

The following information relates to questions 7 and 8.

Fellini Ltd has an accounting year end 31 December 19X7. The bank statement at 31 December 19X7 shows an amount overdrawn of £465.

From a review of the company's cash book and bank statements the following facts are ascertained.

(i) Cheques totalling £896, sent out by the company before the year end do not go through the bank statements until the beginning of the next year.

(ii) A credit transfer from a customer for £1,060 which appears in the December bank statement has not been recorded by the company.

(iii) Bank charges of £154 have not yet been recorded by the company.

(iv) The lodgements of £570 paid into the bank on the last day of the year, do not appear in the bank statements until the beginning of the next year.

7 What figure for cash at bank should appear in the company's balance sheet as at 31 December 19X7?

A £115 Dr
B £139 Dr
C £301 Cr
D £791 Cr

8 Assuming that after the necessary adjustments have been made for the above items, the cash book figure is reconciled to the bank statement figure, what was the *original* (unadjusted) cash book balance?

A £115 Dr
B £115 Cr
C £1,697 Dr
D £1,697 Cr

9 The following information relates to D Ltd

	£
Opening balance on sales ledger control account	87,300
Opening balance on provision for doubtful debts account	4,365
Sales on credit for the year	332,840
Cash received from customers (after allowing for settlement discounts of £20,900)	327,660
Bad debt to be written off (not previously provided for)	4,000

The provision is to be maintained at 5% of trade debtors at the year end.

The amount to be charged to the profit and loss account in respect of bad and doubtful debts is:

A £3,014
B £3,379
C £4,059
D £4,986

10 Which of the following is the same as internal store?

(1) Primary store
(2) Main store
(3) Secondary store

A (1) and (2)
B (1) only
C (2) only
D (1) and (3)

QUIZ 4

1 Which of the following statements are true?

(1) Depreciation is a cash expense.

(2) The 'Limited' in Limited companies is included because these companies are limited in their powers by the object clause in their Memorandum of Association.

(3) Debiting a wrong expense account rather than the correct one is an error of ommission.

(4) A company's selling costs should never be included in its stock valuation.

A (1), (2) and (3)
B (2), (3) and (4)
C (3) and (4)
D (4)

The following information relates to questions 2 and 3.

The Tufty Club makes up its accounts to 31 December each year and has an accounting policy for subscription income of recognising subscriptions in arrears only when the cash is actually received, but recognising subscriptions in advance in the accounting period they relate to.

Information for the year ending 31 December 19X8 is as follows.

Total cash received from subscriptions (including £200 outstanding from the previous year)	£5,800
Subscriptions received in advance as at 31 December 19X7	£ 160
Subscriptions received in advance as at 31 December 19X8	£ 180

2 What amount will be included in the income and expenditure account of the club in respect of subscriptions for the year ending 31 December 19X8?

A £5,960
B £5,780
C £5,800
D £5,980

3 In respect of its policy for recognising subscriptions in arrears, which of the four fundamental accounting concepts of SSAP 2 is the club following?

A Accruals (matching)
B Going concern
C Disclosure
D Prudence

4 Which one of the following costs would be included in the calculation of prime cost in a manufacturing account?

A Cost of transporting raw materials from supplier's premises
B Wages of factory workers engaged in machine maintenance
C Depreciation of lorries used for deliveries to customers
D Cost of indirect production materials

5 On 31 January 19X8 a company's cash book showed a credit balance of £150 on its current account which did not agree with the bank statement balance. In performing the reconciliation the following points come to light.

	£
Not recorded in the cash book	
Bank charges	36
Transfer from deposit account to current account	500
Not recorded on the bank statement	
Unpresented cheques	116
Outstanding lodgements	630

It was also discovered that the bank had debited the company's account with a cheque for £400 in error. What was the original balance on the *bank statement*?

A £200 Cr
B £600 Dr
C £564 Dr
D £1,600 Dr

6 When comparing shareholders and debenture holders, which of the following statements is untrue?

A Shareholders are members of a company. Debenture holders are creditors of a company.

B Shareholders receive dividends. Debenture holders receive a fixed rate of interest.

C Share capital is always secured on company assets. Debentures can be secured on company assets.

D Shareholders cannot enforce a dividend. Debenture holders can take legal action for non-payment of interest.

The following information relates to questions 7 and 8.

The Anthropology Club makes up its accounts to 30 September each year and has 500 members at any time. Subscriptions are payable in respect of calendar years at a rate of £75 for 19X7 and £85 for 19X8. At 30 September 19X7 four members were in arrears with their 19X7 subscriptions. One year later this amount had been settled but two members were in arrears with their 19X8 subscriptions. Subscriptions receipts during 19X8 totalled £42,630.

7 At 30 September 19X7 what amount should be shown in the club's balance sheet as 'subscriptions in arrears'?

A £75
B £150
C £225
D £300

8 What amount should be credited to the club's income and expenditure account in respect of subscriptions for the year ending 30 September 19X8?

A £31,875
B £41,250
C £42,533
D £42,660

9 At 30 September 19X7 the balance on Giorgio Ltd's provision for doubtful debts was £6,400.

During the year ended 30 September 19X8 bad debts, previously provided for of £250 were written off. At 30 September 19X8 debtors balances are £156,000 and the company wishes to have a provision of 5% of this amount in its year end balance sheet.

The profit and loss account charge for bad and doubtful debts for the year ended 30 September 19X8 is

A £250
B £1,400
C £1,650
D £1,900

10 Which of the following statements are true?

(1) A utility program is an example of applications software.

(2) Integrated software means less entry of data for the operator.

(3) An off-the-shelf package is likely to be more expensive than a tailor made package.

(4) A real time system is likely to be more expensive than a batch processing system.

A (1), (2) and (4)
B (1), (3) and (4)
C (2) and (4)
D (1), (2) and (3)

QUIZ 5

1 Automat Limited purchases a machine for which the supplier's list price is £18,000. Automat pays £13,000 in cash and trades in an old machine which has a net book value of £8,000. It is the company's policy to depreciate such machines at the rate of 10% per annum on cost.

What is the net book value of the machine after one year?

A £11,700
B £16,200
C £18,900
D £19,200

2 Which one of the following records is *not* a book of prime entry?

A Bank statements
B Petty cash book
C Journal
D Sales returns day book

The following information relates to questions 3 and 4.

> Womble & Sons have an accounting year ended 31 December 19X8. At that date the balance on the sales ledger control account was £65,000, but the total of the individual accounts in the sales ledger came to £63,620.
>
> Upon investigation the following facts were discovered.
>
> 1 The sales day book total for week 49 had been overcast by £300.
> 2 A credit balance of £210 on Orinocco's accounts in the sales ledger had been incorrectly treated as a debit entry, when balancing off his account.
> 3 A purchase ledger contra of £1,500 had been entered in Bungo's account in the sales ledger but no other entry had been made.

3 The adjusted balance on the sales ledger control account is:

A £62,780
B £63,200
C £63,620
D £64,700

4 The adjusted balance on the sales ledger is:

A £62,780
B £63,200
C £63,620
D £64,700

5 Dior Ltd has prepared the following information in respect of its year end stocks of finished goods.

	Direct costs of materials and labour	*Production overheads incurred*	*Selling and distribution overheads expected to be incurred*	*Expected selling price*
	£	£	£	£
Product I	4,560	2,400	860	7,900
Product II	1,090	860	470	1,450
Product III	8,325	3,950	1,050	13,200
	13,975	7,210	2,380	22,550

At what amount should finished goods stock be stated in the company's balance sheet?

A £13,975
B £20,090
C £20,170
D £21,185

6 On 1 July 19X7 the Crazy Golf Club had the following balances in its books.

	£
Building fund assets:	
12% convertible loan stock	15,000
Building society account	7,000

During the year the club received a donation towards the building fund of £3,000 which was paid into its bank account and also received interest of £560 on its building society account. What is the balance on the building fund account at 30 June 19X8?

A £27,360
B £25,000
C £22,560
D £22,000

7 On 31 March 19X8 the Birdwatchers Society had the following balances in its books.

	£
Binoculars, cameras and tripods	5,000
Camping equipment	3,000
Stock of reference books	500
Subscriptions in arrears	200
Subscriptions in advance	50
Life membership account	2,500
Deficit for the year	150

During the year one life member died, who had paid a subscription of £500. The society transferred life membership to the accumulated fund on his death. No other members have died during the year. What was the balance on the accumulated fund at 31 March 19X7?

A £8,200
B £8,500
C £5,800
D £6,650

The following information relates to questions 8 and 9.

The factory cost of finished goods produced by Widget Manufacturer Ltd during the year ended 31 March 19X8 was £800,000. The opening stock of finished goods had been valued at £44,800 and the closing stock at £67,200 both inclusive of factory profit of 12% on cost. Goods are sold at a mark up of 20% on factory transfer price.

8 What is the sales figure for the year?

A £2,096,640
B £1,160,640
C £1,048,320
D £933,120

9 To the nearest pound, what figure should be included in the profit and loss account for the provision for unrealised profit in stock?

A £2,400
B £2,688
C £3,733
D £5,733

10. A spreadsheet is made up of cells usually labelled A1, A2,............B1, B2.........etc. Which of the following could be entered in a cell?

(1) 229
(2) Table
(3) + A1 + 3*B2

A (1) and (2)
B (1) and (3)
C (2) and (3)
D (1), (2) and (3)

QUIZ 6

1 Each unit of Donny uses 3kg of raw material. The production and stock budget for December is:

Opening stocks:	raw material	9,000 kgs
	finished goods	3,000 units
Closing stocks:	raw materials	4,000 kgs
	finished goods	2,000 units

Budgeted sales for December are 6000 units. During the production process it is usually found that 20% of Donnys are scrapped as defective and this loss occurs after the raw materials have been input.

What will raw materials purchases be in December?

A 10,000 kgs
B 13,750 kgs
C 18,750 kgs
D 23,750 kgs

2 Which of the following statements are false?

(1) Prime cost is the total of all variable costs.

(2) A manufacturing account only records the change in all types of stock.

(3) An adjustment may be necessary in the manufacturing account for unrealised profit included in stock.

(4) If the value of work in progress has fallen during a period the cost of finished goods produced would always also fall.

A (2) and (3)
B (1), (2) and (3)
C (1), (2) and (4)
D (1), (2), (3) and (4)

3 Extracts from P Limited's records for last month are as follows.

	Budget	*Actual*
Production	7,000 units	7,200 units
Direct material cost	£42,000	£42,912

What is the total direct material cost variance?

A £288 favourable
B £288 adverse
C £912 adverse
D £1,200 adverse

4 The cost card for product Zed is

	£
Materials 3kg	6.0
Labour 2½ hours	7.5
Variable overhead	2.5
Fixed overhead	5.0
	21.0
Standard profit	9.0
Standard selling price	30.0

Budgeted production for the month was 5,000 units although the company managed to produce 5,800 units selling 5,200 of them and incurring fixed overhead costs of £27,400.

Which of the following combinations of profits is correct

	Absorption costing	*Marginal costing*
A	£46,800	£49,800
B	£48,400	£45,400
C	£48,400	£51,400
D	£45,400	£45,400

Information for questions 5 to 8.

Catfish plc makes one product with a selling price of £60. The unit cost for Catfish is detailed below.

	£
Materials 2 kg at £3	6
Labour 2 hours at £10	20
Variable production overhead	10
Fixed production overhead	5
Variable selling expenses	4
Fixed selling expenses	2
	47

These costs were based on a budgeted level of production of 15,000 units. Actual production data for last month was as follows.

Production	16,000 units
Sales	14,500 units
Fixed production overhead incurred	£85,000
Fixed selling expenses	£28,500

All variable costs were as budgeted and no stock had been brought forward at the end of the previous month.

5 Using absorption costing the amount of over or under absorbed overhead was

A £5,000 under absorbed
B £5,000 over absorbed
C £10,000 under absorbed
D £10,000 over absorbed

6 The net profit for last month using absorption costing was

A £183,000
B £184,000
C £188,500
D £190,000

7 The net profit for last month using marginal costing was

A £172,500
B £173,500
C £176,500
D £184,000

8 If sales volume increased by 1,000 units (and all other factors remained unchanged), profits under marginal costing would

A increase by £13,000
B increase by £19,000
C increase by £20,000
D increase by £24,000

9 For a company that does not have any production resource limitations, in what sequence would the following budgets be prepared?

Budget

1. Cash budget
2. Sales budget
3. Stocks budgets
4. Production budget
5. Purchases budget

A Sequence 2, 3, 4, 5, 1
B Sequence 2, 3, 4, 1, 5
C Sequence 2, 4, 3, 5, 1
D Sequence 4, 3, 2, 1, 5

10 The Central Processing Unit is made up of:

(1) the arithmetic and logic units and output devices

(2) input devices, output devices and backing store

(3) the main store, the control units and the arithmetic and logic unit.

A (1)
B (2)
C (3)
D (1), (2) and (3)

QUIZ 7

1 Which of the following statements are true?

(1) Standard costing can be used to assess actual costs.

(2) This year's current standard should be next year's expected standard.

(3) Ideal standards are the usual basis for a standard costing system.

(4) Standard costing can be used to calculate the value of closing stock.

A (1), (2) and (4)
B (1) and (4)
C (2) and (4)
D (1), (2), (3) and (4)

2 Which of the following statements are false?

(1) Absorption costing is more appropriate for short-term decision making than marginal costing.

(2) Marginal costing is recommended by SSAP9.

(3) Contribution is an important idea in absorption costing.

(4) Marginal costing is sometimes referred to as period costing, due to its treatment of fixed costs.

A (1) and (3)
B (2) and (3)
C (1), (2) and (3)
D (1), (2), (3) and (4)

The following information relates to questions 3 to 5.

Archibald Leach Ltd., a company using marginal costing, had the following results in 19X6 and 19X7.

	19X6	*19X7*
	£	£
Sales	20,000	19,800
Variable costs		
Materials	(8,000)	(7,400)
Labour	(6,000)	(5,000)
Fixed costs	(2,000)	(2,400)
Profit	4,000	5,000

Archibald increased the 19X6 selling price of his product by 10% for 19X7.

3 The effect on profit of the change in volume of sales was

A £ 600 decrease
B £ 800 decrease
C £1,000 increase
D £2,000 decrease

4 If material prices per kg were the same in 19X7 as in 19X6, materials usage per unit affected profit in 19X7 compared with 19X6 by

A £200 increase
B £200 decrease
C £600 increase
D £600 decrease

5 A decrease in selling price of 20% on 19X6 levels could have been expected to increase sales volume by 20%. Assuming no other changes in variable or fixed costs per unit, the profit Archibald would have expected for 19X7 is:

A £(400) loss
B £nil
C £400
D £4,000

6 X Ltd is preparing a cash budget for its first year of operations. Budgeted sales for the first four months are as follows.

Month	*Sales* units
January	10,000
February	12,000
March	15,000
April	20,000

Each unit requires 1 kg of material at a cost of £1 per kg. X Ltd wishes to maintain a finished goods closing stock balance of 10% of the subsequent month's sales. Payment terms to suppliers are: 50% of balance due is paid one month after purchase, with the balance paid two months after purchase.

The payment made to suppliers in April is

A £11,750
B £13,900
C £15,500
D £16,750

The following information relates to questions 7 and 8.

Banks Ltd made the following purchases and sales of Ernies in the four months to 31 December 19X8.

	Purchases	*Sales*	*Cost* £
September 15th	1,000		4,500
October 1st	500		2,500
October 10th		700	
November 5th	800		3,800
December 8th		1,000	-
December 10th	1,500		7,875
December 30th		750	-

7 Using a LIFO method of valuation, the value of the closing stock of Ernies at the year end is

A £6,250
B £6,634.50
C £6,637.50
D £7,087.50

8 Using the data in question 6, the value of the closing stock using an end of period weighted average method of valuation is

A £6,250
B £6,634.50
C £6,637.50
D £7,087.50

9 The following data relates to Virgo plc.

Budgeted 19X8 sales revenue (£8/unit sales price)	£40,000
Stock of raw materials at 1 January 19X8	50,000 units
Stock of raw materials at 31 December 19X8	45,000 units
Change in finished goods stock during 19X8	nil

Four units of the raw material are required to produce one unit of finished product. The amount of raw materials units to purchase during 19X8 is

A 5,000 units
B 15,000 units
C 20,000 units
D 25,000 units

10 A spreadsheet model may derive numerical data from a variety of sources. Which of the following sources may be used?

Sources

(1) Keyboard input
(2) Other data in the model (use of formulae)
(3) Data on a disk file
(4) Standing data within the spreadsheet package

A Source (1) only
B Sources (1) and (2) only
C Sources (1), (2) and (3) only
D Sources (1), (2), (3) and (4)

QUIZ 1

1. D	2. C	3. D	4. D	5. C	6. A	7. A	8. B
9. D	10. B	11. A	12. C	13. A	14. C	15. C	

1 D Prudence

2 C Note the question stated *equity capital* not *equity share capital.*

3 D 800,000 x 50p x 5% = £20,000.

4 D The effect of each error is to overstate cost of sales and therefore understate profit. The total understatement is therefore £2,900 which means that corrected profit is £(27,200 + 2,900) = £30,100.

5 C

		£	£
Amounts due to creditors at 1 January (balancing figure)			16,970
Purchases in year			83,200
			100,170
Less:	cash paid to creditors in year	79,500	
	discounts received	3,750	
	contra with debtors control	4,000	
			87,250
Amounts still unpaid at 31 December			12,920

6 A The amount of £370 has effectively been debited twice in error.

7 A The sale was valid. The stock was overstated by £570 reducing the reported cost of sales by that amount.

8 B £2,400 x 20% = £480.

9 D

10 B Credit purchases = £(27,850 + 720 - 970) = £27,600. Therefore total purchases = £(27,600 + 3,900) = £31,500.

11 A Stock is valued at the lower of cost or net realisable value. In this case, net realisable value is

£80 - £15 - £12 (= 80% x 15) = £53 NRV.
£53 x 85 = £4,505.

12 C

13 A

	£	£
Rent		1,400
At 31 December 19X6 rates prepaid £1,700 x 3/12		425
Rates 1 April 19X6	900	
Less rebates	(200)	
Rates to 31 December 19X6 x 3/6	450	
		1,150
		2,975

14 C Salesmen's basic salaries are usually fixed. Their commission increases with turnover.

15 C

	January	*February*	*March*
	£	£	£
Credit sales	14,000	18,000	20,000
Less 5% trade discount	700	900	1,000
Net credit sales	13,300	17,100	19,000

	Cash received
	£
From March sales £19,000 (100 - 5%) x 20%	3,610
From February sales £17,100 (100 - 2½%) x 50%	8,336
From January sales £13,300 x 30%	3,990
	15,936

QUIZ 2

1. D	2. D	3. A	4. B	5. D	6. D
7. D	8. C	9. A	10. A	11. D	12. B

1 D Definitions A, B and D are all taken from the CIMA *Official terminology.*

A is the definition of cost allocation, which is part of cost attribution
B is the definition of cost ascertainment
Cost apportionment is also part of cost attribution.

2 D

	£
Overhead absorbed = $\frac{£15,000}{20,000 \text{ hours}}$ x 19,500	14,625
Overhead incurred	14,000
Over-absorption	625

3 A Continuous stocktaking is defined in the question. Perpetual inventory is a stock recording system whereby each movement in or out of stock is recorded as it occurs, and so stock records for every item are always up to date. ABC inventory analysis is a stock control system which categorises stock items into three categories, according to the proportion and value of total stock usage of the item. The stock items in category A which represent the largest proportion of stock usage by value (but the smallest number of items) merit the greatest amount of stock control effort. Low value or small-usage items in category C merit the least amount of stock control.

4 B £25,185 + £5,440 = £30,625. The only direct costs are the wages paid to direct workers for ordinary time, plus the basic pay for overtime. Overtime premium and shift allowances are usually treated as overheads. However, if and when overtime and shiftwork are incurred specifically for a particular cost unit, they are classified as direct costs of that cost unit. Sick pay is treated as an overhead and is therefore classified as an indirect cost.

5 D

	Dept A	*Dept B*	*Total*
	£	£	£
Direct materials	5,000	3,000	8,000
Direct labour	1,600	1,000	2,600
Production overhead	1,600	800	2,400
Full production cost			13,000
Other overheads (20%)			2,600
Cost of the job			15,600
Profit (25% of sales = $33\frac{1}{3}$% of cost)			5,200
Sales price			20,800

6 D

	units
Planned increase in stocks of finished goods	4,600
Budgeted sales	36,800
Budgeted production (to pass quality control check)	41,400

This is 92% of total production, allowing for an 8% rejection rate.

Budgeted production $= \frac{100}{92} \times 41{,}400 = 45{,}000$ units

Budgeted direct labour hours = (x 5 hours per unit) 225,000 hours

7 D Probably the easiest way to solve this question is to draw up a stores ledger control account.

STORES LEDGER CONTROL ACCOUNT

	£		£
Opening stock b/fwd	18,500	Creditors (returns)	2,300
Creditors/cash (deliveries)	142,000	Overhead accounts (indirect materials)	25,200
		WIP (balancing figure)	116,900
		Closing stock c/fwd	16,100
	160,500		160,500

8 C

		Units	£/unit	Value FIFO £	Units	£/unit	Value LIFO £
Purchase	1/1	4,000	2.50	10,000	4,000	2.50	10,000
	31/1	1,000	2.00	2,000	1,000	2.00	2,000
		5,000		12,000	5,000		12,000
Sales	15/2	(3,000)	2.50	(7,500)	(1,000)	2.00	(2,000)
					(2,000)	2.50	(5,000)
		2,000		4,500	2,000		5,000
Purchase	28/2	1,500	2.50	3,750	1,500	2.50	3,750
		3,500		8,250	3,500		8,750
Sales	14/3	(500)	2.50	(1,250)	(500)	2.50	(1,250)
		3,000		7,000	3,000		7,500

9 A The intercept on the vertical axis gives the amount of the standing charge.

10 A

	£	
$\frac{£15,000}{10,000}$ x 12,000 =	18,000	absorbed
	21,000	incurred
Underabsorption	3,000	

11 D Expected hours to make output $= \frac{5,400}{30} + \frac{3,800}{40}$ = 275 hours

Efficiency ratio $= \frac{\text{expected hours to make output}}{\text{actual hours taken}} = \frac{275}{266} \times 100\% = 103\%$

12 B Budgeted labour hours in period $= \frac{5,550}{30} + \frac{3,760}{40}$ = 279 hours

Production volume ratio $= \frac{\text{expected hours to make output}}{\text{budgeted labour hours}} = \frac{275}{279} \times 100\% =$ 99%

QUIZ 3

1. B	2. D	3. D	4. D	5. D
6. B	7. D	8. D	9. A	10. A

1 B (1) True
(2) False - depreciation recognises the cost to business of using a fixed asset
(3) False - employer's NICs are part of salary costs already
(4) True - debits will still equal credits

2 D
- A Incorrect, as the wrong figure will be posted correctly
- B Incorrect, as no entry is posted at all
- C Incorrect, as postings come from day books
- D Correct, as this matter is dealt with in the control account but apparently not in the personal account

3 D

CREDITORS

	£		£
Cash	94,275	Balance b/d	10,748
Discount received	1,270	∴ Purchases	100,204
Balance c/d	15,407		
	110,952		110,952

4 D Legal fees for the purchase of a freehold warehouse can count as capital expenditure and added to the cost of the building. The remaining costs are normal running costs of a business.

5 D is correct. £3,950 rates + £5,650 rent = £9,600. Costs should be matched with benefits received for the accounting period.

Rent		£
1 June 19X7 to 31 December 19X7	$= \frac{7}{12} \times £5,400$	3,150
1 January 19X8 to 31 May 19X8	$= \frac{5}{12} \times £6,000$	2,500
		5,650

Rates		£
1 June 19X7 to 31 March 19X8	$= \frac{10}{12} \times £3,900$	3,250
1 April 19X8 to 31 May 19X8	$= \frac{2}{12} \times £4,200$	700
		3,950

6 B

	%		£
Sales	100	Purchases	75,000
Cost of sales	80	Increase in stock	(5,600)
Gross profit	20	Cost of sales	69,400

$$\therefore \text{Sales} = \frac{100}{80} \times £69,400 = £86,750$$

7 D

	£	£
Balance per bank statement		(465)
Less: unpresented cheques	(896)	
Add: uncleared lodgements	570	
		(326)
		(791)

Items (ii) and (iii) are already included in the bank statement balance.

8 D

BANK CONTROL ACCOUNT

	£		£
Credit transfer	1,060	∴ balance b/d	1,697
Balance c/d (from Q7)	791	Bank charges	154
	1,851		1,851

9 A

SALES LEDGER CONTROL ACCOUNT

	£		£
Balance b/d	87,300	Discounts allowed	20,900
Sales	332,840	Cash receipts	327,660
		Bad debts expenses	4,000
		Balance c/d	67,580
	420,140		420,140

PROVISION FOR DOUBTFUL DEBTS

	£		£
To P & L account	986	Balance b/d	4,365
Balance c/d (5% x £67,580)	3,379		
	4,365		4,365

∴ Net P & L account charge £4,000 (bad debt expense) less £986 provision no longer required = £3,014.

10 A Secondary store (3) refers to storage external to the CPU. Answer A therefore is correct.

QUIZ 4

1. D	2. B	3. D	4. A	5. B
6. C	7. C	8. B	9. C	10. A

1 D (1) False. Depreciation is not cash
(2) False. Ltd means limited liability
(3) False. An error of omission is when no entry at all has been made or the double entry has not been completed
(4) True

2 B

SUBSCRIPTIONS ACCOUNT

	£		£
∴ To income and expenditure a/c	5,780	Balance b/d	160
Balance c/d	180	Cash	5,800
	5,960		5,960

3 D

4 A Item A is a part of the cost of raw materials. Items B and D are production overheads. Item C is a selling and distribution expense.

5 B

CASH ACCOUNT

	£		£
		Balance b/d	150
Transfer from deposit account	500	Charges	36
		Balance c/d	314
	500		500

	£
Balance per cash book	314
Add unpresented cheques	116
Less uncleared lodgements	(630)
Less error by bank	(400)
Balance per bank statement	(600)

Note that on the bank statement Dr is overdrawn

6 C

7 C 4 members x £75 x $\frac{9}{12}$ (to 30 September 19X7) = £225.

8 B

	£
30 September 19X7 to 31 December 19X7 $\frac{3}{12}$ x 500 members x £75	9,375
1 January 19X8 to 30 September 19X8 $\frac{9}{12}$ x 500 members x £85	31,875
	41,250

9 C

PROVISION FOR DOUBTFUL DEBTS

	£		£
Debtors account	250	Balance b/d	6,400
Balance c/d (5% x £156,000)	7,800	∴ To P & L a/c (answer C)	1,650
	8,050		8,050

10 A Statement (3) is incorrect. Packages are generally a lot cheaper than custom-built applications. The time and expense of designing an application from scratch is incurred only once, even though the application is sold to several customers.

QUIZ 5

1. B	2. A	3. B	4. B	5. B
6. A	7. C	8. C	9. A	10. D

1 B The cost of the machine is £18,000. Automat has paid £13,000 in cash and has evidently agreed a trade-in value of £5,000 for the old machine. (The asset's NBV is irrelevant.) After one year, the net book value of the new machine is 90% of £18,000 = £16,200.

2 A

3 B

	£
Sales ledger control balance	65,000
Overcast of sales daybook	(300)
Purchase ledger contra	(1,500)
	63,200

4 B

	£	£
Sales ledger		63,620
Correction of misposting	210	
Correct posting	210	
		(420)
		63,200

5 B

	Direct costs	*Production overheads*	*Production cost*	*Selling price*	*Selling costs*	*Net realisable value*
	£	£	£	£	£	£
Product I	4,560	2,400	6,960	7,900	860	7,040
Product II	1,090	860	1,950	1,450	470	980
Product III	8,325	3,950	12,275	13,200	1,050	12,150

Stocks are valued at the lower of cost and net realisable value.

		£
From the table above	Product I	6,960 (cost)
	II	980 (net realisable value)
	III	12,150 (net realisable value)
		20,090

6 A

	£
Balance b/f	22,000
Donation	3,000
Interest (building society)	560
Interest (loan stock - 12% x £15,000)	1,800
	27,360

7 C

	£
Assets	
Binoculars, cameras and tripods	5,000
Camping equipment	3,000
Stock of reference books	500
Subscriptions in arrears	200
	8,700
Liabilities	
Life membership	(2,500)
Subs in advance	(50)
Net assets	6,150
Funds	
Balance b/f	5,800 (balancing figure)
Deficit for year	(150)
Transferred from life fund	500
Balance c/f	6,150

8 C

	£
Opening stock	44,800
Goods produced £800,000 x 112%	896,000
Closing stock	(67,200)
Cost of sales at transfer price	873,600

Sales = £873,600 x 120% = £1,048,320

9 A

	£
Provision b/f (£44,800 x 12/112)	4,800
Provision required (£67,200 x 12/112)	7,200
Profit and loss account	2,400

10 D

QUIZ 6

1. B	2. D	3. A	4. B	5. A
6. B	7. C	8. C	9. A	10. C

1 B The only complication is the 20% scrap rate.

Materials	*Kg*	
Opening stock	9,000	
Closing stock	4,000	
	5,000	towards production

Finished goods	*Units*	
Opening stock	3,000	
Sales	6,000	
Closing stock	(2,000)	
	5,000	units to produce
	= 6,250	units if 20% to be scrapped

	Kg
Requirement: 6,250 units x 3 kg per unit	18,750
Kg from stock	(5,000)
Necessary purchases	13,750

2 D All statements are false

(1) False. Prime cost is the total of all direct costs.

(2) False. A manufacturing account has other functions too.

(3) False. Unrealised profit is a P & L item. The manufacturing account is concerned with the cost of producing finished goods

(4) False. It would not fall if there were simply fewer *units* of WIP.

3 A

	£	
Standard direct material cost = 7,200 units x £6 per unit	43,200	
Actual direct material cost	42,912	
Total direct material cost variance	288	favourable

4 B (i) *Marginal costing*

	£/unit
Sales	30.0
Materials	6.0
Labour	7.5
Variable overhead	2.5
Total variable cost	16
Contribution per unit	14

	£
Total contribution £14 x 5,200	72,800
Fixed cost	27,400
Profit	45,400

(ii) *Absorption costing*

	£	£
Sales (5,200 at £30)		156,000
Materials (5,200 at £6)	31,200	
Labour (5,200 at £7.5)	39,000	
Variable overhead (5,200 at £2.5)	13,000	
Total variable cost		83,200
Fixed overhead (5 x 5,200)		26,000
Over-absorbed overhead (W)		(1,600)
Profit		48,400

Working	£
Overhead absorbed 5,800 x £5	29,000
Overhead incurred	27,400
Overabsorbed overhead	1,600

5 A

Overhead absorption rate	=	£5/unit
Actual activity	=	16,000 units produced
		£
∴ Overhead absorbed	=	80,000
Overhead incurred	=	85,000
		5,000 under absorbed

6 B

	£/unit	£
Sales (14,500 units)	60	870,000
Materials	6	87,000
Labour	20	290,000
Variable production overhead	10	145,000
Fixed production overhead	5	72,500
Variable selling expenses	4	58,000
Fixed selling expenses	2	29,000
Under absorbed production overhead		5,000
Over absorbed selling overhead *		(500)
Profit		184,000

* £(2 x 14,500) = £29,000 absorbed - £28,500 actual

7 C

	£/unit	£
Sales	60	
Materials(6)		
Labour	(20)	
Variable production overhead	(10)	
Variable selling expenses	(4)	
	20	
Contribution 14,500 x £20		290,000
Fixed costs: production		85,000
selling		28,500
Profit		176,500

8 C Contribution/unit = £20
∴ 1,000 units x £20 = £20,000

9 A A sales budget and budgeted changes in finished goods stocks are needed to prepare a production budget. The production budget and budgeted changes in raw materials stocks are needed to prepare a purchases budget for raw materials. A purchases budget is needed to prepare a cash budget.

10 C

QUIZ 7

1. B	2. C	3. A	4. B	5. C
6. B	7. C	8. B	9. B	10. C

1 B (1) True. Standard costs are a basis for budgeting.
(2) False. The expected standard should be an improvement on current
(3) False. Expected standards are more common
(4) True. This is true of a standard costing system

2 C (1) False. Fixed overheads are not relevant for short-term decision making, as they are normally sunk costs in the short term
(2) False. Absorption costing is recommended by SSAP 9
(3) False. Contribution is important in marginal costing
(4) True. All fixed costs written-off in the period in which they arise

3 A If the sales volume in 19X7 was the same as in 19X6 then the sales value would be £20,000 + 10% = £22,000. The actual sales value for 19X7 was only £19,800 ie 10% below £22,000, therefore there was a 10% reduction in the volume of sales. The effect on profit would be a 10% fall in contribution (£600).

19X6	£
Sales	20,000
Variable costs	14,000
	6,000 x 10% = £600

4 B If material prices were the same, then the expected material cost for the lower sales volume in 19X7 would be £8,000 x 90% = £7,200. The actual material cost was £7,400 therefore profit fell by £200 as a result of the increase in materials usage.

5 C

	Selling price up 20%
	£
Sales (£20,000 x 120% volume x 80% price)	19,200
Variable costs (£14,000 x 120% volume)	16,800
Fixed costs	2,000
Profit	400

6 B

	£
February purchases = (90% x £12,000) + (10% x £15,000) =	12,300
March purchases = (90% x £15,000) + (10% x £20,000) =	15,500
	27,800

Payments to be made in April = 50% x each of these purchases
= 50% x £27,800
= £13,900

7 C

	Receipts			Issues			
	Units	£/unit	£	Units	£/unit	£	
Opening stock	1,000	4.50	4,500				
1 October	500	5.00	2,500				
10 October				500	5.00	2,500.0	
				200	4.50	900.0	
5 November	800	4.75	3,800				
8 December				800	4.75	3,800.0	
				200	4.50	900.0	
10 December	1,500	5.25	7,875				
30 December				750	5.25	3,937.5	
Closing stock				750	5.25	3,937.5	£6,637.50
				600	4.50	2,700.0	
	3,800		18,675	3,800		18,675.0	

8 B Average value of receipts = £18,675/3,800
= £4.91/unit

Average value of closing stock = £4.91 x 1,350 units
= £6,634.50

9 B Amount required = sales + closing stock - opening stock

(1) Sales = £40,000/£8 per unit = 5,000 units finished goods needed
∴ 20,000 units raw materials are required

(2) Opening stock = 50,000 units raw material

(3) Closing stock = 45,000 units raw material

Amount required = 20,000 + 45,000 - 50,000
= 15,000 units of raw material

10 C Source 4, 'standing data within the spreadsheet package' is not a source of data. The spreadsheet *package* itself contains no standing data at all: it is merely a modelling system that starts as an 'empty sheet'. Any data for a model must first be input, or derived by a formula from other data in the model. A spreadsheet model, made with the use of the spreadsheet package, is saved as a *file* of data, if it is given a unique name.

FURTHER READING

You may like to obtain further practice in tackling multiple choice questions on accounting fundamentals. BPP publish the *Password* series of books, each of which incorporates a large collection of multiple choice questions with solutions, comments and marking guides. The relevant *Password* titles for this paper are Basic Accounting and Costing. These are priced at £6.95 each and contain about 300 questions.

To order your *Password* books, ring our credit card hotline on 081-740 6808 or tear out this page and send it to our Freepost address.

To: BPP Publishing Ltd, FREEPOST, London W12 8BR Tel: 081-740 6808

Forenames (Mr / Ms) ____________________

Surname ____________________

Address ____________________

____

Post code ____________________

Please send me the following books:	*Quantity*	*Price*	*Total*
Password Basic Accounting		£6.95	
Password Costing		£6.95	

Please include postage:

UK: **£1.50 for first plus £0.50 for each extra book** ....

Overseas: **£3.00 for first plus £1.50 for each extra book** ....

I enclose a cheque for £__________ or charge to Access/Visa

Card number | | | | | | | | | | | | | | | | |

Expiry date ____________ Signature ____________________

Whether you are placing an order or not, you might like to look at the reverse of this page. It's a Review Form, which you can send in to us with comments and suggestions on the kit you've just finished. Your feedback really does make a difference: it helps us to make the next edition that bit better. So do fill in the Review Form and return it to us at the freepost address above.

CIMA: ACCOUNTING FUNDAMENTALS

Name: ______________________________

How have you used this kit?

Home study (book only) ☐ With 'correspondence' package ☐

On a course: college ______ ☐ Other ______

How did you obtain this kit?

From us by mail order ☐ From us by phone ☐

From a bookshop ☐ From your college ☐

Where did you hear about BPP kits?

At bookshop ☐ Recommended by lecturer ☐

Recommended by friend ☐ Mailshot from BPP ☐

Advertisement in ______ ☐ Other ______

Have you used the companion text for this subject? **Yes/No**

Your comments and suggestions would be appreciated on the following areas.

Study guide and quiz

Content of solutions

Errors (please specify, and refer to a page number, if you've spotted anything!)

Presentation

Other